Praise for Nik Ripken and
The Insan

The Insanity of God is a book you ~~may want to put down~~ but you won't. You can't. Time and again you will have to stop, go aside, and weep. At times you will weep for our suffering brothers and sisters around the world who experience persecution for King Jesus as normal Christianity. At other times you will weep for joy at how the gospel continues to run wide across the globe in spite of demonic opposition. And, you will also weep as the anemic and tepid "Christianity" of the American Church is exposed for the shameful counterfeit it too often is. I was literally "undone" by this book. I will not be the same for reading it. Be warned: neither will you!"

Daniel L. Akin
President, Southeastern Baptist Theological Seminary

What can I possibly say about this book? It completely and utterly wrecked me. Half the time I found myself sitting in heartbreaking silence on the verge of tears, and the other half I found myself wanting to shout and dance over some of the stories. No one will read this book and be the same person after the last page. If you want a front row seat to the raw, potent, heart transforming power of Jesus, this book is a must read.

Jeff Bethke
Author, *Why I Hate Religion, But Love Jesus*

This is a book that every well-meaning Christian ought to read. It gives the most comprehensive overview of what life is like for the true followers of Jesus who are willing to pay the whole price for following Him. Extremely touching at times. It makes you cry and it makes you laugh. But remember they are your brothers and mine. Therefore we have a responsibility of standing with them as part of the body of Christ worldwide.

Brother Andrew
Founder, Open Doors International
Author, *God's Smuggler* and *Secret Believers*

The Insanity of God is a compelling, convicting and life changing book. This true story grips you from the introduction and keeps you reading page after page. You will weep as you read about persecution around the world. You will fall under conviction as you read about the commitment of Christians in dark places who risk their own lives to share the good news of Jesus. You will be encouraged as you realize that the power of the gospel supersedes evil and the malevolent intentions of men. In the end you will come away with a renewed sense of faith in God who truly is enough, even in the face of extreme persecution.

Dr. Mac Brunson
Pastor, First Baptist Church Jacksonville, FL

In his book, *The Insanity of God,* Nik Ripkin takes us on a journey of extreme emotional highs and lows to demonstrate that our limited understanding of events in our lives is only one piece of God's larger puzzle of fulfillment and salvation. This book puts our daily struggles into perspective and leaves us inspired and ready for the next challenge.

Dr. Ben Carson
Benjamin S. Carson, Sr., M.D. and Dr. Evelyn Spiro, R.N. Professor of Pediatric Neurosurgery, Johns Hopkins School of Medicine
President and Cofounder, The Carson Scholars Fund
Author, *Gifted Hands*

The story is gripping; the crisis is universal.

John Eldredge
Author, *Wild At Heart* and *Beautiful Outlaw*

We are in danger of rapidly losing what it means to feel compassion for those held in the grip of sin on this broken planet. After glancing at a few fleeting photos and hearing the usual review of "today's tragedies" on each evening's network news, we casually top off the evening with a little "weather and sports" before plodding off to an undisturbed sleep. But for Jesus, the very sight of those crushed beneath the boot of the Adversary was nothing short of gut-wrenching. He was compelled to do something about it! Now Nik Ripken takes you on a personal, real life journey with Jesus into the dark, back-alleys of human depravity where only Christ's love can overcome. With remarkable clarity, this gifted writer transports you into a world where, through the blood-stained glass of persecution, the light of Christ shines brightly.

Tom Elliff
Former President, International Mission Board

In *The Insanity of God* we are reminded of the power of the gospel to save using biographical sketches that most of us in the American church will struggle to comprehend. Deeply moving, intensely powerful and challenging describes the stories contained in these pages. I cannot recommend it strongly enough. This book will help you walk closely with Jesus and challenge you to take great risks for the sake of His name.

Micah Fries
Lead Pastor, Frederick Boulevard, St. Joseph, MO

Nik and Ruth Ripken have long been heroes of mine as I have watched and admired them from afar, drawing personal inspiration from their passion, faith, and resilience that comes from the Resurrection Lord they serve. More than once I have been encouraged to keep going, because they kept going, overcoming challenges that would crush lesser souls. In this, I am not alone. Around the world, I have met countless young missionaries who trace their pilgrimage back to the influence of Nik and Ruth.

The Insanity of God merges the Ripkens' story with those of hundreds of other heroes of the faith who did not consider their present sufferings worth comparing to the glory that will one day be revealed in them. These stories bear telling, and hearing, and reproducing. You need to hear these stories that the Ripkens have rescued from this world's prisons, gulags and shadows. I pray that they will do for you what they have done for me: encourage you to shake off your slumber and press on to the high calling that is ours in Christ Jesus.

David Garrison
Author, *Church Planting Movements*

A touching, deeply stirring book about the seriousness of the Great Commission. This book rekindled my passion to do all that God is leading me to do for the nations, to expect and attempt great things. I am grateful for the grace that drips off every page of this great work.

J.D. Greear
Lead Pastor, The Summit Church

If there's one thing many desire, it's going deeper and knowing the God of the Bible intimately. When one takes the trip of following Jesus to the ends of the earth, having previously counted the cost, died to self, surrendered fully to His call, they may then know the reality of 2 Timothy 3:12, "all who desire to live godly in Christ Jesus will suffer persecution." The Insanity of God will stretch you to new places of trusting God for the impossible in reaching the nations, at any cost.

Johnny Hunt
Pastor, First Baptist Church, Woodstock, GA

In this life-changing book, Nik Ripken recounts his adventures as one who walked in faith, hoping against hope, obeying God's call regardless of its costs in hardships, pains, and bewilderments. To the list of the heroes of faith in Hebrews 11, we may add our contemporaries who took God's Word seriously, and at any cost! I heartily recommend this epic story as a necessary "vitamin" to help Christians live out their faith in this terribly secular age, demonstrating that we walk by faith, and not by sight.

Bassam Michael Madany
Middle East Resources

Nik Ripken has told a great story, and in doing so he has made it clear that the question every believer must answer is whether we have the courage to bear the consequences of obediently exercising our freedom to be salt and light to all peoples, wherever they live. Perhaps Nik has put it best when he says, "Perhaps the question should not be, 'Why are others persecuted?' Perhaps the better question is, 'Why are we not?'"

John Maxwell
New York Times Best-selling Author

This is not a book. It's a soul earthquake. You don't read it as much as you experience it, and when it's done with you, you'll never be the same. Ripken's story is one of those that shows up once in a generation, and everyone I know needs to read it. 'The Insanity of God' may very well be the book of the century.

Johnnie Moore
Vice President, Liberty University
Author, *Dirty God: Jesus in the Trenches*

Once I picked up *The Insanity of God* I literally could not put it down! After multiple occasions of participating in the Ripken's persecution workshops with our team at East-West Ministries, I thought I was prepared for what I was about to encounter in The Insanity of God. I was wrong. Nik Ripken is truly one of the best, most captivating story tellers that I have ever met. In The Insanity of God, these stories literally come to life, carrying the reader on a dramatic, life-changing missionary journey with Nik and Ruth—across Africa and eventually around the world. But these are not simply their stories, these are God's stories. Reading The Insanity of God led me to a wonderful, fresh encounter with Jesus—and with His calling upon my life to "go and make disciples of ALL nations," especially those in greatest spiritual darkness where persecution of witness for Jesus is most intense. As I read these compelling stories of resurrected faith, I laughed out loud and I wept aloud as well. I felt as though I was right there—literally witnessing each miraculous story unfold right before my eyes. These are God's stories, powerful stories, like those recorded in the Book of Acts, played out in the lives of real, every day men and women all around the world. Men and women whose extraordinary faith in the resurrected Jesus enabled them to endure unspeakable persecution and yet not lose heart. Most of all, these faithful believers did not allow their tormentors to silence their witness for Jesus and for His gospel. The Insanity of God ushers one into a fresh encounter with the Jesus and with the power of His resurrection, with the joy of being called to suffer for His Name, and with a compelling call to "Find Jesus! Find the gospel" —and then to follow Him and serve Him with resurrection faith and resurrection obedience anywhere He leads.

Kurt Nelson
President and CEO
East-West Ministries International

If you think being a God-follower will make life safe and secure, buckle your seat belt. *The Insanity of God* will jolt you into a new reality and change your life—for the better. Discover the thrill and adventure of following Jesus like you never have before! This book will awaken a new boldness in your spirit. Don't miss out on this amazing message!

Drs. Les Parrott and Leslie Parrott
Authors, *Saving Your Marriage Before It Starts*

The Insanity of God tells an incredible story of faith lived out in the most difficult of circumstances. It showcases the power and glory of God no matter the context, challenge, or opposition. The Ripkens haven't just lived this story, they have been students at each step of the way, learning from those who have suffered most and sharing those lessons with all of us. As a result, you will not be the same person on the last page of this book as you were on the first. You will be struck anew with the unquenchable power of a great God to build His kingdom and bring glory to His name. May we read, may we learn, and may we go forward in the power of Him who brings light to the darkest of places!

Thom S. Rainer
President, LifeWay Christian Resources

Priorities: Survive or thrive? Peace or freedom? Death or life? Where can one find that Jesus is really enough? Read *The Insanity of God* and you'll be surprised how your worldview might change. You might even pray for the persecution of the church by praying that believers in persecution will never stop loving and sharing Jesus. Insane . . .

Steve Ridgway
CEO, Open Doors USA

A captivating spiritual diary! Join a journey of discovery how God is spreading his kingdom in the midst of adversity, suffering and even the most atrocious persecution. It shares the experiences made in gathering the wisdom of 700 followers of Christ in 72 countries who are walking with Jesus in hard places. A challenge to radical discipleship! And a helpful source on how to cope with persecution.

Prof. Dr. Christof Sauer
International Institute for Religious Freedom
Editor, "Suffering, Persecution, and Martyrdom"

It's true. God's thoughts are not our thoughts and His ways are not our ways (Isa. 55:8). *The Insanity of God* is an account of Nik Ripken's life-long and very personal journey of discovery into the ways of God related to persecution and suffering. You've heard that fish are not aware of the water they swim in. Nik chronicles how God has revealed to him the water we all swim in related to persecution in our sojourn in the Kingdom of God on this earth. "All who desire to live godly in Christ Jesus will be persecuted" (2 Tim. 3:12). This book explains why. Just as a pearl is formed from a simple grain of sand with layer upon layer of deposits until it becomes a large and lustrous thing of beauty, God has worked in Nik's life to reveal the beauty of His ways and thoughts which are different from our own. Inspiring. Engaging. Insightful.

Curtis Sergeant
International Mission Board
Director of Church Planting, Saddleback Church

Jesus' call to discipleship is to come and die. Few Christians take the call literally, but it's not outside the realm of possibility given the current state of the persecuted church. *The Insanity of God* is not for "safe" Christians, or those interested in pursuing comfort over the cross. Be warned, this book is a threat to mediocre, cautious, lukewarm faith.

Ed Stetzer
Billy Graham Distinguished Chair,
Author, *Subversive Kingdom*

The Insanity of God is one of those rare books you'll want to give to everyone you know. But you may feel the need to apologize to those you give it to, knowing it will shake their world! Give it to them anyway. Its message is one every believer needs to hear, and for those who are looking for evidence that God still loves this world, you'll find it here.

Jeff Taylor
CEO, Open Doors International

The Ripkens' simple faith and willingness to follow Jesus wherever He said to "Go!" led them to wrestle with and discover some of the deepest truths of the faith. In some of the darkest places on earth members of the persecuted church experience a fellowship with Christ and life in abundance that few of us have known. As a follower of Christ, a husband, a father, and a missionary I was alternately encouraged and convicted by what I read. I am humbled to call the people in the pages of this book my brothers and sisters. This is a book I will read again and again and share with others.

Ryan Williams
Executive Director, Leadership Development,
Campus Ministry, CRU

THE
INSANITY
of
OBEDIENCE

THE
INSANITY
of
OBEDIENCE

WALKING WITH JESUS
IN TOUGH PLACES

NIK RIPKEN
with BARRY STRICKER

PUBLISHING
NASHVILLE, TENNESSEE

978-1-4336-7309-2

Published by B&H Publishing Group
Nashville, Tennessee

Published in association with Yates & Yates, www.yates2.com.

Dewey Decimal Classification: 231.1
Subject Heading: PERSECUTION \ CHRISTIAN LIFE \
WITNESSING

8 9 10 11 12 13 • 23 22 21 20 19

This book is dedicated to Ruth alongside three unique and special sons. I love you deeply.

For decades Somali believers have been beaten, kicked from their homes, hounded out of their country, killed for their faith in Jesus, with their killers going to the extreme of hiding their bodies. Brothers and sisters, we honor you through this book. Thank you for what you have taught us and the faith which you have modeled. They can kill you and hide your bodies; but nothing nor anyone can cause us to forget how you walked with Jesus. We remember. We will not waste your sacrifice. We will sing your songs, tell your testimonies, and continue to share Jesus with those for whom you also gave your lives.

Contents

"I am sending you out like sheep among wolves."

—Matthew 10:16

Foreword
by Brother Andrew

Warning: this is a difficult book. Not because it is hard to read, but because it makes me uncomfortable. Radically uncomfortable!

This book will turn your life upside down. In fact, I recommend you read it on your knees. Because if missionaries (career as well as short-termers), mission-sending agencies, church leaders, those who support missionaries and mission agencies, plus all who pray for missionaries truly take this book to heart, there will be an incredible harvest for the kingdom of God.

Yes, the insights in this book are that radical. And, this radical message is for every follower of Jesus Christ.

When I read Nik's first book, *The Insanity of God*, I didn't like the first half very much. I'm just being honest. Like most people I like stories of success and victory. Nik had a testimony of defeat—how else do you describe beginning your ministry in a nation with 150 believers and ending it six years later with just four? No, we want stories of triumph—start with four and grow a church to 150 or better 1,500, or 15,000. That's a story that sells. Then everyone wants to know your secrets of success and imitate your "formula."

Yet it was in defeat, following the death of their teenage son on the mission field, that God took Nik and his wife Ruth on a journey of discovery. God didn't lead them to a seminary or a mega-church leadership conference. Rather he took them to more than seventy countries were Christians are persecuted, often severely. Nik met believers who spent years in prison because of their faith or who had family members martyred. Under such oppression the church survived, often thrived, and in China exploded in unprecedented growth.

For over a dozen years Nik has done in-depth interviews with more than 600 believers in persecution. In the process he's learned what victorious faith looks like in spite of circumstances. That journey of discovery forms the second half of Nik's first book. It left me wanting more. I needed to know what this means to us. How do we, particularly in the free West, take this incredible body of knowledge learned in the crucible of suffering and apply it to our missionary efforts? That's the question this book answers.

To explain the impact of Nik's books on me I need to tell a personal story. In my office I have a photo. It was taken in 2002 in a hotel in the midst of a radical Muslim region. Two men are with me smiling for the camera. They are dressed simply in indigenous clothing. They had come secretly to my hotel after midnight to tell me their story. For security reasons I identify them only as S and Q.

S was a handsome young man with a nicely trimmed black beard. His English consisted of saying, "Hi, my name is S." So we spoke through a translator. S was raised in a very religious home. His grandfather was an imam. His father was an imam. Two of his brothers were imams. He memorized the entire Qur'an in Arabic even though that was not his native language. S became an imam, taught religion at a government school, and regularly led prayers at the neighborhood mosque.

The teaching job gave S access to a library where he made a valuable discovery. Among the many books covering Islam were volumes about Hinduism, Buddhism, and Christianity. Another imam, recognizing S's hunger for knowledge, initiated a discussion about which religion is true. It soon became evident that this imam was a secret follower of Jesus Christ. After several conversations comparing Islam and Christianity, S was introduced to the New Testament. S began reading the Gospels and met the person of Jesus. "I realized that there is no one like Christ after God," S explained. "Christ is the true revelation of God. In reality, He is God."

It had been two years since S had become a follower of Christ. He had given up serving as an imam and teacher of Islam so he was struggling to earn a living. To complicate matters, one of his brothers had learned of his conversion and vowed to kill him. So for the past two months S had lived in hiding. So what was he going to do? With a big grin my new friend announced "I want to be an imam for Jesus!"

One of my colleagues met with S two-and-a-half years later and learned that he was now working covertly in a region where a fierce fundamentalist Muslim group was in charge. In the midst of radical Islam S initiated clever conversations to determine which individuals might be interested in learning about Jesus. He had led many to faith in Christ, including one of his brothers, and now made the rounds of several underground congregations that secretly met in homes. He had just married a woman fourteen years younger—she had been promised to him when she was just three. Patiently he had told her of Jesus, until she had come to faith.

Two weeks after that meeting I received a phone call. S had been captured by Muslim fundamentalists. Despite our prayers, we never saw him again and we believe he died sharing his faith. He simply could not keep quiet about Jesus.

Q was just as bold in working for Christ and the death of S did nothing to dampen his passion. He traveled the same route as S and took over care of those house churches. Like S he led people to Christ while narrowly evading a couple of attempts on his life. But after a few years, his "luck" ran out. Q was also captured and killed.

I look every day at that photo and grieve the loss of these two dear brothers. But I also marvel at their example. You see, I am free to share Jesus with my neighbors. I can cross the street and knock on their doors. They may slam the door in my face, but I won't be kidnapped or killed for talking about Jesus. Yet, how often do I go and talk to my neighbors about Jesus?

By contrast, S nd Q woke up every morning eager to tell people about Jesus, knowing it could cost them their lives that very day. Eventually they paid the price. I'm convicted because they followed the way of Jesus. It's the hard way. It's the way of the cross.

So here's the challenge. Am I more free because I live in a democracy and enjoy religious freedom, yet I'm hesitant to talk about Jesus? Or were S and Q more free even though immersed in the culture of radical Islam, living under Sharia law, knowing people were eager to silence their witness? These two men spread the gospel in an area most of us would consider impossible for any missionary work. Indeed, western missionaries cannot go into this particular region. Still these two men planted churches. I ask you, who was more free?

The faith of S and Q shames me and inspires me. Nik has six hundred more examples. The depth of his research brings the lessons of the Persecuted Church to all of us. We must listen and learn from this part of the body of Christ that suffers just because they follow Jesus. These men and women have put the focus back on the Great Commission. Their words and actions conclusively demonstrate what I have always believed—no doors are closed to the gospel. In fact, as Nik shows, Jesus is already working in areas where we think it simply isn't safe to go.

The radical findings and conclusions discovered by Nik from his experiences and the research he accomplished should challenge us all to the core. In this book, you can understand why Nik calls the response to those findings and conclusions *The Insanity of Obedience*. However, Nik shares with us that "obedience" is exactly what the Lord calls each of to, regardless of our location or our circumstances. You will find out that the answers as to how one comes to obey are not easy. But, the Church, as I can testify in my country of Holland, is not growing where living out the faith is easy. That's why we need to study Nik's books (and others such as *Radical* by David Platt). We need to get back to the radicalness of the gospel message. If every Christian took the messages found in *The Insanity of God* and *The Insanity of Obedience* seriously and applied them diligently, the result would be a revolution. Not a revolution of guns, but of love. We might even win the world.

Prologue

Recently, we led a training meeting with some believers in China. In public remarks, I commented on the significant spiritual harvest among the Chinese. I enthusiastically described how that harvest had been an encouragement to the global Body of Christ. My tone was almost boastful. That was not my intention, of course; I was simply overwhelmed by the work of the Spirit in drawing people to faith.

After my remarks, a Chinese house church leader asked me to join him for a meal. With unflagging gentleness, this church leader firmly challenged the number of believers in China that I had cited. His comment took me off guard; after all, I had used the most conservative estimate quoted by Westerners! I defended my figures and I explained to my host the source of my statistics. He listened to me patiently. Then, with a smile, he agreed it might be possible to support the numbers which I was using. At the same time, he suggested a different way of interpreting the numbers being bandied globally.

I will never forget what he said next: "Of that large number of believers that you described in your talk, two-thirds of those people are what we would call 'members.' Only one-third of those people are who we would call 'true followers of Jesus.'"

I was puzzled by that distinction and I asked my new friend to explain the difference in those two categories.

He said, "Probably two-thirds of the people you mentioned regularly attend a house church. Most of those people have been baptized. Most of those people contribute financially to the work of a house church." He paused before continuing: *"But we do not consider church members to be true followers of Jesus until they have led other people to Christ and until they have helped plant more house churches."*

I found myself moving into the mode of researcher as I began to absorb his comment, but then I stopped short, seized by the implications of what this church leader was suggesting. The next question which entered my mind was intensely personal: *Am I simply a member of the church or am I a true follower of Jesus Christ?*

That crucial question is at the heart of this book: are we simply members of a church or are we true followers of Jesus? This central question brings to the surface many other important questions. Is there anything in our lives we are holding outside of God's authority and control? Is there any place in the world where we are unwilling to go for Him? Is there any person we are unwilling to love or forgive?

Essentially, are we simply members of a group or are we true followers of Jesus and part of His Body?

The book you hold in your hands is an invitation to ask crucial questions and a challenge to deal with the implications of our answers.

I walked down the steps of the small airplane which had landed in a desert area separating two Central Asian countries. I expected to be met by a European doctor. Much to my surprise, though, I was immediately "accosted" by five men dressed in conservative Muslim clothing. Pulling away from their physical grasp, I tried to make my way into the tiny airport to book a flight out of this dangerous environment. I felt certain I had just walked into a trap, and I was sure my life was in jeopardy.

Just before I entered the small terminal building, one of the men whispered to me, "We are followers of Jesus."

The men led me to a small hotel room. After serving tea and exchanging pleasantries, they said to me, "We know how to be Muslims in a Muslim country. We even know how to be communists in a Muslim country. What we do not know is how to be followers of Jesus in a Muslim country. We were praying at one a.m. this morning and the Holy Spirit told us to go to the airport, meet the first plane that landed, and greet the first white man who exited that plane. God sent us to meet you. He has sent you to teach us what you have learned from other believers in persecution—how to follow Jesus in a place like ours that seems to be controlled by evil."

This book is for those men.

I was secretly sharing with believers from Muslim backgrounds outdoors in the bush of a North African country each evening. We talked together late into the night for a week. There were twenty men and seven women in the group. On the third night of our conversation together, as we focused on vibrant stories of survival in the midst of persecution, one of the young ladies in the group blurted out, "When our families beat us, are we allowed to fight back?"

The young believing men in the group were paralyzed by the question. As the other women gathered around their sister and held her tight, the whole group looked to me for an answer to her question.

This book is for her.

They came to us from a college campus in what we call "the Bible Belt" of America. They talked fervently about their ministry to international students, especially students from Muslim backgrounds.

They talked about the struggle of ministry, and they talked about reasons to celebrate. They talked about their excitement in seeing a handful of Muslim college students give their lives to Jesus.

They then described how they had taken their new believing friends to a Western-styled church, introduced them to church leaders, witnessed their baptisms, and welcomed them into the local fellowship. They also admitted that it felt like these new followers of Jesus were treated like "trophies." Sometimes, in fact, the pictures of these new believers were even plastered on the church websites.

Then, with broken hearts, they said to us, "All of these students who have come to Christ from Muslim backgrounds have now disappeared. We heard that many were forced to return to their home countries. We heard that the young men were placed under the authority of their most conservative uncle and that the young women were taken home and married off to older Muslim men. What are we supposed to do? What did we do wrong? Help us!"

This book is for them.

Another group told this story: "Dr. Nik, we had a growing ESL (English as a Second Language) class on our church campus with international women from countries hostile to the Christian faith. Everything was going so well and it seemed that many of our students were just about to express faith in Jesus. Then they all disappeared. They simply stopped coming to class. When we went looking for them, we found evidence that a religious leader had come from another city and threatened them against ever returning to this church property."

The class leaders' question was sad and heartfelt: "What do we do now that we have lost our ministry to these people?"

This book is for them.

I rode in a van for eighteen hours across China. Waking up from a long sleep, I found myself in a compound surrounded by approximately 150 leaders of a house church movement. Before I could even introduce myself, the gathered group said to me, "Forty percent of our group has already been in prison for three years. That means that 60 percent of our group has yet to go to prison. Will you teach us, Dr. Nik, how to prepare to go to prison?"

This book is for them.

The house church elder explained that the Holy Spirit woke him up in the middle of the night and told him to gather together the fruits, vegetables, and meat that the house church had stored up to care for people in need. The Holy Spirit told the man to take this load of food, by horse and sled, to a pastor's family who had been left to die in a one-room hut in the frozen tundra.

The man reminded the Holy Spirit that it was thirty degrees below zero outside and that there was no way that he would survive the trip. The man reminded the Holy Spirit that the wolves would probably eat his horse and then eat him.

Then the words of the Holy Spirit rang in his ears: "You do not have to come back; you simply have to go."

This book is for him.

I listened as some "Bible women" in China taught about church planting and evangelism. Their boldness was almost scary. Their ability and willingness to share the Good News of Jesus Christ everywhere they went was inspiring. Wanting to understand more about leadership in this house church movement, I listened to these women explain: "God has chosen men to pastor the house church with a mixed audience." Then, with sheer joy radiating from their faces, they added, "Look how good God is! God has given men the ministry of the church and He has given women responsibility for the rest of the world!" These women exulted in the grace of God in allowing them to be "sheep among wolves" out in the world for His sake, and they considered this command a high and holy privilege.

This book is for them.

Current trends in the Western evangelical church are alarming. When we were young church planters in sub-Saharan Africa, we were taught to measure what was called the "front door" and the "back door" of church planting. The "front door" measured how many new people came into the church. The "back door" measured how many people left the church. The goal was to end up with a positive figure; the hope was that there would be more people coming in than going out! Large losses, we were told, indicated a weakness in the area of discipleship. In the early days, we were told that a "back door" loss of, say, 20 percent was unacceptably high.

Today, that "back door" figure for the American, evangelical church hovers around 76 percent! Between the late high school years and the middle years of college, more than 72 percent of the church's young people are leaving through the "back door."[1]

This book is for them.

Even more, this book is for all of us who love the church, the beloved Bride of Christ!

The book that you hold in your hand dares to ask the questions: Are we willing to walk with Jesus in the hard places? Are we willing to live among—and to love—those who have little or no access to the gospel? This book is offered to Christians who are tired of merely being "members" of a church and who want to be "true followers" of Jesus.

Thank you for giving this book a hearing! As you read, we pray that you will hear the laughter and the joy in the background of stories which often have a tough edge to them. As you turn the pages, we pray that you will imagine families at worship in their homes, fathers baptizing their wives and children, and brothers and sisters in Christ finding joy in the high honor of suffering for Jesus.

Ultimately, this is not a book about persecutors and persecution. Instead, this is a book about Jesus. This is a book about the Body of Christ obediently carrying His love and grace to a lost and broken world. This is a book about who we can be as true followers of Jesus.

In our first book, *The Insanity of God*, we sought to answer the questions, "Why give your life to Jesus and then naturally share your story and His story across the street while also getting on a plane, taking your love for Him to the Nations?" Be assured, Jesus' story is to be vocalized while we feed the hungry, clothe the naked, heal the sick, while also being His peacemakers to the Nations.

This book, *The Insanity of Obedience*, dares to answer the questions, "What do we do after crossing the street and getting off the plane?" There will be some "do this but don't do this" in the book, but it is also a spiritual guide for experiencing the battle between the principalities and powers while squarely on the side of the Good News. Have no doubt; this is a dangerous stance to take. If you want all this life, this temporal world has to offer, put the book down. If you are determined to be defined by the Resurrection, read on.

1

Our Marching Orders

At the risk of sounding a bit "preachy," allow me a moment to restate the obvious—for what we have heard the most often might well be the very command we ignore the most. As the Gospel of Matthew comes to a crescendo, Jesus gave His followers a final word of instruction. We often refer to these words as the "Great Commission." With stark simplicity, Jesus set out the calling and the mission of those who would follow Him. "Go," He commands, "and make disciples of all nations" (Matt. 28:19). From that day until now, Jesus' followers have endeavored to fulfill that assignment. Whatever else the church takes on, it is broadly understood that both "going" and "making disciples" are essential and defining tasks. The church cannot be the church unless it is going and making disciples.

Interestingly, Jesus' final instruction was nothing new; it is utterly consistent with His overall ministry. Early on, as Jesus invited Simon and Andrew to follow Him, He explained that He would make them "fishers of men" (Mark 1:17). Later, Jesus designated twelve apostles. They were appointed "that they might be with him and that he might send them out to preach" (Mark 3:14). He called them close, and then He sent them out. Consistently, this invitation *to walk closely with* Jesus is linked with the command *to go out with* Jesus. In fact, it becomes clear that an intimate relationship with Jesus necessarily leads to a life of ministry and service and mission for **all believers**. *God is a sending God.* Repeatedly, He draws people close and then He sends them out. In the Gospels, we encounter this same pattern over and over again.

When Jesus sent His followers out, He gave explicit guidance. He also explained clearly what would happen to His followers as they obeyed Him. In Matthew 10, Jesus gave the Twelve "authority to drive out evil spirits and to heal every disease and sickness" (Matt. 10:1). He told His followers exactly what message to proclaim (v. 7). He also gave them specific instructions about their upcoming journeys (vv. 5–15).

Some of His instructions sound uncomfortable and even potentially dangerous. For these specific and short trips, Jesus told His followers to take no money as they journeyed. He told them to take no bag. He told them to take no extra clothing or shoes. Evidently, Jesus wants His followers to experience God's sufficient provision firsthand.

As challenging as some of Jesus' specific instructions were, however, what He had said to this point was downright encouraging compared to what He said next. "I am sending you out," He explained, "like sheep among wolves" (Matt. 10:16).

Like sheep among wolves. With that simple, startling phrase, Jesus defined the identity of His followers: they are like sheep. At the same time, He clarified the identity of the people they would meet in the world: they are like wolves. It is not especially difficult to ascertain what will happen to sheep in the presence of wolves. Even if we have no personal experience with either sheep or wolves, we plainly see how this scenario plays out. Frankly, it is not good to be a sheep in the presence of wolves. Sheep don't normally survive in the presence of wolves! Even so, Jesus wanted His followers to understand both their true nature and the true nature of the world in which they would journey. Jesus wanted His disciples to understand both the content of the gospel and the context in which it was to be shared. What He offered was a simple statement of fact.

And notice this: Jesus did not ask the sheep to behave like wolves, and He certainly did not suggest that the wolves would behave like sheep!

After setting this image before them, Jesus did not give His followers the opportunity to revisit their earlier commitment to Him. He did not ask them if, in the light of these new words, they *still* were serious about following Him. After all, they had already answered His call, and obedience to Him was the necessary next step. With some notable objections, His followers obeyed. They went.

And ever since, His followers have continued to go.

Jesus said plainly that He was sending His followers out "like sheep among wolves" (Matt. 10:16). Then He told them even more. He told them that they would be handed over to the local councils, flogged in the synagogues, and brought before governors and kings as witnesses. He told them that they would be arrested, betrayed, and hated (vv. 17–22). In a word, His followers would be persecuted (v. 23). Jesus made it clear that this impending persecution was not merely a possibility; for those who would obey Him, persecution is a certainty.

In response to His instructions, Jesus' followers set out on this grand and frightening adventure, and, sure enough, they experienced everything that Jesus had promised. They went out as sheep among wolves, and they experienced what sheep typically experience in the presence of wolves. Predictably, the sheep were true to their identity.

Just as predictably, the wolves were true to theirs. And the inevitable result is precisely what Jesus has promised: persecution.

If there is any possible way to do it, we generally want to relegate passages like Matthew 10 to the distant past. We want to keep passages like Matthew 10 as far as possible from our own experience. Obedience to these ancient words, in today's world, would potentially be seen as unbalanced—even insane. Especially within the church today, we might be encouraged to avoid taking Jesus' instructions too seriously.

All the same, we claim that we are utterly devoted to Scripture. With great respect, we study to understand the world of these earliest followers of Jesus. We read about their suffering and we celebrate their costly obedience to Jesus' call. Jesus clearly told His followers long ago that they would suffer, and they did suffer. We know the story of these faithful followers is true.

As true as this story of ancient persecution is, however, we long to believe that these verses are merely "history." We want very much to believe what happened to these earliest disciples is not what will happen to us. We want to believe Jesus' words in Matthew 10 do not apply to believers today—at least, not to all believers!

We desperately cling to the possibility that these hard verses do not apply to us.

But what if Matthew 10 is not merely "history"? What if Matthew 10 is a true word intended for Jesus' followers of every time—a true word intended for even our time? *What if Matthew 10 is about you and about me?* What if "sheep among wolves" is an accurate description of both our calling and our world today? What if Jesus' followers—His followers today—really are like sheep? And what if the world—the world today—really is filled with wolves?

Opening ourselves to the truth of God's Word is dangerous. Popular theologies would tell us suffering can be avoided, that there is a way to be both faithful and comfortable at the same time, that there is a way to be both obedient and safe, that persecution is the destiny of believers who live only at certain times or in certain places, that God will reward obedience with success and security. Popular theologies would tell us that, even if we are sheep, it is possible to minimize our exposure to a world filled with wolves.

God's Word—lived out in present active tense—however, tells us something very different. Jesus would have us understand that His followers—His followers long ago and His followers today—are, in fact, sheep. Jesus would have us understand that our world—our world long ago and our world today—is filled with wolves. And knowing the certain outcome of that encounter between the sheep and the wolves, Jesus would have us understand, even in this kind of a world, He fully intends to accomplish His purposes. Jesus will use these sheep to complete His great plan.

Judging by what eventually happened to Jesus Himself, we come to understand that persecution and suffering and sacrifice are necessary parts of His ultimate strategy, even today.

This book retells the story of that strategy. This book tells the story of modern-day followers of Jesus who understand what it means to live as sheep among wolves. This book tells the story of Jesus' settled intention to accomplish His purposes using unlikely things like persecution and suffering and sacrifice and martyrdom. This book is about the unlikely followers of Jesus who model the characteristics of sheep.

Jesus' instruction is compelling in its clarity. It is not a suggestion; it is a command. "Go!" He says. "I am sending you!"

But what He says next is quite a surprise: "I am sending you out like sheep among wolves."

We have the high privilege of answering Jesus' call to go. But let us be clear about this: we go on His terms, not ours. If we go at all, we go as sheep among wolves.

Why then, given that Jesus led His disciples every day to be with Him "to seek and to save what were lost" (Luke 19:10), did He feel it necessary to one more time command us with the Great Commission of Matthew 28?

Can it be that which Jesus lived and commanded the most is what we ignore obeying the most?

Today are we willing to follow Jesus to the tough places; anywhere and anytime He still commands?

More than Talking Points

- Is this command of Jesus always defined by His desire today to "seek and to save" those who are lost? Who are you seeking today?
- One enlightened brother said every Body of Christ who have a heart for the Nations needs four types of people: (1) Those who go, (2) Those who send, (3) Those who raise support for those who go, and (4) Those who welcome the Nations in their midst to their homes. Evaluate the obedience level of your church by these statements. Evaluate your commitment.

Part I
_____

God's Command to Go to the Nations

2

Where's the Parachute?

It is surely a truism to say that we are not where we thought we would be.

Though we came to faith in different ways, my wife (Ruth) and I clearly heard Jesus' command to follow Him. We took the words of Scripture at face value and we simply assumed that the Great Commission was intended for us; we heard Jesus' words of invitation and instruction personally. Through the training of denominational schools and through a variety of experiences in ministry, and because we were convinced of God's personal call for us, we prepared to serve overseas.

Our first assignment was in Malawi. There, we joyfully lived in a setting where God was visibly and dramatically at work. Our ministry involved both planting new churches and strengthening churches which had already been established. As far as we were concerned, we could have remained in Malawi for decades. Our work there felt satisfying and rewarding. We sensed that we were a part of what God was doing, and we found joy in our service.

Much to our heartbreak, however, our time in Malawi was relatively short. After debilitating struggles with malaria, we were forced to relocate. We found ourselves living in a different part of Africa, serving for several years in the Transkei, a then-black homeland within South Africa. At that time, South Africa was defined by the official policy of radical racial separation called apartheid.

During our time in Transkei, Ruth and I began a serious study of the New Testament book of Acts. We had read and studied Acts many times before. But this time, we experienced a life-altering encounter with God's Word. Individually and as a couple, we sensed a clear command from God to begin serving in a part of the world where the gospel had not yet been broadly proclaimed. With the help of our supervisors and through our own journey of prayer, we were drawn to work with the people of Somalia. We moved to the Horn of Africa and began working among the Somali people.[2]

While, as most people, we had challenges and sorrows in our lives before, nothing had prepared us for what we experienced in Somalia. For the first time in our journey, we truly lived "as sheep among wolves." For the first time we were serving as sheep among wolves—where the wolves were the vast majority. Honestly, we did not really mind being sheep among wolves. But our experience in Somalia was like flying from Kenya in a C-130 transport aircraft with a single instruction: "Jump!"

It would have been a better experience if someone had given us a parachute.

Despite our best intentions and despite years of grueling work, we experienced little in the way of spiritual success. In fact, our time in Somalia was defined by heartache, loss, and failure. Our disappointment in ministry was surpassed only by the personal losses that affected our family. Near despair, we returned to the States wondering where to turn next.

During a long and painful season of soul-searching and prayer, God placed before us the opportunity to grapple with some of our personal and professional struggles from a completely different direction. We desperately wanted to discern healthy and God-honoring ways of bearing witness to Jesus in hard places such as Somalia. That search led us to consider other hard places in the world where Jesus' followers had already been living out their faith for a long time. With significant spiritual and financial support from many different people, we began to develop a plan to sit at the feet of believers around the world who knew how to live and to thrive in settings of intense persecution. We also longed to hear the stories about believers who had died in settings of persecution. In a word, we wanted to learn about the experiences of sheep in a world filled with wolves.

Our intention was to go to these believers in persecution as learners, not teachers. Our intention was simply to listen and to learn. And that is exactly what we did.

Originally, we made a list of forty-five countries known for persecution of believers in Jesus and we began to make plans for visits. We made contacts with people in those countries. We also made contacts with people who had been forced to leave their countries because of their faith. Painstakingly, we planned travel itineraries and we arranged interviews. Traveling from country to country, we simply listened for days in each country to stories of faith and faithfulness.

Now, more than fifteen years later, we have conducted, recorded, documented, and analyzed more than six hundred personal, in-depth interviews with believers from seventy-two different countries. Interviews continue even now and the numbers of both interviews and countries visited grow month by month. Obviously, these life stories have radically changed us.

What we heard was powerful and profound. Some of what we heard was expected and predictable; some of what we heard was shocking and unexpected. Much of what we heard was almost impossible to believe. We have been horrified to learn of the cruelty that some believers have endured. We have been moved by stories of selfless sacrifice. We have been amazed by the steadfastness of God's people. And we have been reminded over and over again of God's faithfulness, grace, and power.

Through our pilgrimage, we have been challenged biblically to believe that God can use even unspeakable pain for His purposes. And we are able now to say with confidence that God uses persecution and suffering for His purposes. Exactly *why* God uses persecution and suffering is a holy mystery, but the fact that He *does* use persecution and suffering is a certainty!

Crucifixion and resurrection are central themes of the gospel story. Believers in persecution bring these themes into present active tense today as they live out their faith in harsh and horrible environments.

At the same time, we have also been able to distill lessons and truths from these hundreds of interviews, as we have reflected on them in light of our three decades of overseas service. As we listened carefully to suffering, yet victorious, believers around the world, we noticed common themes—lessons learned. At first, this surprised us. From distant corners of the globe, we realized that the same stories with biblical insights were being told. Over time, we began to connect the dots and we were able to discern crucial truths. Clearly, we still have much to learn, but we began to garner valuable insights about persecution, about the ways of God, and about how the church is planted and thrives—especially in persecution.

Admittedly, we were ill-prepared when we began our work in Somalia. While places like Somalia will always remain a challenge, what we have learned—and what we are learning—is invaluable. It is our hope and prayer that the truths of these interviews will help you as you seek to respond obediently to God's command and call in your own life.

Even further, it is our prayer that this book will help you cross the street and go to your neighbors and that it will help you cross the oceans as you journey to the Nations.

The foundation for this book has been incarnated through a workshop which we have shared with hundreds of groups all over the world these past fifteen years. As time has passed, we have done more and more interviews. Additional insights have been gained, and the material presented in the workshops has developed. The contributions of those who have attended the workshops have also been valuable; questions and comments constantly refine our thinking. This book is the result of our fifteen years of experience working with this material. We offer it here not as any kind of "final answer." Instead, we offer this as a work in progress. We also offer this material as a resource which we hope will help all of us think more clearly about Jesus' command for all of us to go and make disciples and His injunction to be "like sheep among wolves" as we do represent Him in tough places.

This book is comprised of five major sections:

Part I deals with God's command to be His people on mission and with our response to His command. Exactly who does God command to be on mission? And what kind of a response does He expect?

Part II chronicles the birth of faith within settings of persecution. Is it possible for faith to be born in settings of hostility and opposition? And, if so, how exactly does that happen?

Part III describes how faith grows from small groups of believers into succeeding generations. As faith is born, how does it then move from one family to extended families and communities?

Part IV considers the role of the overseas worker (the book of Acts calls them "sent out ones," as the word *missionary* is not found in the Bible) and matters of local leadership. What are the leadership dynamics that foster healthy growth?

Part V describes and celebrates the miracle of victorious living in settings of persecution. Is it possible for believers not merely to survive in settings of persecution, but also to thrive? And, if so, how?

The life questions we will struggle with in this book are both compelling and crucial:

- What does it really mean to follow Jesus?
- How might followers of Jesus best "go and make disciples"?
- What role do persecution and suffering play in this assignment that Jesus has given His followers?
- Is the Bible merely past history, or is it also the living, life-giving story of God's activity today?
- What would it mean to the church to have its Bible lived out in present active tense today?
- When you read that persecution for followers of God was normal in the Bible and normal today, what is your response? Do you see it as normal?

As interesting as our interviewing work has been, the ultimate goal is more than simply learning about our brothers and sisters in Christ who live in other places, often defined by persecution. Through our research, we are trying to discern some answers to key missiological and theological questions. Those are big words for "how do we get off the couch, walking and working with God, especially in the tough places?" We know that God's purpose is to extend an invitation of grace to the entire world, but we are intrigued with the significant role believers play in that divine purpose. We are seeking to discern how exactly human beings can come along with God and partner wisely in His work.

- How might believers cooperate with God as He reaches out to a broken world? Even in a world filled with persecution and suffering, is it possible for believers to work together to foster more and greater faith?
- Are we willing to admit—and then to learn from—the mistakes we, especially as Western believers, have made? (We hope that you will be able to learn from and avoid our mistakes! We have Ph.D.'s in what not to do.)
- Can we discern some specific strategies God desires to bless?
- Are there specific times or situations when persecution is most likely? And when persecution does come, how might believers respond? How *should* believers respond?
- Can we humbly learn from the examples of other, non-Western believers?
- How does the gospel spread in a predominantly Muslim, Hindu, or Buddhist context? How does the gospel spread in a communist or atheistic context?
- Is it possible in persecution for a first-generation faith to be passed on to the succeeding generations, and, if so, how exactly can that happen? Is it even possible to assist in the spread of the faith from one generation to the next?
- What vital role does baptism play in the birth and growth of the church?
- Is it possible to translate cultural expressions of the faith from one culture to another? And if so, how can that be done? Do we all have to come to Jesus in the same way, singing the same songs, or wearing the same clothes?
- Are we willing for our Bible to be read, believed, and experienced in the present active tense?
- As followers of Jesus, will we allow ourselves to be seized by both the content and the context of the New Testament?

These questions, and hundreds like them, are profoundly important. Interestingly, many believers today assume they know the answers to these important questions. This book, however, will call some of those familiar answers into question in light of what believers around the world have taught us. Based on extensive research and illustrated by anecdotal stories, this book will attempt to tell the story of what we have discovered as we have traveled the world. Believers in persecution have, indeed, been our teachers, and, here in this book, we joyfully share what we have learned from them.

With all humility, we desire to partner with God in His grace-giving work. Some of what we thought we knew to be true turns out to be exactly that; it is true. Many of our convictions have been confirmed and strengthened. But, often, we have been compelled to rethink our assumptions and reexamine our perspectives. In some cases, our assumptions were simply wrong. As God has shown us new things, we have tried to be open to His guidance.

When Ruth and I married in 1976, we heard about another couple beginning their married life together at the same time. As the story goes, the husband would often speak on the topic "How to Raise Your Children." There was only one problem: at that time, they had no children of their own! This speech was filled with all kinds of wonderful advice and insight, none of which had even been applied.

After having a few children, the speaker reworked his talk and gave it a new name: "Some Suggestions on How to Raise Your Children." In this second version, his dogmatic advice was softened to "suggestions."

A number of years later, after struggling through years of parenting, this man changed his speech once again. This time it was entitled "Feeble Hints to Fellow Strugglers."

This story represents well our pilgrimage. We offer this book to you as "feeble hints to fellow strugglers."

We are grateful to have you join us on this journey. And we invite you to sit with us at the feet of believers around the world as we ask them to tell us what they have learned about God's will and God's ways in this broken world. Even as we grapple with tough truths, we pray that we will also be able to hear the laughter in the midst of the tears, witness faith that transcends earthly sorrows, and know with assurance that if the resurrection is true, that changes everything.

Consider These Questions

- Where are you intentionally being among the "wolves"? At work, deliberately during recreation, or having families who do not know Jesus in your home?
- What percentage of your time is spent being "sheep among sheep," or as "sheep among wolves"?
- How in this world does one love wolves? Especially those who harm and slay God's lambs?

3

Did I Sleep Through This Class
in Seminary?

When we began our interviews with believers in persecution, Russia was the first destination. Over the course of several weeks, I heard marvelous testimonies of God's provision through long seasons of unspeakable suffering. Believers in Russia who told me their stories were rather matter of fact both about their pain and about God's ability to use their pain for His purposes. Often, what I heard in the stories sounded miraculous to me; the stories I heard sounded almost "biblical" to my ears.

My storytellers, however, seemed so accustomed to God's well-timed intervention they reserved the word *miraculous* for even more dramatic actions of God. They seemed completely casual about the stories they were recounting. It is not that they took God's activity for granted, because they did not. Rather, they seemed to know God so well, and God seemed so close and so real they were not surprised when He acted in very personal and needed ways.

In their understanding, God's intervention was not really miraculous; God was simply acting the way God acts! His activity was expected, natural, and completely in character. Often they reserved the word *miraculous* to describe a person's conversion.

After hearing stories like these for several weeks, I was simply amazed. As my time in Russia was drawing to a close, I found myself with a group of pastors. In light of all that I had heard, my heart and head was full.

I said to the gathered group: "There is one thing I don't understand. You have told me so many remarkable stories about what God has done. You have told me about unspeakable suffering. You have told me about grievous persecution. And you have told me about God's power to work. Why haven't you written these stories down? Why haven't you published these stories? Why haven't your stories been recorded in some way?"

The pastors seemed genuinely confused by my questions.

Finally, an older pastor took me aside. He gently took my arm and he led me to the large picture window in the home—a picture window that was facing the east.

The old pastor began by making reference to my family: "You have told us that you have some sons, Dr. Ripken."

"Yes, that's true," I responded.

"Tell me, Dr. Ripken," the pastor patiently asked, "how many times have you awakened your sons before dawn and taken them to the east-facing part of your home? How many times have you said to them, 'Boys, get ready! Look out this window, because the sun is about to come up in the east! Boys, I woke you up early today because I wanted you to see it! It's about ready to happen!' Dr. Ripken, how many times have you awakened your boys and said that to them?"

"Well, sir," I answered. "I have *never* done that. In fact, my sons would think I was crazy if I did that."

The old pastor nodded as if a profound point had been made. However, I could see no connection to our earlier conversation. I was completely baffled.

Sensing my confusion, he went on to explain, "You would never do that with your sons because the sun coming up in the east is normal and ordinary. It is an everyday event. It is expected. Well, that's the way persecution is for us. That's the way God's activity is for us. We don't write much about these things—we don't even talk much about these things—because these things are as normal as the sun coming up in the east."

It was a startling thought for me. From my perspective, persecution was something exceptional, unusual, out of the ordinary. From my perspective, persecution was a problem, and it was something to be avoided. From the perspective of my pastor friend in Russia, however, persecution was not exceptional at all. It was usual. It was ordinary. Persecution was simply to be expected for followers of Jesus. And God's ability to intervene and use persecution for His purposes was expected as well.

I was in the Ukraine a few weeks later. Once again, my heart and head was full. I had heard more stories about persecution and suffering and God's provision. Once again, I asked a similar question: "Why haven't you written these stories down? Why can't you see how dramatic and amazing these stories are? I have never heard of God doing these sorts of things before! Why haven't your stories been recorded?"

This time it was a Ukrainian pastor who took me aside. He was much more gruff than the Russian pastor had been. In response to my questions, he simply said, "Son, when did you stop reading your Bible?"

"What do you mean?" I protested.

He emphatically repeated his question: "When did you stop

reading your Bible? Everything we have told you about has already happened in God's Word. God's people have been experiencing these things for a long time, and God has been taking care of His people for a long time. Why would we write down stories that have been known and experienced by God's people for centuries? These kinds of things have been happening from the beginning. The Bible is full of stories just like our stories! When did you stop reading your Bible?" I was so embarrassed and felt so biblically inept, I could have hidden in a thimble.

Again, his perspective was so different. His perspective was so unusual. His perspective was so . . . biblical.

Most people simply assume that their view of the world is exactly the way the world is. Perhaps that perspective is simply part of the human condition. If, for example, we happen to live in a part of the world where overt persecution of believers is rare, then we assume persecution is rare. This assumption seems obvious and clear. Many of our brothers and sisters in Christ around the world, however, have a very different point of view.

One of the great struggles for followers of Jesus is to develop and embrace a biblical worldview which, in most cases, is radically different than the worldview we already have. Nowhere is this struggle more acute than when it comes to persecution.

According to Paul Marshall of Freedom House, 80 percent of the world's believers *who are practicing their faith* live in persecution.[3] Before offering this shocking statistic, Marshall goes to great lengths to define what he means by "believers." It turns out that he is talking about people who would not only use the word "Christian" to define themselves, but specifically about people who have a genuine relationship with Jesus. Marshall is talking about people who consider themselves to be "born again," people for whom faith in Jesus is formative in life. Using that definition of a believer, Marshall claims that 80 percent of the world's believers live in persecution.

If his claim is even close to the truth, then we are compelled to rethink our definition of "normal." If 80 percent of a group experiences something, then perhaps what they are experiencing is normal. According to the Bible, persecution is normal, simply a natural byproduct of faith. Much to our surprise, today's world reflects this precise biblical perspective of persecution.

Marshall's statistic continues to be debated in mission and advocacy circles, but it certainly fits the story we encounter in the book of Acts. In fully half of the chapters in Acts, we find believers either in jail for their faith or experiencing intense pressure for expressing their faith openly. In the world of Acts, suffering for the faith is neither exceptional nor unusual. If anything, persecution appears to be both normal and expected.

Generally speaking, persecution increases as people respond more and more to the activity of God, which is precisely what we find happening in the book of Acts. It is also what we find happening in many parts of the world today.

Quite simply, as people come into relationship with Jesus, persecution follows. Our interviews suggest that *access* to the gospel, by itself, is not a direct correlate of increased persecution. The clearest predictor of persecution is *response* to the gospel. Often, of course, response to the gospel increases with greater access, but access, by itself, does not necessarily lead to increased persecution. What leads to greater persecution is, typically, greater response.

That might seem to be an obvious point, but it leads to an intriguing observation. If our goal were simply to reduce persecution, that could easily be done. The way to reduce persecution—or the way to eliminate persecution completely—is simply to keep people from coming into relationship with Jesus. If our goal were simply to stop persecution, then followers of Jesus could accomplish that goal easily and quickly by refusing to share Jesus—by refusing to live as sheep among wolves.

Obviously, that is something that we are not willing to do!

Hopefully, believers are not willing to stop sharing their faith. Even so, this is a good reminder that the primary cause of persecution is people coming into relationship with Jesus. Perhaps it is good to be reminded that, given our calling and our mission, the reduction (or elimination) of persecution is not our ultimate goal.

Jesus, clearly, has a different point of view. Jesus' ultimate priority for His followers is the sharing of the good news of grace. As the good news is shared, Jesus assures us that persecution will come. The goal, therefore, is not to reduce or eliminate persecution, but to see persecution the way that Jesus sees it. And Jesus sees persecution as an inevitable result of the obedience of His followers. According to Jesus, faithful obedience, in every case, will *cause* persecution. Generally, the greater the response to the activity of God, the greater the persecution.

It is often hard for us to see things in different ways, but both God's Word and the testimony of believers around the world would tell us that persecution is normal. Persecution is fully expected by Jesus. And persecution can (somehow) be used for His purposes. Sheep living among wolves may, in fact, be slaughtered, but those slaughtered sheep may also (by God's grace) be used to accomplish holy purposes. These are mysteries worthy of our consideration.

Persecution itself is difficult to understand. It seems obvious, in fact, to assume that any threat or intimidation or attack is technically "persecution," but it is not always that simple. In Somalia, we discovered that there were many kinds of *apparent* persecution that had very little to do with Jesus. For example, believers in Somalia were often attacked because of their association with Westerners (specifically, Western Christians). Believers were killed because of who they worked for or because of the outsiders with whom they worshipped. Persecution soared when local people were found in possession of literate religious materials, even though they were typically unable to read. It is heartbreaking to recall the Somali believers who were killed because Westerners had employed them to evangelize their own people and had taught them to use Western modes of evangelism. As tragic as those attacks were, these causes for persecution are quite different than actually being persecuted "for Jesus' sake." It is important to define what persecution for Jesus' sake entails and what persecution for other, secondary reasons is. All believers, Western and local, need to make sure that when persecution arrives, it is for Jesus' sake.

To be painfully frank, being persecuted for Nik is not the same as being persecuted for Jesus. It was a costly lesson to learn, but we came to understand that when believers were persecuted for secondary reasons, we would never again choose to participate in the practices which precipitated such a secondary persecution!

Workers from the West should strive to create the best possible spiritual environment and foster the growth of a believing community *before* serious persecution arrives. In the setting of a believing community, persecution can glorify God, strengthen believers, and validate the gospel. In fact, when those who are outside the kingdom of God witness believers who are willing to suffer and die for their faith, they are attracted to God who is the "author and finisher" of our faith. In that context, the end result can be a significant increase in both people coming to faith and multiple bodies of Christ being birthed. But those good results can happen only within the context of a believing community.

In the face of persecution, several different responses are possible. In our interviews, we identified a progression of faith responses as people described their persecution experiences and their reactions to their persecutors.

"God, save us!" This is often the initial and normal response to persecution. Understandably, a suffering believer would think first of personal survival. Predictably, a suffering believer would ask for God's

help. Practical prayers for rescue are common. The first response to persecution is often, "God, save us!"

"God, judge them!" Again, this is a typical and frequent response to persecution. Based on God's commitment to justice, this prayer acknowledges both God's awareness of what is happening and His ability to make things right. The believer in persecution would almost naturally ask for God's judgment on the persecutors: "God, judge those who are persecuting me! God, may Your judgment come upon them!"

There is certainly nothing wrong with these first two prayers. They are natural and normal responses. Spiritually, problems arise when we limit ourselves to these first two responses, when we get stuck within these two prayers and refuse to grow spiritually. Many organizations who report on persecution focus on the rescue of believers in persecution and the punishment of the persecutors. We suggest, despite these normal (human?) focuses, there are deeper truths to be discovered within persecution.

If we allow ourselves to grow in Christ through persecution, we will come to pray this next prayer.

"God, forgive them!" Echoing Jesus' words on the cross, this next and deeper level of response signals a shift in the heart of the believer being persecuted. The desire for personal survival and even the hope for justice move into the background. In keeping with Jesus' teaching in the Sermon on the Mount, the suffering believer begins to pray for his or her persecutors (Matt. 5:44). The suffering believer, very much like Christ, prays for the persecutors to be forgiven: "Father, forgive them, for they do not know what they are doing" (Luke 23:34).

Four of my dear friends, all Somali believers, were killed on the same day. These murders were planned and deliberate. These children of God were slaughtered in less than an hour. Their murderers hid their bodies in order to deny them a proper burial. I remember walking through the rubble of Mogadishu after these events, having asked my guards to stay a few yards behind me. I was broken and angry as I cried out to God. These were my words: "God, it is time for You to bring judgment on these people. They are killing the people who love You and cherish Jesus. There is not a person in Somalia deserving of the blood of Jesus!"

In the emotion of that moment, I heard the voice of God clearly. He said, "Neither do you, Nik. You are not deserving of the blood of Jesus either. Even while you were a sinner, Christ died for you" (see Rom. 5:8). I argued with God. I told God that I was offended that He would compare the condition of my soul to those of these persecutors! Yet the Holy Spirit told me that it was a fair comparison. The Holy Spirit reminded me of the generations of my family with access to the gospel of Jesus Christ. The Spirit reminded me that Somalis had not had that opportunity and that, even now, they had no real choice to say yes or no to Jesus.

"God, forgive us as we forgive others!" Living out these challenging words from the Lord's Prayer, the suffering believer comes to understand that there is a theological connection between his or her own personal sin and the sin of the persecutor. A profound and personal awareness of God's forgiveness results in a heart that is willing to extend His same forgiveness to others. The suffering believer dares to ask God for the kind of forgiveness the believer is willing to extend to others.

This is an immensely difficult prayer to pray. Unless we are willing to extend a radical and free forgiveness to others, this, in fact, is a frightening thing to pray. In our interviews, we met believers who were willing to extend startling forgiveness to their oppressors and then humbly pray, "Lord God, forgive me in the same way that I have forgiven my persecutors."

"God, glorify Your name!" In this final level of response, the believer in suffering acknowledges exactly what Jesus has promised—that God can use even persecution for His purposes. What becomes

most important is not the personal circumstance of suffering or even God's judgment of the persecutor, but the ultimate outcome that is made possible and assured by God.

In the face of persecution, this is a radical—and biblical—prayer to pray! We might think again of Jesus on the cross and recall His conviction that the Father would use even the grievous pain of the cross for ultimate good. The suffering believer is drawn into this mystery and prays that God would somehow be glorified *even in and* *through the persecution.*

There is an additional truth embedded in this last prayer. This last prayer highlights the believer's responsibility to glorify God regardless of the setting or environment. Sometimes, we act as though we can bring glory to God only when the circumstances are right or, perhaps, only when we live in a setting of political or religious liberty. **This final prayer, however, reminds us that believers can choose to glorify God regardless of their setting.** Suffering believers told us plainly about their commitment to glorify God even in environments of severe persecution.

No one, of course, should seek persecution. It is one thing to believe that God can use suffering for His purposes; it is another thing altogether to seek suffering for its own sake. The lesson here is *not* that any believer should seek persecution. Even if we are rightly convinced that God can use persecution for His purposes, we would be wrong to seek it on our own. When persecution does come, however, believers are certain that God can use it. Seeking persecution is evidence of psychological instability, and that should be immediately addressed. A healthy understanding of persecution, on the other hand, leads to a confident trust in God to use it for His purposes.

In sum, persecution is not necessarily good or bad; it simply is. How believers respond to persecution gives it its value, and that response also determines whether or not persecution leads to a meaningful result.

One does not run away from persecution due to fear, nor does one run toward persecution due to pride or psychological imbalance.

Believers also understand that persecution, when it comes, needs to come for the right reasons. By way of illustration, the Twelve in Matthew 10 were assured of persecution, but they were also assured that persecution would come *because* they were bearing bold witnesses to Jesus, and not because of any lesser cause. As we noted before, the easiest way to avoid persecution is to be silent with our faith, but that is not a choice that we can make without denying Jesus' hold on our lives. So we are left with a clear choice: we can be faithful to our calling and deal with the persecution that will inevitably come or we can avoid persecution by ignoring or disobeying Jesus' instructions to go and make disciples.

Quite simply, obedience will result in persecution. Persecution can be avoided only if we are disobedient and we fail to cross the street or cross the oceans. The choice is frightening in its clarity. At the same time, the choice is one that every believer must make. The hope that we can somehow be obedient *and* avoid persecution is a naïve and misplaced hope.

These are the truths that we are learning from our suffering brothers and sisters around the world. For us, these were often startling truths and new lessons; for those who had lived with persecution for a long time, these were simply the ways of the world.

As we struggled to understand the persecutors and persecution, we were led to a greater comprehension of the nature of good and evil. Representing the forces of evil, Satan strives to deny entire people groups and nations access to Jesus. *It became clear in our interviews that the ultimate goal of the persecutors is always to deny people access to Jesus,* and our interviews indicated that persecutors would do whatever was necessary to reach that goal.

Persecutors seek to deny human beings the two great spiritual opportunities: first, access to Jesus and, second, opportunity for witness. Choosing Jesus as Lord and Savior and then sharing His love and grace with others is the clearest way to stand against and oppose evil.

As strange (and as horrifying) as it sounds, we came to realize that believers could be unwittingly complicity with the persecutors by simply refusing to share their faith. Just like persecution, the refusal to share the faith denies people access to Jesus. It was a startling thought to realize that the persecutor's use of violence to inhibit the faith and the believer's refusal to speak openly of Jesus yield the same result. In both cases, *people are denied access to Jesus.* How tragic that the silence of believers could yield the same result as the violence of persecutors! On the other hand, when we share our faith boldly and refuse to silence our witness, we are powerfully identifying with believers in persecution.

When we witness to the resurrection of Jesus Christ, we identify with those in chains. When we refuse to witness, we identify with those who place the chains on followers of Jesus.

With which group do we wish to identify?

Most people, of course, would assume that reducing persecution is a worthy goal. That seems like common sense. However, our interviews told us something quite different. On the one hand, persecution decreases as people stop coming into relationship with Jesus. Obviously, believers cannot stop sharing their faith, even if that choice would reduce persecution. On the other hand, God has assured us that He can use even persecution for His purposes.

In the Old Testament book of Genesis, Joseph is put in prison. He is imprisoned unfairly. If we had any say in the matter, we would likely rescue Joseph from jail, and we would likely insist on that rescue happening quickly. In fact, we would probably insist on that rescue happening immediately. In today's world, we might petition governments and international entities to assist in the rescue of this brother or sister wrongly accused and in prison.

In the Genesis story, however, God is content to leave Joseph in jail for a long time. Somehow, God gives purpose to this time of suffering in Joseph's life. Our typical assumption is that the highest goal would be to lessen Joseph's suffering, to reduce his time in prison, and to put an end to his persecution. The astute biblical question is, "How do we know when to leave Joseph in jail?" To have politically or militarily delivered Joseph from Pharaoh's prison prematurely would be contributing to the starvation of both the Jews and the Egyptians. Dare we suggest God uses persecution for the deliverance of both believers and nonbelievers!

God, however, seems to have a very different agenda. Imagine how the Bible story would change if Joseph had been rescued from prison before he had the opportunity to interpret Pharaoh's dreams. In light of the story we encounter in Genesis and in contrast to the alternative story that we might imagine, we are compelled to wonder if it is possible that God has a higher purpose than lessening Joseph's suffering. And as we think of suffering believers today, we are compelled to wonder if it is possible that God may have a higher purpose than lessening the suffering of these persecuted believers.

Believers in persecution remind us of a possible lie inherent in Western Christian cultures. We sometimes thank God that we live in countries where we are "free to worship." It is interesting that public prayers are rarely uttered thanking God that we are "free to witness"! Significantly, witnessing to the death and resurrection of Jesus Christ has little to do with political freedom. Believers are as free to share Jesus in Saudi Arabia as they are in St. Louis. Believers are as free to share Jesus in Somalia as they are in Kentucky.

Being a witness for Jesus has little to do with political freedom. On the contrary, our willingness to witness has everything to do with obedience and courage.

We can easily convince ourselves that being a positive witness for Jesus is a matter of political freedom. In truth, however, being a positive witness for Jesus is a simple matter of obedience and courage. Our witness may, in fact, result in persecution—but we always have the freedom to share even when there are negative (and perhaps devastating) consequences to that sharing.

When persecution does come, the reaction from both individuals and organizations is fairly uniform. Most believers are drawn to five specific responses.

First, we want the persecution to stop. In fact, this might be our first and greatest hope. This response is so obvious that even calling it into question seems ridiculous. The assumption is that persecution is a "bad thing," and we simply want it to end. So we pray for persecution to end and we work for persecution to end.

Second, we are inclined to rescue the persecuted. We want to remove them from harm and to put them in a safe place. We might even want to ensure their safety by extracting them to another country. Again, this often seems like a completely obvious response. The assumption, again, is almost beyond question: if I care about someone, then I want that person protected from harm. According to Scripture, strategic extraction *can* be an appropriate step, but not in most cases. For example, through a vision, God led Joseph to take the young Jesus to Egypt for a season. Then in a second vision, God led Joseph to take the child Jesus back to His own homeland. Sometime later, Jesus Himself gave instructions to His followers and suggested that sometimes they should flee to other towns and cities. Extraction, when it did happen, was to be strategic. At the same time, extraction was not always the proper response. Rescuing and church planting are not the same goals.

Third, we desire that the persecutors be punished. Once again, this is a response that most people would barely question. We assume that, since persecution is evil, it deserves to be punished. We have been in numerous meetings led by well-known Western Christians that have focused on a call for military intervention on behalf of believers in persecution. Our commitment to stop persecution and punish "the bad guys" likely says more about the condition of our own hearts than about the needs of believers in settings of suffering.

Fourth, we tend to believe that Western forms of democracy and the concomitant civil rights will usher in the kingdom of God and create an environment where persecution will simply not happen anymore. We tend to believe that spiritual brokenness can be healed through political means. Wars have been fought—and continue to be fought—based on the belief that Western styles of government and the kingdom of God are, essentially, synonymous. This is a dangerous, nonbiblical assumption.

Fifth, we tend to focus on raising financial support so that believers in persecution might be rescued and helped. Interestingly, we tend to rely on the power of financial resources to accomplish the highest goals and aims of both individual believers and mission organizations.

All five of these responses are perfectly normal. They all "make human sense." These are all common responses to persecution at both personal and organizational levels. In fact, these responses are so normal and so common that they are almost beyond question.

Significantly, however, all five of these responses fail on biblical grounds.

First, Jesus has clearly told us that persecution is normal and expected. The only way to stop persecution, in fact, is to be disobedient to His call. How can we pray that persecution will stop when the only way to stop persecution is by refusing to share Jesus and keeping people from coming to Jesus as their Lord and Savior? How can we pray for persecution to stop when Jesus has told us that it is an inevitable and unavoidable result of obedient witness? Working to stop something that Jesus told us would happen—or praying for it not to happen—puts us in a strange place!

Second, is it possible that God has purposes that are tied to the suffering of His people? To put it simply, as attractive as extraction might sound, is it possible that Joseph should be left in jail? In our desire to be helpful, could we find ourselves working against the ultimate purposes of God?

Third, how does our desire that the persecutors be punished fit with Jesus' clear instruction to love our enemies and to pray for those who persecute us? Persecuted believers in China have told us time and time again that being in prison was a tremendous evangelistic opportunity. Churches were started among prisoners. Beyond that, persecutors often encountered the grace of God through the witness of imprisoned believers. Suffering believers did not pray that their persecutors would be punished; they prayed that their persecutors would come to experience God's grace! Persecuted believers discovered that the best way to deal with persecutors and to stop their persecution was *to pray and witness so that their persecutors would become brothers and sisters in Christ!*

Fourth, as much as we might cherish Western, democratic forms of government, it is humbling to know that the vast majority of movements toward Christ today are in countries and among people groups where persecution abounds. There is less kingdom growth in the Western, democratic, and so-called "Christian" countries today. The horrible fact is, in almost every Western environment Christianity is in decline.

Fifth, while we must find creative ways to stand with our brothers and sisters who are in settings of persecution, our primary way of identifying with them is by being consistent witnesses in our own environments. *It is impossible to replace witness with money.* We identify with those in chains for their witness by sharing Jesus in our own particular environment. We identify with their persecutors by keeping

Jesus to ourselves. Financial resources will never replace the faithful witness of God's people

As noted above, many suffering believers told us that the best response to persecution is to work for the salvation of the persecutors. In salvation, they explained, persecutors will cease to be persecutors and they will become brothers and sisters in Christ! For these suffering believers, the goal was not the punishment but the salvation of their persecutors.

Typically, we want the persecution to stop.

Typically, we want suffering believers to be rescued.

Typically, we want the persecutors to be punished.

Typically, we equate Western forms of democracy with the kingdom of God.

Typically, we try to do with money what we should do with witness.

And in those perfectly normal responses, we can find ourselves out of step with the purposes and plans of God.

Much to our surprise, believers in persecution did not ask us to pray that their persecution would cease. *Instead, they begged us to pray that they would be obedient through their suffering.* And that is a very different prayer.

More Hard Questions for Discussion

- Perhaps this is a brand new thought, but is it possible that persecution is simply the normal way of living for those who choose to follow Jesus? And, then, is it possible that God can bring some greater purpose out of suffering and persecution?
- Perhaps the crucial question is not: How can I keep persecution from happening? Perhaps this is a better question: Why am *I* not being persecuted? If Jesus said that His followers should expect persecution, then why am I not being persecuted?

- What if the worst persecution today was having little or no access to Jesus? Am I a persecutor when I keep my faith to myself, only within the environment of the church?
- Why is there little persecution in the West?

We would be wise to think on these things, and we would be wise to pay careful attention to what Jesus said.

4

Defining the Conversation

Let's take a few moments to define our conversation. Several foundational truths have already surfaced in our discussion, but it would be helpful to highlight them specifically.

First, according to Scripture, persecution is normal. Believers who live in contexts where persecution is rare find this truth to be startling and unsettling. But both the testimony of Scripture and the witness of believers around the world claim that persecution is the expected and inevitable result of people coming to faith in Jesus. That was certainly true in New Testament times. It is equally true today.

Second, persecution happens because people give their lives to Jesus. This is the primary cause of persecution. This does not, of course, excuse the actions of the persecutors. Yet it must be remembered that persecution is a by-product of faith!

Third, believers who respond faithfully to Jesus' call to go and make disciples will precipitate persecution, suffering, and martyrdom.

These results, of course, are not specifically desired. And these results are not to be sought. One does not run toward (or away from) persecution. Believers do not intentionally set out to make things hard for themselves or for others. All the same, sharing our faith necessarily results in persecution, suffering, and martyrdom for ourselves and/or for others. Even in suffering, our focus is not on the persecutor and persecution; rather, our focus is on Jesus and on witness. What moves us forward is the joy of seeing lives and families transformed.

Each generation of believers must determine when to leave Joseph in Pharaoh's prison, even when it might be in our power to gain his release. Serving Jesus today, as in New Testament times, requires spiritual insight, psychological strength, and godly wisdom.

Often, when believers think about sharing their faith, they think about opposition to the message that is shared. In the sharing of the faith, believers might fear rejection and ridicule and argument. And those might all be very real fears; those things might, in fact, happen when we share our faith. What we do not often consider, however, is the hardship that is certain to come *when the message is received!*

If we listen carefully to Jesus' own words, we are compelled to consider that cost as well. According to Scripture, persecution is perfectly normal, and it is the inevitable result of faithful witness. Clearly, there is a high cost for not sharing our faith: there is an eternal consequence for those who have never heard. At the same time, there is a high cost for sharing our faith as well! The inevitable result of bold witness is persecution. While we simply cannot choose to remain silent, we cannot ignore the high cost of witness either.

At the same time, here is another truth to consider. Most of the peoples of the earth who have little or no access to Jesus essentially live in an Old Testament environment. Because they do not currently have access to Jesus, they are already suffering! These people are already living under oppressive governments. Lot's story within Sodom and Gomorrah is their story. In a sense, Job's story is a common story for those living today in Old Testament-like environments. They are already hostage to religious systems that offer little in the way of love and hope in this life, let alone in the life to come. When these people do become followers of Jesus and experience hard times for the sake of the gospel, their response is often one of joy. They were suffering before they met Jesus; now, at least, their suffering has been given meaning!

Western readers can barely imagine what it is like to go from the Old Testament to the New Testament in one generation through a relationship with Jesus Christ! Imagine getting on an airplane in the New Testament and getting off a plane in the Old Testament.

For the sake of clarity, let's define some of our key words.

Persecution is a negative reaction to the incarnate presence of Jesus among His people. This negative reaction can take many forms and it can come from many different sources. Persecution can come from society as a whole, from the government, from an ideological entity, or from families and individuals. Persecution may be overt (open) or covert (hidden). It can be physical or psychological. Persecution can be actual or merely threatened. Regardless of its form, however, the ultimate goal of persecution is to silence witness. At its worst, persecution denies people access to Jesus.

Now, in truth, that ultimate goal of denying people access to Jesus is not always expressly understood even by the persecutors. Persecutors might simply be concerned about order or control. If we were in a position to ask the persecutors to explain what they were doing, they might talk about the need to control dangerous movements or the need to keep new ideas in check. Their specific concerns might be political or economic. Their *expressed* intentions, however, may not tell the whole story. It is quite possible for the actions of the persecutors to embody a larger purpose—an evil purpose that they might not even understand themselves.

Scripture is quick to identify an Evil One who opposes the purposes of God. Whether or not persecutors can articulate the spiritual dimension of their attacks, it is clear that this Evil One ultimately desires to use persecution to silence witness and to deny people access to Jesus. And the Evil One can use the actions of the persecutors for that purpose even if they do not fully understand the spiritual dimension of their behavior.

In chapter two, we hinted at the multiple definitions of the word *Christian*. Paul Marshall is helpful at this point. First, he points out that the word *Christian* can be used in a variety of ways. It is not always easy to differentiate between the various definitions, but the categories that Marshall proposes are extremely helpful.[4]

Census Christians are people who, if asked about their religion, would say, "Christian." This designation might not relate at all to anything that these people believe or practice. Often, this is a cultural answer. If asked about their religion in certain geographic areas, for example, many people might answer, "Of course I'm a Christian. Isn't everybody?" These people, according to Marshall, are "census Christians." On a census, these people would check the "Christian" box. What that designation actually means is anybody's guess.

Member Christians claim some sort of identification with a particular Christian institution or organization. Again, this does not mean that these people necessarily participate or even that they show up at their church. These people simply have some sort of personal connection with a church and they identify themselves with that church. They might say, "I am Catholic," or "I am Baptist," or "I am Methodist."

Practicing Christians actually participate in the life of a church. They typically attend worship services. In some fashion, these people are involved in the forms and rituals of the faith. Often their connection with the church is limited to weddings, baptisms, and funerals.

Believers (or Committed Believers) are people for whom the Christian faith is central and shaping. These Christians strive to live out their faith and communicate their faith to others. To use the language of the evangelical world, these people have a personal relationship with Jesus. Often they will use the language of John 3 and talk about being "born again."

Hidden Christians are people who believe secretly. Fearful of persecution, these people keep their faith to themselves. In some settings, these believers might keep their faith secret from government officials and employers. In other settings, they might keep their faith secret from even family members and friends. These believers might not even experience specific acts of outward persecution, but the fear of persecution has caused their faith to be completely inward. For the most part, their faith, though real, is hidden. In most cases, they have not "joined" a church, though this might be an artificial measurement since, in many settings, there is no official institutional church to join.

In this book, when we speak of "believers" or "Christians" or "followers of Jesus," we will generally be using Paul Marshall's fourth and fifth definitions: the people he refers to as "believers" or "committed believers" and the people he calls "hidden Christians." We are speaking of people who know who Jesus is and people for whom the Christian faith is central and shaping. In our research we use these last two definitions for our use of who is considered a Christian, a follower of Jesus.

Importantly, when Paul Marshall claims that 80 percent of the world's believers are living in persecution, he is focusing that statistic on his last two categories. The kind of persecution that he refers to happens specifically because Christians are true followers of Jesus and not for some other reason.

Not all persecution ends in death. Some does, however. The word *martyr* describes those who have died for their faith as believers. Missiologists David Barrett and Todd Johnson claim that over the past twenty centuries of the Christian faith, some seventy million believers have been murdered for their faith and can rightly be called martyrs.[5] Barrett and Johnson further claim that currently more than four hundred believers are killed every day for their faith. Our research cannot verify but a one-digit percentage of this large number. While there is significant debate about the accuracy of these numbers, the definition of *martyr* that Barrett and Johnson use is helpful for our discussion.

Their basic definition is that Christian martyrs are "believers in Christ who have lost their lives prematurely, in situations of witness, as a result of human hostility."[6] This definition has five essential and distinct components:

1. *Believers in Christ:* Barrett and Johnson include the entire "Christian" community in this grouping. This broad category includes professing Christians, crypto-Christians (hidden Christians), affiliated Christians, and unaffiliated Christians. Using this extremely broad definition of "Christian," Barrett and Johnson claim that there are two billion Christians in the world today. Using the same definition, they claim that since the time of Christ, over 8.3 billion people have believed in Christ. Our research leads us to question the use of this broad definition of "Christian," and our research also leads us to a much more limited view of martyrdom.

2. *Lost their lives:* The Christians numbered among the martyrs have actually been put to death. There are many levels of persecution, but martyrdom results in death.

3. *Prematurely:* For Barrett and Johnson, this word is important. Martyrdom, they point out, is sudden, abrupt, unexpected, and unwanted. It is a death that happens before it "should" happen; it is, in that sense, premature. Had martyrdom not

happened, these people would have lived longer. All the same, "premature" is a troubling phrase. In the teaching of our workshop, we typically ask the question: "What death would not be considered 'premature'?"

4. *In situations of witness:* By definition, the word *martyr* suggests the idea of witness. In traditional usage, a martyr is a person who bears witness to Christ in his or her own death. A "situation of witness," however, is not necessarily public testimony or proclamation. A "situation of witness" can also refer to a lifestyle of witness or simply a way of life. According to Barrett and Johnson, this way of living, with or without a verbal testimony, can comprise a situation of witness. In a telephone interview with Dr. Barrett, he indicated that a "situation of witness" would necessarily include some form of testimony to the resurrection of Jesus Christ.

5. *As a result of human hostility:* The martyr's death, according to Barrett and Johnson, happens at the hand of a persecutor. A human being is involved in the martyrdom.

In addition to these five essential elements, we would add that *the witness of the martyr stands the test of time.* That means at least two things. First, the martyr's way of living will not later be revealed to be untrue or inauthentic. As people look back and consider the life of the believer who has died, they will see that there was, in fact, true belief. Second, whether we can measure it or not, the death will serve as testimony. The death will encourage and even bear fruit, and it will do those things over time. There will be evangelistic impact in the setting where the martyrdom takes place, within the group that sent out the believer, or in both settings.

While these definitions and clarifications are helpful, it is important to note that there are substantial questions about the number of martyrs reported by organizations year after year. If we use Paul Marshall's fourth and fifth definitions of Christian—meaning those who publicly profess Christ and share their faith with others—*we can find no substantial evidence to support the claims of popular publications today that point to hundreds of thousands of martyrs annually.*

In fact, when we have asked these publications for documentation and support for their claims, and for lists of countries where these deaths are taking place, we have received no answers. In a typical year, references are made to "150,000 plus martyrs." But we have been unable to find evidence to support that claim. So while the persecution of followers of Christ is rampant, martyrdom is not. Our desire here is not to cause dissension within the family of God, but it appears to us that this kind of unsubstantiated claim keeps our focus on the acts of the persecutors and prevents us from talking about how our own lack of witness denies millions of people access to Jesus.

Several other words are important for our discussion. Volumes have been written concerning each of these words. Our intent here is to briefly capture the essence of these important words within environments of persecution.

Church is the called-out, baptized, gathered-together people of God. Church will be defined by community-belonging, it will act on Jesus' call to be people on mission, it will reproduce itself (which will result in both new believers and new communities of faith), it will finance itself, it will provide care and support for those who make up the church, and it will choose its own leaders and polity. The categories and activities highlighted in Acts 2 are a helpful guide: a church will be committed to worship (usually inside of homes), and missions which lead to a fulfilling of the Great Commission from across the street to the ends of the earth. Though quite Western terms, church includes fellowship, education, and a lifestyle of discipleship which is an interchangeable term with evangelism. When did Jesus disciple His disciples and when did He evangelize them?

A ***house church*** is typically a small body of ten to thirty believers who meet together in homes. Organization of house churches can vary significantly, but leadership is normally fluid and adaptable. When a house church grows to be a certain size, it will typically divide into smaller groups. House churches were the norm in New Testament times, and they are the norm in many settings today.

Unengaged and unreached peoples are those who have little or no access to the gospel. They are typically unreached not because they have rejected the gospel, but because they have had little or no access to it. These people number in the hundreds of millions. Typically, there are no gospel workers among them. They have no Bible or Bible portions, and no "*JESUS* film." In general, their access to the Good News is almost nonexistent.

Missionary is not a Bible word, but it is a word that has come to define the response to Jesus' command to go out with His message. A missionary or a *missionary group* is an individual, a family, or a team committed to proclaiming the gospel. In this book we will occasionally use this nonbiblical (but popularized) word to describe a person who proclaims the gospel to people who have never heard and people who have little chance of hearing. Often workers who share their faith are required to learn other languages and cross cultures; often, that is required even in our home countries. In general, we will avoid using the word *missionary* in this book. Instead, we will typically substitute the words "worker," "sent out one," or "overseas worker."

The root idea of "mission" is the sending activity of God. In one sense, certainly, Jesus sends His followers to their families and friends and neighbors. In a deeper sense, however, Jesus ultimately sends His followers to proclaim His grace throughout the entire world, starting in Jerusalem through Judea, on to Samaria and then to all the people groups, especially in places where His grace has not yet been proclaimed. Scripture is clear in helping us understand that, in this sense, *every believer is a sent out one.* The command to be on mission is a command common to every follower of Jesus. It is a command to be both local and global.

A *church planting movement* (CPM) is a rapid and exponential increase of indigenous churches. These churches are, by definition, planting new churches. In turn, these new churches are planting even more new churches. The growth in a CPM is exponential. Exponential growth ($2 \times 2 = 4$; $4 \times 4 = 16$) contrasts with incremental growth ($1 + 1 = 2$; $2 + 1 = 3$).[7]

Throughout this book, we will make reference to various people groups in relation to their culture of origin.

Muslim Background Believers are followers of Jesus who live in (or who have come out of) a predominantly Muslim context. We will refer to them as MBBs.

Hindu Background Believers are followers of Jesus who live in (or who have come out of) a predominantly Hindu context. We will refer to them as HBBs.

Buddhist Background Believers are followers of Jesus who live in (or who have come out of) a predominantly Buddhist context. We will refer to them as BBBs.

Christian Background Believers are followers of Jesus who live in (or who have come out of) a predominantly historical Christian context. We will refer to them as CBBs. Many CBBs, for instance, predate Islam in many Islamic countries.

Other terms and identifications will be defined as we use them, but these preliminary words are crucial for our discussion, and they will be used throughout the book.

Thinking Together

- Can you imagine the Old Testament being present today? Where in your city might it be? What would it be like to exit a plane into an Old Testament-like environment?

- Can you imagine experiencing church without a church building? If house churches are the New Testament norm, what may God be saying to us?
- How would you define faith and church quickly and clearly to a nonbeliever?

5

The Need for Willing
and Tough Workers

Despite the significant effort of believers to share their faith, hundreds of millions of people in our world today remain unreached, and many are unengaged with the gospel. As we move further into our study, it is helpful to consider some of the obstacles that stand in the way of a viable witness to those who have never heard of Jesus. To put it plainly, these are obstacles that keep hundreds of millions of souls unreached.

In response to Jesus' command to share His grace with the whole world, many believers have obeyed His initial command to "Go." As we will see later in our study, "going" is easier than "staying." Often, the challenge is not merely to go, but to develop a viable long-term Christlike presence among those who have yet to hear the gospel clearly. What is required of us is not a casual or temporary response to Christ's command, but a radical lifelong commitment. The result of that kind of commitment is the gospel taking root deeply within the host culture, wherever it may reside.

What are some of the obstacles that might keep the gospel from taking root in a host culture?

1. Preoccupation with a Spiritual Harvest

The New Testament word for evangelism conveys the activity of "telling" or "proclaiming." Somewhere along the line, well-meaning believers added to that basic instruction the seemingly mandatory element of *harvest*. Obedient proclamation was seen as the necessary first step. Then, added to that first step was a measurable result to the proclamation. Some kind of spiritual harvest was both expected and required. It was not enough simply to proclaim the gospel; a measurable response to the gospel was expected. That measurable response allowed workers to evaluate their efforts and to demonstrate success. Some kind of a measurable spiritual harvest was needed.

While a spiritual harvest is greatly to be desired, we would be wise to remind ourselves of the difference between what God requires of us (obedience) and what God Himself might or might not grant (results that human beings can see and measure; what we might call a spiritual harvest). The task of the believer is simply to share the gospel so that all peoples have an opportunity to hear the Good News. The believer's task is to be part of a community who baptize and disciple those whom God brings to faith. Beyond that, believers are compelled to leave results in God's hands.

Our task remains to provide access to Jesus to all men and women, boys and girls from every people group. This access includes the opportunity to hear the gospel, to understand, to believe, to be baptized, and to be gathered into house churches.

If we expect (or even demand) a spiritual harvest, then we will be inclined to gravitate toward places where response to the gospel is more likely or to places where response is already happening. At the same time, we will likely avoid places where response to the gospel is less likely. These tendencies will clearly result in the unengaged and unreached people remaining unengaged and unreached.

Astoundingly, the vast majority of overseas workers today reside in environments which are already defined as "Christian" and therefore have a significant believing witness.

A harvest mentality affects churches and sending agencies as well as overseas workers. Two of our colleagues from Kenya visited the same church while they were stateside. One of the workers serves among a fairly responsive people group; the other worker serves with Somalis. They lived in the same city.

In his report to the church, the first worker described significant numbers of people who were being converted. He talked about churches that were being planted, and he shared that these new churches were already planting additional churches.

The second worker, in his report, explained that he had seen only one Somali man accept Jesus. At the same time, he sadly shared that he was aware of three other "seekers" who had recently returned to Islam.

It is not hard to imagine which worker received additional financial support from the church that year! In general, believers desire to see a harvest and, sadly, we often connect a visible harvest with the faithfulness of overseas workers. In other words, we simply assume that workers who work hard, pray hard, and do a good job will produce the fruit of a spiritual harvest.

Among a Muslim people group in the Horn of Africa in the late 1990s, the rate of persons coming to know Jesus was approximately one person *per year* per church-based evangelical agency. Over the past fifty years, eight of every ten "seekers" have eventually returned to Islam.

What, exactly, is the result of long-term service? What, exactly, is the result of faithfulness? Certainly, the result is not always a harvest. Sometimes there is not even, it seems, the promise of a harvest in our lifetime.

The point is not that a harvest of souls is contrary to the will of God! At the same time, focusing on the seemingly fruitful areas of the world, to the detriment of those areas that have never heard of Jesus, is not a balanced biblical approach. That choice is also not obedient.

The requirement of obedience is simply to "go and make disciples" of all people groups. The apparent harvest—or the absence of a harvest—should remain in God's hands.

It is even possible to make the case that the military invasions of places like Somalia, Iraq, and Afghanistan are, in large measure, indicative of a failure by the Body of Christ to sacrifice and obey in taking the gospel of Jesus to those hard places. As a result, the cost in blood for the disobedience of the church might be greater than the cost in blood for obedience. Even further, the financial cost of disobedience is much higher than the cost of obedience. *(Note: These statements are not intended to be controversial, and they are certainly not meant to impugn the work of the military. Our point is simply this: the price that the peoples of the world pay when followers of Jesus are disobedient to take the gospel to all peoples is staggering.)*

2. The Knowledge of Only One Way to Do Church

More than 80 percent of the unreached people in the world are oral communicators. By definition, that means they cannot read or write at a functional level. These people live in oral cultures. A Somali nomad explained his situation this way: "Show me how to put your church on my camel before you talk to me about your Jesus."

Many of the unreached dwell in areas where there are none of the traditional resources and forms related to the Western church. In fact, even when those traditional forms are present, they are often dangerous to believers who dwell in those environments. But without church buildings, corporate worship, pews, and hymnbooks from believers' environments, how and where does someone meet God? Sharing the faith is a natural part of a believer's life. But how does the absence of literate Bible studies, corporate worship, clergy-led baptisms, and the Lord's Supper affect those who are called to minister in unreached settings?

Obviously, we understand that God can work in *any* setting, but sometimes we have trouble figuring out exactly how that can happen. Sometimes workers simply take what they know and have gathered among themselves through two thousand years of Christian history and try to superimpose those traditions into a new, host environment. That approach is typically ineffective, and it can lead to profound frustration.

Along with this kind of frustration is an inherent desire to transfer Christian attributes, especially the Fruit of the Spirit, to the unreached. Obviously, the unreached are people who have never experienced a believing environment. Yet, we somehow expect these unreached people to exhibit attitudes and behaviors they have never seen! Often we have witnessed heartache on behalf of our colleagues because they wanted the unreached to exhibit the attributes of love, joy, peace, long-suffering, and kindness even though the unreached had never known or been around anyone who knew the Author of those attributes.

One of our professors was wise in his counsel: "Don't be surprised when unreached people act like unreached people!" Discovering new ways, or returning to a more oral, biblical way, of "doing church" is mandatory in unreached settings, and that is something most believers and sending bodies find extremely difficult. How can we "do church" in a setting where "church" will look completely different? How can "church" be planted in settings where the traditional literate forms and foundations in the Western world simply do not and should not apply?

3. The Need for Security

Institutions grow and perpetuate themselves by generating funds through the promotion of their programs and personnel. How, then, do churches, sending boards, seminaries, and mission publications handle ministries that cannot be talked about openly? How do they celebrate publicly when the normal statistical categories do not fit? Sometimes, the need for an institution to promote itself and its work takes precedence over the needs of the ministry, resulting in unfortunate consequences. Sadly, there is a "trophy" mentality that leads to unwise publicity concerning converts from resistant cultures. There is a human and institutional need to take credit for the spiritual fruit that only God can produce.

For example, should the story of the baptism of a businessman who is an MBB be published, when doing so may cause his death? That may seem like a silly question. At the same time, the sending institution will want very much to tell the story of this great "success," even though doing so will likely cause unspeakable damage to the individuals involved. This might seem like an easy decision, but sometimes those who make such decisions are unclear about the possible consequences. They live in the New Testament and should remember that all of this takes place in a world of instant communication within the Old Testament. It may sound trite, but we often proclaim openly what should remain secret and secure in our prayer closets. Perhaps we should adopt the biblical model of communication between believers and believing communities: when such a need existed in Bible times, *personal letters were written and hand-delivered from believer to believer and from church to church.*

Much of our secure communication, or what *should* be secure communication, is often on the websites of the persecutors within hours. *Even further, the way that we talk about believers in persecution—and the wide distribution of that information—often ends up causing even more persecution.*

We would be wise to notice a frequent theme in the Gospels. Especially in the Gospel of Mark, we read about Jesus' ministry, and that ministry was often followed by His instruction "to tell no one." This is not normally the way that we do ministry. In fact, we feel compelled "to tell everyone!" We long to publicly celebrate *our* successes and *our* conversions. However, to borrow a phrase from the medical world, we must do our work in such a way, especially with new converts, that we "do no harm."

In Matthew 16:13, Jesus asked His disciples an important question: "Who do people say the Son of Man is?" The disciples offered several answers: "Some say John the Baptist; others say Elijah; and still others, Jeremiah or one of the prophets" (v. 14). Jesus then asked a more personal and pointed question: "But what about you? Who do you say I am?" (v. 15). Simon Peter boldly announced, "You are the Christ, the Son of the living God" (v. 16). Jesus blessed Peter for his answer, and He explained that his answer was a "God-given answer." Then, much to our surprise, Jesus "warned his disciples not to tell anyone that he was the Christ" (v. 20).

Given our tendency to report everything openly and in every setting, we find Jesus' warning in Matthew 16 utterly shocking. After all, we conclude, is it not our specific purpose to tell the world that *Jesus is the Christ*? Yet, at least in this case, we find Jesus instructing silence in the context where first generational faith was being born.

But if we are silent about our work and silent about the results of our witness, how does a ministry raise funds, recruit personnel, and garner prayer support? This is a terrible tension in ministry! Many sending agencies, and those who report on persecution, are unable to operate under this kind of ambiguity. One unfortunate way of dealing with this tension is simply to avoid areas of the world that cannot accept traditional methods of church planting and reporting. Another way of dealing with the tension is simply to ignore the potential consequences and publish openly—even on the Internet—reports about the work. And we might even do that while Jesus is clearly saying to us: "Tell no one." Yet another harmful practice is to go to the tough places without the support and prayer coverage from our sending bodies and families mandatory for the task.

Because this struggle is so difficult, churches, workers, and agencies tend to focus on "Christian" areas and more responsive countries where security concerns are not quite as acute. Our typical (and understandable) desire to keep workers out of harm's way is coupled with our need to talk about our work, and those formidable forces can exceed our desire for the lost to hear about Jesus.

The conclusion may be obvious by now, but if the lost are to hear about Jesus, we will be required to send workers into harm's way, and we will be required to remain silent publicly about the work that is being done.

4. Ignorance about the Christian Faith

To be Somali is to be a Muslim. If we were to ask most Somalis if they are Muslim, they will simply laugh. The question makes no sense to them. Within Islam, there is no division between church and state. Islam is both an economic and political institution as well as a religious entity. Often, if new overseas workers ask believers who were former Muslims what nationality they are, the reply is usually laced with sadness: "I have no country now; I am a Christian." In their minds, ceasing to be a Muslim also means ceasing to be a part of their former nation. Since they have never seen before, for example, a "Somali Christian," living in a believing Somali community, that category is not even a possibility.

This worldview is deeply entrenched. By extension, Muslims also typically believe that to be an American is to be a Christian.

That kind of connection is problematic. The Western presence in Islamic nations has presented a skewed picture of who "Christians" are and how they live. The assumption is not even questioned: *these soldiers, these diplomats, these nongovernment organization (NGO) workers must be "Christians" because they are from the West.* To the extent that these expatriates from the West engage in alcohol consumption, adultery, and the eating of unclean foods, they become the picture of "a typical Christian" in the minds of those who live in those countries.

The thirty thousand American troops who came into Somalia during "Operation Restore Hope" were, in the view of the Somalis, "Christians" on a "crusade" against Muslims. Words like "Christian," "church," and "missionary" are just a few examples of words that are politically loaded with negative and harmful meanings in Somalia and similar areas. Followers of Jesus in these environments begin their ministries with an almost insurmountable deficit because many of these good words have already been tied to negative understandings.

Because of this viewpoint, strongly enforced over time, many unreached people start with a faulty understanding of what it means to follow Jesus. For believers desiring to share their faith in tough environments, this is a huge and difficult obstacle to overcome.

5. Harsh Physical Climate

One of our colleagues mapped Africa by climate and temperature. On that same map, he noted the location and number of overseas workers. Through his mapping exercise, he discovered a direct correspondence between higher temperatures and fewer workers. On a second map, he colored in the location of unreached peoples, especially adherents of Islam. He then discovered a direct correspondence between higher temperatures and greater numbers of the unreached.

Many of the unreached live in environmentally challenging regions of the world. Reaching the unreached will require intentionally leaving behind what many Western believers find to be comfortable. In one Horn of Africa country, the temperature typically averages 52 degrees centigrade (125 degrees Fahrenheit) three months out of the year. It is clearly a challenge to incarnate Christ in that climate. Extreme climate becomes yet another obstacle in the sharing of the Christian faith with unreached people. The financial cost of a small air conditioner in a bedroom window can be prohibitive; yet the cost of *not* providing it can result in a worker being unable to get a good night's sleep for months on end.

6. Difficulties in Caring for and Supporting Personnel

Living among unreached people carries a high personnel cost. Special struggles often include communal living, isolation from the greater believing community, a harsh climate, and extreme spiritual warfare. Often schools and good hospitals are not available.

Many churches and agencies do a credible job in calling out the obedient. Many churches and agencies do well in equipping and sending out their personnel. However, many of those sent ones do not receive the care and support they need in order to function and serve in hostile environments.

Over the years, we have witnessed godly workers serving among the unreached. Sometimes their service lasts only between six months and a year. There are many reasons for these short terms of service, but sometimes the isolation, the persecution, the danger, and the lack of a spiritual support system cause stress and burnout. Often these environments offer no place to pray and no place to play. Burnout is a constant threat. The stress on marriage is immense. Being a Western woman in a Muslim environment can cause godly women to distrust every male—even her husband and her colleagues!

Reaching the unreached and the unengaged will require intentional and significant personnel care on a regular basis. It will also require intervention care when special crises arise. Even further, it will require referral care when normal care is just not enough. Taking care of overseas workers is costly and difficult, but it is essential. In our experience, for every hour we spent giving member care to our colleagues in open countries, we spent ten hours caring for those in environments hostile to the Gospel of Jesus Christ.

7. The Pain of Persecution

At the beginning of our work in the Horn of Africa, a colleague and mentor pointedly told Ruth and me, "If you are 'successful' in sharing Jesus with your people group and some of these unreached people actually come to faith in Jesus, you will get someone killed." We didn't pay much attention to those hard words at the time. In all fairness, however, we had not yet learned that faithful obedience to Jesus' call necessarily causes persecution, suffering, and martyrdom.

It is sobering to report now that many of the believers we discipled were murdered for their faith. To this day, we grapple with the wisdom of our actions that may have played a part in their deaths.

Seventy percent of the local believers from one particular religious entity have been extracted from their environment by well-meaning evangelical agencies, churches, and individuals. As we noted above, it is generally not wise to embrace an "extraction theology" within persecuted environments. All the same, 60 percent of the believers left in such a setting will experience extreme persecution and possibly martyrdom. Overseas workers are driven to despair as new converts are beaten, expelled from families, shot, and killed.

How is it possible to emotionally and spiritually live with the negative consequences of witness that are often more costly for the one receiving the witness than for the one giving it?

For anyone preparing to work among the unreached, this honest challenge is worthy of consideration,

The heart of the issue here is biblical:

Is Jesus worth that?

Is Jesus worth that for the witness-bearer?

Is Jesus worth that for the one choosing to believe His claims?

Is Jesus worth persecution?

Even more, is Jesus worth the death of a person who embraces the faith?

If you do not believe that Jesus is who He claims to be, if you do not believe that Jesus is the Way, the Truth, and the Life, if you do not believe that Jesus is the very Son of God and the only way to heaven, then please do not go out among the unreached. Do not get someone killed for something that you are not eternally sure about.

There are many reasons why the unreached are unreached, and there are many reasons why the unreached *remain* unreached.

Obviously, the first step in overcoming these obstacles is to be obedient and to go. Going is an excellent first step. But going is not quite enough. What is required next is *staying* in the midst of an unreached people group with long-term, viable ministries and approaches.

The challenge is to pay that high price that includes even the certainty of persecution.

Going Even Deeper

- Discuss the cost of reaching the unreached. Discuss the cost of not going.
- Think creatively about how to care and support those who live in the toughest places on the planet—which might be inner city USA.
- Is your country of origin a Christian country or a Christian influenced country?

6

Cleaning Out the Clutter

While we think about the challenging task of going and staying, we also grapple with decisions about our priorities and our focus while we serve. Even with a sincere desire to be radically obedient, it is not always easy to make decisions about what matters most. The Great Commission is a clear word of instruction. Jesus has told us frankly that sharing the gospel is at the heart of His command to obedience. That God has a special concern for the lost is beyond debate. Even so, His special concern is not always *our* special concern, even as we are striving to be obedient!

Consider the priorities that inform our living. Typically, those priorities are clearly reflected in our conversations and gatherings; our priorities are reflected by the way we use our time and money. To illustrate the struggle of determining priorities, imagine a group of overseas workers or even a group of believers in a stateside church.

What occupies our attention? What are we most concerned about? What are the most frequent topics for discussion when we gather?

What do churches care most about? What matters most to individual believers? What is on the overseas workers' agenda? In other words, where do we place our focus?

At the risk of being overly simplistic, this chapter seeks to explore three basic ingredients present in most mission endeavors. These three elements are all important. These three elements, by definition, live in creative tension. But, with every decision and with every action, groups and individuals determine the relative importance of these elements. The question is not: Are these three elements important? Clearly, they are all important. The question is: Where will we place our focus? What will be the dominant and driving force of our work? What will motivate us and shape our decisions?

The following diagram represents the overseas worker's task. *Focus is essential.* In fact, the absence of a clear focus will lead to worker burnout, unrealistic administrative parameters, and, most alarmingly, unresponsiveness to a lost world. In our diagram, the base of the triangle represents the overarching task of carrying out the mission strategy. Our main focus is the top point of the triangle. The three indispensable elements, represented by the triangle's vertices, are worker concerns, concerns emanating from the sending entity, and the needs of the lost.

FOCUS

"Mission"

Foundation for Carrying Out the Mission Strategy

Again, the intent is not to imply that any of these elements are unimportant; they are all important and they will all play a crucial role within our shared desire to make the Good News available to every person on this planet. On the contrary, the intent is to understand what can happen to mission harmony, intentional strategy, and maintenance of a godly support system as our focus changes.

Furthermore, the intent is to illustrate how the lost are affected by the different choices we make. Decisions about our focus will have significant impact on the lost and their needs.

MODEL #1: FOCUS ON THE OVERSEAS WORKER

Worker Concerns

"Mission"

Sending Body/Agency   **The Needs of the Lost**

This first model represents mission endeavors (and individual believers) that are defined by an inward focus. What matters most, in this model, is the needs of the workers. The focus is on the well-being of the "sent out ones." Psychologist Abraham Maslow proposed a theory called the hierarchy of needs. Adapting his basic theory, security, housing, transportation, the cost of living, schooling for workers' children, and matters such as those are the most important considerations in this first model. Again, it is clear that those things are important. But should these matters be our primary concern?

The priority represented in this model is almost never stated as our focus. Yet this priority seems to take center stage as we manage our time and make decisions about our work.

Imagine a gathering of overseas workers. Imagine conversations in that meeting that focus almost completely on transportation, housing, budgets, cost of living concerns, and the education of the overseas workers' children. In that setting, gaining competence in ministry and growing in the ability to communicate cross-culturally can easily become secondary to these other matters related to the care and well-being of the workers. And perhaps unintentionally, local believers, observing this hierarchy of values, would conclude that well-developed support systems are the key for sharing Christ with a lost world. Based on the conversations that consume much of the workers' time, the impression given is that the mission endeavor is "all about me and mine."

MODEL #2: FOCUS ON THE ADMINISTRATION

Sending Body/Agency

"Mission"

The Needs of the Lost   **Worker Concerns**

This second model does not look inward; instead, it focuses on the sending entities that provide for the sheep. In this model, church or denominational identity, mission structures, policies, committees, and administration are afforded primary importance. In most settings, our sending entities provide resources, gather information, and train workers for effective service. They also provide many other services. Obviously, these kinds of sending concerns are crucial. Yet, when the concerns of the sending entity are the primary focus, the results that follow are predictable.

For example, in this model, workers can (sometimes unintentionally) be encouraged to climb the corporate ladder. Success is often measured by numbers; important concerns may include the number of new believers, the number of churches planted, the number of church buildings built, and the number of baptisms. There may even be an emphasis on how closely the new works are identified with the sending entity. The language used in these gatherings might often focus on who is in charge or on matters of authority, policy, and procedure tied to the home office or church. In this model, strategy typically flows from the top down. Ministry can be reduced to flow charts, formulas, and action plans. What is most convenient for administration takes precedence over almost everything else. Field-based initiatives are not always highly valued and creativity is inadvertently stifled.

Perhaps there is a prophetic word that needs to be heard about global plans that originate in places other than the hearts of overseas workers touching lost souls. When the needs of the sending entity are the highest priority, a shared and mutually owned vision within the group is rare. Even worse, new vision can be hijacked or new ideas sidetracked in the attempt to make them fit a particular management approach or a specific theological presumption. These administrative concerns can easily take precedence over creating a new vision for a lost world.

Workers living in this second model may have to struggle on two fronts. On the one hand, there is unavoidable spiritual warfare at the edge of lostness. A model that focuses on the sending body will be less likely to attend to those kinds of spiritual struggles. On the other hand, this second model will often result in conflict between the needs of those who sacrificially send and the needs of those serving on the field, not to mention the needs of lost people. Often, conflict of this nature can be intense and costly. The danger of this model is that the needs of the sending agency or the sending church ultimately assume priority over the needs of the lost world.

Again, the concerns of the senders are not insignificant. These concerns are foundational and vital for effective missions. However, they are not—and must not be—the primary focus.

MODEL #3: THE NEEDS OF THE LOST

The Needs of the Lost

"Mission"

Worker Concerns   **Sending Body/Agency**

This may seem obvious, but it is necessary to make the point. The needs of the lost must remain the primary focus. The lost need to hear, to understand, to believe the gospel, to be baptized, and to be gathered into house churches. Responding to the needs of the lost is our God-given task. As we obediently answer God's command, nothing can be more important than the needs of the lost.

The need for the lost to hear the good news always exceeds the needs of the witnesser.

The focus of this third model encourages workers to prepare for spiritual warfare and to look ever outward. Workers will not rest until every person on this planet has access to Jesus. In this model, the resources of the entire evangelical world are brought to bear upon the lost. Words like "networking," "prayer," "fasting," "worldviews," "advocacy," "strategy," "persecution," and "sacrifice" are the common language of gatherings that reflect this model. In this model, the world's lostness causes workers and sending entities to be broken before God and broken before their colleagues. In this model, workers willingly take on a servant's role, submitting their own needs to the needs of the lost. The vision for reaching the lost holds them in its grasp and, then, creative and responsive sending bodies develop approaches that grow out of ministry encounters. When the lost are the focus, what constitutes a worker's task and what defines a church becomes increasingly clear. Entry and exit strategies are clearly defined.

When the lost are the focus, those who are sent out and those who are sending live in harmony committed to the shared task. Sending bodies and agencies impact the lost by enabling, calling out, sending out, and nurturing workers. Workers enable and reinforce the sender's ability to send as they report what God is doing at the edge of lostness. The ministry assignment shapes decisions as everyone involved strives to address the needs of the lost. *The nature of the task determines the focus.*

Clearly, these three essential elements (worker concerns, concerns of the senders, and the needs of the lost) live in creative tension. And, again, these three elements are all important. The needs of the workers are important, but those needs cannot be as important as the need of the lost to hear a clear presentation of the gospel. Sending concerns are important, but those concerns must serve to focus our attention on a world without Christ.

Ultimately, however, the needs of the lost are our highest priority. Jesus, in the parable of the lost sheep in Luke 15, invited His followers to mimic the character of the Father in focusing on that which is of utmost importance: the one lamb that was lost.

The question is simple, but essential: *What is at the top of our triangle?* If we are not sure or if we cannot tell, then we would be wise to pay attention to a few basic questions:

Having an Honest Dialogue

- Based on budgets, time, and resources, what does our church or denomination care most about? Who do I care about?
- How many spiritual conversations do we have each week?
- How is success ultimately measured?

As simple and as personal as those questions are, the answers clearly reveal our focus.

7

Lies, Lies, and More Lies

Ruth and I have shared the contents of this chapter a multitude of times in many churches. We have never escaped unscathed. This chapter reveals what we say to each other and what we believe in those dark hours of the night. At the same time, these are not often the things that we talk about out in the open. Often church people applaud Ruth and me when we reveal to them some insight from another culture. Yet when we apply the same cultural insights to our own Western church, the response is not quite as positive!

It will be easy to be offended by this chapter. All the same, having insight into our own culture is possibly one of the highest signs of spiritual maturity. It is our hope that this chapter will ultimately help us have a faith rather than a religion, and a church rather than an institution.

Early in the gospel story, we are told that Jesus "was led by the Spirit into the desert to be tempted by the devil" (Matt. 4:1). At that point, at the very beginning of His earthly ministry, Jesus was led into an extended season of testing. The physical strain of this testing time was extreme: a forty-day fast in a wilderness environment.

Even more demanding, perhaps, was the spiritual struggle. Jesus began to hear the whispers of the Evil One:

> *Is this task something that you can accomplish? Have you heard the specifics of your call correctly? Is this obedience worth your life? Could this all be done some other way? Are you certain that this is the path that you should take? Will you do what you have been called to do? How can you run off and leave your mother alone like this?*

These questions were intended to lead to doubt. And the doubts, then, were intended to distract Jesus from His mission, leading Him ultimately to disobedience. These temptations were intended to pull Jesus in some other direction. When Satan realized how important Scripture was to Jesus, he quickly found a way to quote it himself, subtly twisting it for his own purposes.

We celebrate the fact that Jesus stayed obedient to His calling, and we celebrate His assurance that He can empower us to do that same thing. At the same time, in light of this temptation story, we are forced to acknowledge the destructive power of lies.

In a similar way, God's people today find it easy to listen to the whispers of the Evil One:

> *Is this task that you have been given something that you can actually do? Have you heard the call to obedience correctly? Is this obedience worth your life? Could this all be done some other way? Is there a way to accomplish the task without suffering and persecution? Are you certain that this is the path that you should take? What about your family? What about your children? Will you do what you have been called to do no matter what?*

Frankly, those seem like good, reasonable questions that deserve serious consideration. But, before long, we discover we have been distracted; before long, we realize we have been pulled in another direction. What seemed so clear and so crucial at one time is suddenly neither clear nor crucial. Of course, we would never dream of being disobedient, but we do sometimes look for ways to be obedient *on our own terms.*

God's Word is so clear. God's commands are so direct. God's intentions for His church are so compelling. Yet, if that is true . . .

> *Why is more than 70 percent of the world's evangelistic witness focused on the world's historically Christian countries?*
>
> *Why does the church in the West retain well over 90 percent of God's resources for itself?*
>
> *Why is the bulk of sacrificial offerings directed toward buildings, staff salaries, and educational materials for those already in the kingdom?*
>
> *Why is the church in the West willing to share only the leftovers with the Nations?*
>
> *Why do unengaged and unreached people groups today still lack even minimal access to the gospel?*
>
> *Why do many seminaries in the West, filled to overflowing with capable and committed students, send fewer than 10 percent of their graduates to the Nations?*

Answers to those questions are, of course, complex. But some of those answers are wrapped up in the lies that God's people have heard, believed, and gradually incorporated into our hearts and minds. In this chapter, we will consider some of the lies that might keep us from taking God's command seriously, lies that might cause us to question

His ongoing activity, and lies which might actually prevent us from going either across the street or across the world. The Evil One whispers to us today just as he tempted Jesus almost two thousand years ago.

Lie #1: The Bible is an old book.

This lie begins with a simple fact: the Bible is an old book, a record of what God has done. Wrapped up in that starting point is the implication that God no longer does what He used to do. God's call and God's ways no longer apply to our world today, at least not in the same way that they applied in Bible days. And God's expectation that we obey Him is no longer binding. In summary, *this lie suggests that God has ceased doing in our time what He did in the Bible.*

The "old book" lie suggests that the Bible describes accurately what God has done in the past, but this lie securely anchors God's activity to the past. Admittedly, it is impossible to read Scripture and "miss" the command to be people on mission. According to this first lie, however, that level of obedience belongs to an earlier day. It no longer applies to God's people today. Even more, God's ways are different now. This first lie suggests that the miracles, signs, and wonders that we encounter in Scripture are exciting, but God does not work in that same way today.

When we believe this lie, we claim to honor the Bible, but ultimately we dismiss Scripture as ancient history that merely records the activity of God from another day. We claim to love the Bible, but we end up stripping Scripture of its power and life. This allows us to pick and choose which portions of the Bible might still apply today and which parts can be dismissed without a second thought.

The first lie sounds like this: "Study the Bible, learn it, memorize it, live by its precepts, and even preach it, but realize that today we live in a different time. Obedience to God's command is no longer compelling, and God's ways are no longer miraculous."

A man from an Islamic background told me this story:

I never imagined that I might one day be a believer in Jesus. Even in preschool I was taught to be very strict. I went to a Muslim boarding school. In the boarding school we were taught how and why to hate Christians. In high school and at the university I was very active in Muslim student organizations. As a student and then later in business, I always oriented funds and energy toward Islamization.

Then one day there came a personal crisis in my family.

I prayed five times and even added the midnight prayer. For several days I continued with my prayers. But no light was coming from these prayers. I would use the normal set of Arabic prayers. I was encouraged to express my heartfelt emotions in my local language. I called upon Allah to help his servant. I was alone in my room in my city. I suddenly felt a total exasperation, I felt hopeless, and I felt complete frustration.

Then I heard a voice. The voice said: "I am the Way, the Truth, and the Life." I heard the voice in my own language! I did not know what those words meant. But I heard this voice repeating itself over and over again for the next several days and nights.

After this happened for several days, I said in my prayers, "If you are Lord, show me."

The next morning I met a friend who I had not seen in eight years. He told me that he had been looking for me for the past week. This friend said, "I have been thinking about you." He invited me to have supper at the hotel. After we ate at the restaurant, we noticed that a gospel meeting was starting in a nearby meeting room. I was surprised and shocked. I told my friend that I wanted to leave. But even though my body wanted to leave, my mind would not give my body permission.

Suddenly I heard the speaker in the room say, "Jesus is the Way, the Truth, and the Life."

I gripped my friend and I asked him, "What did that man just say?" My friend opened the Bible and he showed me the fourteenth chapter of John. He read to me the very words that I had heard in my dreams.

I felt a feeling of trembling all over me. I was wrestling fiercely like I wanted to run away, but I couldn't. I kept hearing this voice and I kept reading these words in the Bible until I eventually gave my life to Jesus.

Another man told this story:

I was from an Islamic background. I began to dream about a holy book. This book was not green like my Qur'an; it was blue. Many nights I would dream of this holy book. I heard a voice telling me to find this book and to read about the Messiah. I began to look for the book, but I did not know where to find it.

One day I went to the big market in my city in Central Asia. Suddenly from the crowd a man walked up to me. I had never met him before. He handed me a blue book and he said, "God told me to come to the market today and to give this book to you."

He then disappeared into the crowd and I never saw him again. I took this book, the Bible, to my house and I read it five times in the next month. I had never met anyone like the Messiah Jesus and my heart was changed from Islam to follow Him.

There is obviously more to these stories; these episodes were only the beginning of the journeys for these two men. But even the beginning part of their journeys is a reminder of the power and presence of God today!

Everything that God has ever done in the Bible He is still doing! God's presence and command is still compelling. His miraculous works have not come to an end. Even in seemingly dark places in this world, God is making Himself known, often with signs and wonders that seem to step from the very pages of Scripture. We would be wise not to believe the lie that the Bible was written for another day and time. Why would any of us desire to go to the hard places on this planet, or even across the road, with a God who has ceased being all the biblical record says He is?

What God has done in the past He still does today.

Lie #2: God is moving powerfully overseas. God is doing miracles overseas. But His miracles do not happen within the Western world.

This second lie forces us to grapple with our understanding, or misunderstanding, of the miraculous: what the miraculous is, why miracles happen, and whether miracles continue to happen today. Reports of the mighty acts of God around the world are common. Stories from Central and South Asia tell of hundreds of thousands of baptisms, followed by waves of new church starts. Stories from Africa celebrate incredible movements of revival. Stories from South America speak of remarkable spiritual and numerical growth. In the West, we find these stories both wonderful and exciting. But we also tend to believe that such things can only happen in faraway places. For whatever reason, we tend to believe that God does not do miracles here with us.

The Chinese House Church Movement is a story of the miraculous. Conservative estimates of believers in house churches in China begin at nearing one hundred million people ("members" or "true followers"?). During my visits to China, I have been astounded by the church growth happening in three particular church planting movements.

> In one location, more than 150 house church leaders were being trained. It was shocking to have them ask me, "Is Jesus known in other countries or is He known only in China?"
>
> I began to share with them stories about believers in Africa and believers in America. It was exciting to watch them breaking

out with a spontaneous celebration as they were so excited that Jesus was also known in other countries! But the more I described faith, church, and practices in America, the quieter they became.

Suddenly, the house church leaders began to cry out: "Why, God, don't You love us like You love the believers in America? Why can we not experience the miracles that You grant to the believers in America?"

I could not believe my ears. I asked them to explain their anguish. Their experiences rivaled the stories of the apostles. Miracles of healing were common. Thousands were coming to faith in Jesus. Almost half of their pastors had served multiple years in prison for sharing their faith, and they often planted churches in those prisons! How could they possibly compare those miracles to what I had told them about America?

They were surprised that I did not understand.

"Which is more miraculous?" they asked. "That we can divide our Bibles book by book, giving each pastor one torn-out section of Scripture or that you say that you can own dozens of Bibles, along with music books and study materials?

"Which is more miraculous? That Chinese are being healed by the hundreds of thousands and that maybe a thousand of them will come to discern that their healing has come from Jesus or that you have access even to Christian doctors, nurses, and health care any time you choose?

"Which is more miraculous? That we move from house to house, meet on different days of the week and at different times during the day trying to avoid disruption of the church and arrest or that you can gather for worship all day every day and no one would ever think of arresting you or your pastor?

"Which is more miraculous? That we view prison as our theological training ground or that you can study in special schools set aside just for believers and their training?

"Which is more miraculous?"

It was my time to weep. I realized that what I had called "common" in my own country and in my own faith would be considered profoundly miraculous by most of the believing and persecuted world.

In response to the second big lie, we would be wise to take special care in defining the miraculous. *What we dismiss as common is nothing other than the clear activity of God in our Western church world!* It is crucial that we see it, that we call it what it is, that we live in profound gratitude for all that God is doing, and that we recognize the depth of responsibility that accompanies miracles as great as these.

Lie #3: If God wants me to go to the unreached, He will give me a special call.

This third lie is a subtle attempt to avoid personal responsibility. It sounds good at first: If God wants me to go, He can make that clear. But just beneath the surface is another thought: *Absent of a special call from God, I have no personal responsibility for the unreached, wherever they happen to reside.* This third lie is a painful one to confront because it is so very personal.

In thinking about this third lie, I think of my own life story:

I came to Jesus at the age of eighteen. I had already finished high school and I was working in a factory. I heard God's call to salvation and service one night as I worked, and I gave my life to Christ. Upon the advice of people I trusted, I made my way to a denominational college.

I did not yet have much background in the faith, but I was hungry to learn. I began to read the New Testament and I was quite taken by those first four books: Matthew, Mark, Luke, and John.

I fell in love with the work and will of God. I had little interest in the theological debates that seemed important to others. I simply trusted God and I tried to live my life under the authority of what I was encountering in Scripture.

Reading what I later learned was the "Great Commission" in Matthew 28:18–20 and another passage in Acts 1:8, I thought, This is God's Word and it has authority over me. God says in His Word that I must go to the Nations. So I guess I will have to go to the Nations if I am to be Jesus' follower.

It was so simple and so straightforward. With deep joy, I had read and understood that the entire world was open to me for service and ministry.

That's what God had told me in His Word.

And that is what I believed. And that thought was unchallenged until my experience with a sending agency that sent workers overseas.

By that time, my wife and I had been preparing for overseas service, and we were thrilled at the prospect of following through on the biblical command to "go to the ends of the earth." Ruth and I went through the complicated application process. An interview with the sending agency was one of the final steps. Ruth and I found ourselves in a small room with a group of rather serious men. They looked at Ruth and said, "Tell us about your call to overseas missions."

Ruth was the poster child for overseas work. She was a pastor's daughter, came to Jesus at an early age, felt the "call" to missions, and wrote a paper in the sixth grade about her dream of one day being a worker in Africa. Once she finished her testimony, these men were beaming with pride that their churches could produce such an astute and sensitive follower of God.

Then they turned to me and asked, "Nik, tell us about your call to overseas missions."

I innocently looked up at them and said, "Well, I read Matthew 28:18 and Acts 1:8."

They smiled indulgently.

"That's good," they said, "but within this mission agency, there has to be evidence of 'a divine call' to overseas missions. We need for you to share with us when it was that God called you to overseas missions."

I was quite confused.

"Well, I read the Bible," I said. "I read Matthew 28:18 and I read Acts 1:8. I read God's command to go to the Nations, and I am trying to obey that command and go!"

I glanced over and saw that Ruth was now in tears. She had been raised within the denomination and suddenly I realized that I did not know the secret code words that opened the doors for overseas missions. I simply did not know what to say that would get us on an airplane headed for Africa. Ruth was not going to be allowed to go to Africa and it was going to be my fault.

She should have informed and warned me about the secret, denominational passwords!

With great patience, the men explained once again the agency's position about "a divine call" that would allow the agency to send a family overseas. They talked about a fourfold call: a "call" to salvation, a "call" to ministry, a "call" to missions, and, finally, a "call" to a specific location. My brain was swirling; I couldn't imagine how anyone could keep up with all of these "calls."

Patiently, they asked me what I thought about the sermonette they had just shared. I was still young enough to believe that they actually wanted me to share an opinion.

Not knowing any better, I replied, "I am simply trying to be obedient to what God has commanded me to do. God has said 'Go,' and I am trying to go! It seems to me that this denomination has created a special call to overseas missions that would give people an excuse not to be obedient to what God has already commanded them to do."

That comment didn't go over very well. There was dead silence in the room.

To this day, I am not exactly sure how it happened, but I was approved for overseas service. Ruth and I were headed for Africa . . . with a one-way ticket.

Every culture has filters through which God's voice is discerned. Every person is culturally conditioned to hear God's voice in certain ways. But religious structures and systems sometimes add even more filters and conditions. The longer a religious system is in place, the more requirements develop to guide and inform those who are part of that system.

We claim, rightly, that God's command is vital. We claim, rightly, that God's call is crucial. It is. But our conversations about call should be focused on *where* we have been called rather than on *if* we have been called. Should I be in Jerusalem? Judea? Samaria? Should I be serving at the ends of the earth? Now that's a conversation worth having!

But have I been called? That question should be settled at the very beginning of our walk with Jesus. God's Word is clear that we have, in fact, already been called. We have been called to radical obedience.

Perhaps it is simple obedience that initiates the faithful response, and then perhaps it is a call that defines the destination. Matthew 28:18–20 and Acts 1:8 seem to make it quite clear.

Lie #4: We must reach our own country first. The needs here are so great. There are millions of lost people right here. After we meet the needs here, then we can go to the Nations.

The implication of this fourth lie is that God's people in America are so deeply involved in local evangelism that they could not possibly interrupt that important work to serve in some other place. For most people, a personal commitment to local evangelism is not the honest reason to avoid going to serve among the Nations. This excuse may sound good, but it does not ring true.

Obviously, there is great spiritual need in America. Obviously, there are many people here who need to hear the good news. And, obviously, God's people have a mandate to share with their American friends and neighbors. But to say that we cannot go to the Nations until the needs here are met means that we will never go to the Nations.

That is, perhaps, exactly the point.

This fourth lie is an excuse that many people find quite acceptable. After all, how can anyone argue with the need to help our neighbors meet Christ?

What is really behind this fourth lie? It is crucial that we admit and grapple with a devastating truth.

The greatest hindrance to the growth of God's kingdom globally is racism. Despite our protests to the contrary, there are sometimes deeper reasons behind our "convictions." And these deeper reasons are not unique to any particular group or people. Human beings are naturally drawn to "our own people." But God seeks to transform what is "natural" to us into what is more in line with His character and heart.

Within the Great Commission is one of the strongest words in all of Scripture confronting the sin of racism. Sometimes those who are despised are people who are far away. But more often than not, those who are despised are geographically close. Judea may be a challenge for us. And Samaria? Well, even "the ends of the earth" might be more attractive than Samaria! Some people find it easier to take the good news to a black African than to share with a neighbor who is a person of a different race or different color. These attitudes are deep and they are often deeply held. Crossing the street might be much harder than going to the ends of the earth! And only the power of God can transform our hearts.

Do we honestly believe that Jesus intends for the church to finish the task in Jerusalem before venturing into Judea? Do we honestly believe that Jesus intends for us to send teams into Samaria while ignoring Samaritans living in our own neighborhoods? Do we honestly believe that working hard in Jerusalem sets us free from the responsibility to care about and even go to the ends of the earth? Going just to "our people" and deciding for ourselves just how far God would have us go is the very antithesis of the good news and it is contrary to the nature of Christ.

Lie #5: I have made a bargain with God. If I work really hard in my own church, especially in supporting mission work, then He will keep His hands off of my children and grandchildren.

Once again, my own life story illustrates the power of this lie:

It was one of the hardest things that I ever had to watch, especially early in our overseas career. Our entire family was sick; we were all terribly sick with malaria. We had finally been evacuated from our ministry station to be treated by a down-country doctor in a better hospital. This was the fifth time that our sons had fallen sick with this mosquito-borne disease, and the tenth time for Ruth and myself. They put us in a little concrete-block hospital room and quickly inserted quinine IVs in the arms of my two sons and my wife. I waited on them for the twenty-four hours that it took for the quinine drip to finish. Then it was my turn for twenty-four hours.

We spent the next two weeks recovering in a friend's home before making the long journey back to our place of service. Ten days after arriving home, our oldest son Shane had malaria again.

This was not an academic exercise for us. We have salvation because Almighty God sent His Son. We can never escape the fact that obedience to the call of God affects both individuals and entire families.

We can invite Mohammed and his wife Aisha and their children to come to Jesus only when we too have been willing for our family members to pay the price for following Jesus. Our invitation to others is valid only if we too are willing to enter into shared suffering.

There is perhaps only one thing more difficult than releasing our own lives into the hands of God, and that is releasing the lives of our loved ones, especially our children. What risks are we willing to shoulder, including risks for our wives and children, for the sake of the kingdom of God? When we ask churches in the West this question, there is often a deafening silence; we are still waiting for an answer.

What is the hardest task? Going? That might be difficult, but that is not the hardest task. Staying? Yes, as we have already noted, that is hard. *But the hardest task of all may be sending: giving and blessing our sons and our daughters to serve the Nations.*

Which is harder: dying on a cross or sending the one most loved to die on a cross? Most parents would willingly die on a thousand crosses if that would keep their children from dying on one! But both the sending and the dying are intrinsic to the nature of God.

When the Body of Christ recaptures the true responsibility of sending loved ones to the Nations, it will either experience a profound season of mission renewal, or it will stop sending.

The Western church often idolizes its children. Bargaining with God and holding back our children so that they might experience "the good life" of the American dream is to believe a lie that ultimately causes the church to deny the Nations the best the Father has to offer. And it ushers in the demise of the church itself.

Lie #6: God seems to be calling more single women to the Nations. He must have a special need for single women to serve in this way. Evidently, He does not call as many single men.

A careful examination of the mission community reveals an intriguing reality: *for every single man in overseas service, there are approximately seven single women*.

Why is this so? Does the heavenly Father have a communication problem with single men? Are single women simply easier to convince? Are single men reading past the biblical commands to go to the Nations? Is it that God, for some reason, needs more women than men?

One mission leader, grappling with this trend in his own area of service, often addresses gatherings of college and seminary students. Many of these college students are single. He suggests to the single men that they need to cease praying the prayer that exclaims, "Here I am, Lord, . . . send my sister!" That comment would be funny if it did not ring so true.

Even in the toughest places, even in places wracked by war and famine, single women within the mission community outnumber single men seven to one. That statistic seems consistent across denominational lines and within different areas of the world.

Why does this matter? Consider these not-so-hypothetical scenarios.

Ten single women obediently follow God's command to serve on the mission field. Let's assume they make an initial commitment of two years. During that time, their call is confirmed and they are deeply affected by their experience. But they honestly do not believe that they have been "called" to be single. They return to the United States after two years of service, seeking godly husbands who will walk with them overseas. Anecdotal evidence seems to suggest that only three of these ten women will find such a husband.

Ten single men obediently follow God's command and serve on the mission field. Let's assume that they make an initial commitment of two years. During that time, their call is confirmed and they are deeply affected by their experience. But they honestly do not believe that they have been "called" to be single. They return to the United States after two years of service, seeking godly wives who will walk with them overseas. Anecdotal evidence seems to suggest that *eight* of these ten men will find such a wife.

Why the disparity?

Numerous campus ministers, youth leaders, and pastors have been asked to comment on this social and cultural anomaly. Many have struggled to explain the apparent imbalance in biblical obedience between single men and single women. Two initial observations are emerging. Both of these observations suggest that there is a cultural illness infecting the church in the West.

First, statistics suggest that "the ladders of advancement" found in our churches, seminaries, and denominational structures are generally the territory of males. This is not offered as a moral or theological judgment, simply as an observation. Many of these ladders are not available to women. Therefore, while men climb professional ministry ladders, women become much more familiar with service. Mission fields are typically places with few ladders to climb. Even a proficient and growing worker will rarely be rewarded with additional salary, a promotion, or a new title. Typically, leadership on the mission field may have more to do with longevity than aptitude.

Advancement in a mission setting simply means that a person is given more tasks to perform. This lack of clear and measurable social and work advancement fails to reward men in ways their culture has conditioned them to expect. On the other hand, women who are more service-oriented, and who are already conditioned not to expect advancement and recognition, are perhaps more suited for the mission field.

Second, consider the models that men have for full-time ministry in the United States. Many young men today come from broken homes. Many of these men have never lived with healthy models of male leadership in their lives. Few have ever experienced a father who was able or willing to provide spiritual leadership. Increasingly in the United States, the megachurch is becoming the norm. And what type of leader will often be most visible in that setting? Our model is a polished, well-groomed, articulate, socially adept speaker-leader-teacher-administrator-pastor, standing behind a pulpit or before a classroom of students. This leader can move the masses and dazzle a television audience with wit and humor. The tools of the trade are commentaries, microphones, computers, and carefully crafted words. This world is increasingly white-collar.

Clearly, these gifts are not always well suited for the mission field. The mission field is typically more blue-collar. It often requires—or, at least, results in—callouses on the hands and the heart as the faithful struggle with lostness, persecution, starvation, and flying bullets. Arguments can be made for seminaries. Scholarship is indispensable. But where will today's men learn how to be spiritually and physically tough? Where will they learn how to rewire a generator? Where will they learn to minister in a hostile culture that neither reads nor writes?

In the West the traditional model seems, for men, to be a pastor and teacher. These are the spiritual roles to which many men aspire. Yet in movements across the globe, the roles of evangelist and church planter are the roles most often sought. Such models are often absent in Western church and institutional life. Seminaries are often geared toward the pastor/teacher rather than the evangelist/church planter.

What we need today are fathers and ministers and mentors who can model not only the ability to parse Hebrew verses in the book of Exodus, but who can also carry the Ark of the Covenant across the harsh desert into physical and spiritual battles.

We need men to grow up and show up.

Perhaps the apparent shortage of young, single men on the mission field is linked to our current model of ministry that emphasizes polished presentation more than towels and washbasins.

These observations may be right or wrong, but the fact remains that single women outnumber single men on the mission field by a ratio of seven to one.

Is God really biblically commanding more women than men toward the tough stuff? Surely not.

Lie #7: As a young woman, I was commanded to go to the Nations. I have decided to marry a man who does not share my calling. Surely, God will now call my husband to the Nations.

This is a devious and subtle lie.

Many cultures look upon a single person as less worthy than one who is married. Even more worthy, in many cultures, is a person who is married and has children. In a mission context, the struggle is often expressed in these kinds of thoughts and feelings: Does not my desire and call to be married outweigh my call to the Nations? Indeed, what are godly, single women to do? As noted above, the evidence is clear in suggesting that, in terms of biblical obedience to the command to missions, single women far outnumber single men.

When obedient, godly single women cannot find obedient, godly single men to marry as global partners among the lost, which choice should they make: the Nations or marriage?

Personal experience suggests that within the American church there is a significant population of women who traded in their call of obedience to the Nations for marriage. It is not (always) the case that these women resent the choice that they made, and it is certainly not the case that they regret the children they have borne. What is common, however, is a deep awareness that, early on, God had worked in their hearts and affirmed His call. The awareness reminds many of these women of a command to obedience to be salt and light to those who have little or no access to the Good News. The awareness causes them to wonder if they traded godly obedience for a husband who did not share such an understanding.

In recent years, changes have been noticed. Increasing numbers of single women are embracing God's command to go to the Nations. Though they do not feel that they are specifically called to be single, they value God's command above all else. They determine to share early in any potentially significant relationship that their primary commitment is to God and to the Nations. Ideally, this results in a couple exploring together—and ultimately embracing together—the plans and purposes of God. Sadly, however, that is not always the outcome, and relationships are sacrificed to a higher command. In any case, it is often too late to have that conversation after the relationship has become serious.

Lie #8: Because I serve through short-term overseas trips, I don't really need to serve and minister through my local church.

This lie is essentially a different version of the "His work, my way" model of living. Following the logic of this lie, we have understood enough of God's command to make ourselves a detriment to God's purposes. We are eager (we say) to participate, but we desperately want to participate on our terms.

Thankfully, tens of thousands of Christian volunteers travel the globe each year for seasons of service and ministry. From youth of high school age to retirees, planes and buses are filled with volunteers going to the Nations. Major cities are inundated with these volunteers. Many of these volunteers, blessedly, make every effort to fit in with long-term strategies, while others perpetuate the unfortunate stereotype of the "missionary tourist."

Consider for a moment the mind-set and practice of some

volunteers who regularly go overseas. While clearly being a blessing in the overseas setting, the reaction of their sending church is perhaps less enthusiastic.

Returning home, overseas workers visit their sending and partnering churches. In good faith, they thank the church for sending such helpful and productive volunteers. Later, after the service, it is not uncommon for pastors and lay leaders to say something like this: "Well, I'm glad that these volunteers were of good service to you on the field, but we have never been able to get them to lift a hand in support of local ministries within their home church." In some cases, even regular worship attendance and faithful stewardship from such volunteers is not consistent.

Perhaps serving the cause of Christ overseas can seem glamorous and even exotic. Perhaps people feel more open in sharing a personal testimony in environments where they are not known . . . and where they will not be around long enough to reveal personal character.

On the other hand, perhaps a brief time overseas can be used by God to renew a commitment at home, or to focus a person's attention on ministry close at hand. Perhaps.

But the practice of going thousands of miles from home while neglecting lost, needy, and nearby neighbors points to a believing life that is badly out of balance. Christ has commanded all of His followers to incarnate Him *wherever* they happen to be. Neglecting "Jerusalem" threatens to undermine the entire mission endeavor. Ministry among the Nations simply must be a natural extension of whatever ministry is happening at home. Being a poured-out and broken vessel among the people we know best is essential preparation—even more, it is a prerequisite—for ministry among people we do not yet know. And the kind of maturity and seasoning that comes from extended ministry at home tends to reduce the mistakes that we are all prone to make in mission settings.

God help us if we attempt to do in faraway places things that we would never dream of doing close to home!

Lie #9: The primary way we support work among the unreached in our church is through our financial giving. As long as we give money, we have fulfilled our responsibility for the Nations.

This lie has paralyzed mission endeavors across the globe. Many church members give of their funds sacrificially. Stories abound of widows giving their "egg and quilt money" to mission enterprises. An individual church's giving to mission causes can easily be the largest item in the annual budget. This kind of giving should be applauded.

Even so, if the majority of mission support is defined primarily by the giving of money, as vital as financial support is, there can develop a line between the church and the field. This leads to a "them" and "us" mentality. Missions can become something the church does, rather than defining who the church is.

How can a church determine if it has given in to the lie that can sometimes hide within even sacrificial giving? Listen to how the church talks and prays. Does a church pray "for" the missionaries or does it pray "with" the missionaries? Can church members articulate what missionaries have done with "their" money among the Nations?

> *For decades, overseas workers in a "closed" Muslim country had heard about and prayed for the persecuted around the world. They had heard modern stories of extreme suffering and marvelous faith of biblical dimensions. Often they wept with sorrow, mixed with joy, as they listened to stories from across the globe describing the lives and challenges of those persecuted for their faith. They felt privileged to pray for the persecuted.*
>
> *Then one day, something horrible happened.*
>
> *It was that day when four of their colleagues were shot by*

a Muslim extremist. Three cherished followers of Jesus were martyred.

Global resources within the Body of Christ were immediately mobilized. Prayers flowed and counselors were flown in. Scores of those who had witnessed and survived the event were debriefed by their local and home governments. Spiritual leadership arrived to walk beside these grieving believers. Answers and meaning were sought.

After a long morning of debriefing, the local team returned to the large conference room. Centered in the circle of chairs was a table. On that table were a cup and some flat bread. In the midst of this overwhelming tragedy, this group of grieving "sent out ones" approached the Lord's Table and shared together His Supper.

The Holy Spirit fell with power.

It could be argued that, for the first time in their lives, these overseas workers, rather than remembering the Lord's suffering, entered into the suffering of their Jesus. No longer were the sufferings of Jesus historical or abstract. His sufferings were suddenly real and they were shared. In that holy moment these workers no longer prayed "for" the persecuted. They could now pray "with" the persecuted. Giving and praying "for" something implies a distance, a disconnect. Praying and giving "with" overseas workers implies a shared burden, a shared ministry, and a shared task unto the ends of the earth.

We would be wise to erase the line between the church and the mission field. The offering that God requires most is not only financial; His required offering leads ultimately to the giving of our lives and the willing surrender of children and grandchildren to God's purposes. When those priceless gifts are offered, the local church is finally walking alongside the overseas workers rather than seeing missions as simply another item in the church budget.

Lie #10: The safest place in the world is within the will of God.

"Are our overseas workers safe?" is an oft-asked question. Worker safety is of prime importance. Yet if safety is the primary issue for families, churches, and agencies, then there is only one thing to do: *Stop sending.*

Western culture has attempted to cleanse faith of its rough edges. Our untested assumption is that, surely, God only wants what is best for me, my family, and my country. Given that assumption, when troubles, suffering, persecution, and even death come, we are quick to see those hard things as signs of God's disfavor. It might be that Western Christianity has diminished the heart of biblical faith by removing the suffering and persecution that the New Testament promises are intrinsic to following Jesus.

Many overseas workers find it difficult to engage in church planting among people who are dangerously unreached. These workers are often much more committed to what we might call "rescue work." Workers who serve in Muslim areas will often remove Muslim Background Believers (MBBs) from persecution to a safe place in another country. In reference to the Old Testament story that we mentioned in a previous chapter, many refuse to leave Joseph in jail and strive to provide rescue before modern-day Josephs ever have the opportunity to interpret Pharaoh's dreams.

And, as a result, well-intentioned choices actually work against the ultimate purposes of God.

It is an extremely difficult decision to make, but overseas workers and those who advocate for the persecuted must spiritually discern when to leave Joseph in Pharaoh's prison. At the same time, they must never cease to pray for his—and their own—obedience.

As much as we might want to avoid the obvious conclusion, it may be time for believers in the West to admit that we are afraid. Sadly, when MBBs are asked what they learn from overseas workers, they often respond with the same answer. With great sincerity and sadness, they say, "Western workers teach us to be afraid."

Instilling fear in new believers is not merely a missiological mistake. It also is a sin. By way of illustration, MBBs indicate that overseas workers are afraid of getting local believers arrested or harmed. They indicate that workers are afraid they will lose their visas or work permits. They suggest that workers fear moving, having to learn yet another language, or placing their children in yet another school. In so many different ways, overseas workers tend to struggle with crippling fear.

And it is quite possible that overseas workers have learned this fear from their parents, from their churches, and from their sending bodies.

The belief that personal safety and the absence of risk is of paramount importance and that our need for safety should keep us from risking all for the kingdom of God is a heinous lie that infects mission enterprises all around the world.

What do Chinese house church leaders call prison? They call it their "theological training school."

What do pastors and lay leaders alike call persecution, and even martyrdom, in their environments? They call it "normal."

Fear is devastating. Fear paralyzes. Fear causes people to run and hide. Fear is a black hole that will deplete joy from the soul of a believer. Fear is a deadly enemy of the church.

Your fear is the greatest tool you will ever give to Satan. Overcoming your fear is your greatest tool against Satan.

Following the terrorist attacks of September 11, 2001, about 60 percent of all United States mission volunteers cancelled their planned trips. During that same period, an even higher percentage of pastors cancelled previously made plans for overseas service. Perhaps those kinds of decisions make sense to us, but, at the same time, they reveal the high value that we place on supposed safety and they make clear our unwillingness to take risks to pursue God's call.

This tenth lie is difficult to face. While we understand many of the reasons for fear, we dare not allow that fear to keep us from fulfilling Christ's command. In simplest terms, we can make an obedient choice. We can either choose not to be afraid or we can choose to obey despite our fears. The Evil One can never take from God's children the opportunity to make right and godly choices. God Himself has given that opportunity. We are told clearly in Scripture not to be afraid. And, even if we are not able to keep fear completely in check, we always have the opportunity to obey. Eternally the only safe place for everyone on the planet is within the will of God. Let us be clear; the will of God is not always the safest place to be, but it is the only place to be.

Believers cannot always choose safety, but they can always choose obedience.

These ten lies are formidable obstacles that can prevent us from pursuing Christ's command. These lies can be devastating to the cause of Christ. But these ten lies can also be recognized, refuted, and rejected. God's people have no higher calling than to live in the light of His truth. May that be so, especially when it comes to dealing with these lies that would keep us from obedient faith.

What Is Left to Talk About?

- Would you be willing to risk telling a coveted friend to share with you which of these lies you are listening to?
- What hold does fear have over you? Of what are you afraid?
- Men, are we entitled by God to a life of ease, without suffering or allowing our family to suffer for Jesus? What must change in our religious culture for men to step up?

8

Staying Put

Despite the clarity of the Great Commission, the decision to obey and "go" is often difficult and daunting. Sometimes, an even more difficult decision stands before the overseas worker: the decision to stay.

In 1991, I entered into a time of dialogue with a friend who was also a worker. He had been on the field for a long time; he was experienced and seasoned. We were talking about the work in Somalia, a work that had proved to be expensive, dangerous, and not especially productive (at least, not productive from our human way of measuring things). Some of the comments that my friend made in 1991 are branded on my soul.

My friend claimed there was no way to justify "the waste" of personnel, money, and witness among Somalis. He compared what was happening in Somalia with what was happening in his own country of service. He went so far as to make this audacious claim: "If you give me one of your workers—just one—we will start a church in my country within forty-eight days. If you keep all of your workers in Somalia, after forty-eight *months* there will still be no church. In fact, after those forty-eight months, the Muslims in your people group will still be witnessing to you!"

He then repeated his painful conclusion: "There is no way to justify *wasting* personnel, money, and witness in a place that is so unresponsive."

About a year later, a leader of a sponsoring mission board called me on the phone from the midst of an evangelistic crusade in East Africa. After making some small talk, he reached the point of his call. In essence, this was the question that he wanted to have answered: "How many people have you baptized, how much money have you spent, and is it cost effective for you to be in there?" I knew at this point that this was not just a polite phone conversation!

After I gave him my answer, he told me, "I will leave my hotel in five minutes. When I return this evening after our evangelistic crusade, a few hours from now, there will be more than one hundred and fifty new people in the kingdom of God. What you are telling me is that you have had only one convert in one and a half years, you have spent one million dollars, and you have seen three people martyred? How can you justify staying in that place?"

I replied, "Sir, I do not have to justify our being in the unreached, hard places. We simply have to be obedient to go where God has told us to go."

Ruth and I were aware of the meager spiritual harvest long before those two painful conversations. All the same, those encounters were startling in their clarity. We were serving in a place far removed from a spiritual harvest. In fact, we realized that we were not even at a point of watering or planting or even tilling the soil; we felt we were simply moving rocks so that one day the field would be prepared for the sowing of seed. At times, that preliminary work seemed legitimate. In our confident moments, we would have said that we were being true to God's call.

At other times, we wondered. To be honest, we wanted to quit.

As we evaluated our work, we knew that resources needed to be used wisely. But we could find no place in Scripture where a line was drawn between the cost expended and the number of new brothers and sisters added to the kingdom of God. As far as we were concerned, there was no such ratio. Despite hard words from friends and colleagues, we were driven by a passion to obey, not by the promise of a productive harvest. Yes, we were deeply troubled by the lack of measurable success, but (at least on our good days) we chose to leave those matters in God's hands.

Our initial tentative conclusion has now become a rock-solid conviction: *Followers of Jesus do not need to justify their presence in areas where Christ is not known. They need simply to be obedient.*

This chapter is a brief review of the biblical rationale for continuing to focus on people groups that are, seemingly, not responsive and for remaining in ministry environments which constitute significant risk to national and expatriate believers.

Our mandate is to go into all the world and provide every person with an opportunity to hear clearly about Jesus Christ (Matt. 28:18–20). It is our conviction that, by God's determination, every person has the right to hear, to understand, and to have the opportunity to believe in Jesus. Christ's command to go and share the gospel is not an optional choice for believers or merely an opportunity for a select group of believers. Christ's command to go to the Nations is a command incumbent on every one of His followers.

Our methodology involves not only going, but also sending out those who are commanded by God to go to the Nations. Those who are sent out are to be supported by those who are called by God to stay and fulfill the task of growing and nourishing the existing church (Rom. 10:14–21). Sending is by far the hardest task.

Our resolve is to remain at the task until all Nations and all people groups have had an opportunity to hear. We do not have to come back; we simply have to go!

Often our team members have been told, "You have done enough. It is time to 'shake the dust' off your feet and pull out." As attractive as that option seems, it should be examined in light of what we read in Scripture.

In sending out His disciples, Jesus addresses this exact matter. He refers to situations where witness is not well received. He talks about situations where there is no welcome and where the message is rejected. Within this context, Jesus speaks of "shaking the dust off your feet" (Matt. 10:14; Mark 6:11; Luke 9:5).

In these parallel passages, several things are worthy of note:

- Jesus sends His disciples to every town and village.
- There are serious consequences for rejecting both God's message and God's messengers. These passages in Matthew 10, Mark 6, and Luke 9 carry the weight of warning.
- The stories of sending we encounter here find Jesus' disciples going to the Jewish people. Significantly, the Jewish people were those who had a revelation history; they did not belong to a people group who had never heard!
- Jesus told His disciples that they were to "shake the dust off their feet" if they or the gospel message were rejected.
- The final thing we notice is that, even when there was rejection, Jesus never withdrew His followers from a people group! Even in settings of rejection and persecution, His followers were simply relocated and redeployed into the next village or town. In every case, however, the next village or town was populated by people who were part of the same people group.

The only apostolic examples of shaking the dust off of feet in response to a rejected message are found in Acts 13:50–51 and Acts 18:6.

In the first passage, Paul was indignant at the Jews in Pisidian Antioch who were stirring up opposition to his preaching. Significantly, Paul did not "shake the dust off his feet" in any other towns on this journey where he encountered similar Jewish-instigated persecution (such as Iconium and Lystra). Also, he even returned to Iconium later to encourage the church there (Acts 14:21).

In the second reference, Paul was in Corinth. In response to Jewish rejection of his message, Paul "shook out his clothes" as a sign to the Jews that he was now shifting his evangelistic ministry to the Gentiles.

In evaluating our efforts among the dangerously unreached, and in making difficult decisions about leaving or staying, we should compare the commands found in Matthew 28 and Romans 10. Especially because of our propensity to count heads and record numbers, we are often prone to choose places of service that are more responsive. While this kind of choice may make good sense to our sending entities, it may not reflect biblical obedience. It is entirely possible—more than this, it is quite likely—that God would have His messengers stay among the dangerously unreached despite our struggle to justify such ineffective and unproductive commitments.

Not too long ago, an influential mission leader was reported to have said, "As long as Somalia and other countries are unresponsive and dangerous, I will use my influence to pull our workers out of those places and keep our workers out of those places." This comment is representative of many who would sacrifice the opportunity for all peoples to hear about Jesus for matters such as measurable response, cost, or security.

Clearly, it is not time to pull out from the people groups in places like the Horn of Africa (knowing full well that workers can be forced out of those places) or to withdraw our witness from people groups that have had little or no chance to hear and believe. *The people groups in question have not rejected Christ or His messengers; they have simply not heard clearly about Jesus and His gospel.*

In 1992, we had a conversation with a well-known missiologist. He said to us, "So you are the couple who has the audacity to go to Somalia with the gospel?"

I replied casually, "The Somalis are not responsive to the gospel of Jesus Christ."

Aggressively, this learned man leaned across the desk and chastised me: "How dare you say that these people are unresponsive? They have simply never had a chance to respond!"

In fact, soon after that conversation, the Somalis rejected aid offered by the United Nations. They rejected the assistance and the involvement of the West. They, in fact, rejected a false pre-conceived idea of Christianity. But they did not reject Christ or His message. To this day, Somalis have not rejected Christ or His message. In most cases, they have simply not had an opportunity to hear clearly enough to respond.

In specific areas where persecutors have killed Christ's followers, we must honestly and biblically struggle with God's will in regard to an expatriate presence. As a parallel consideration, we might ask if the Jews *as a people group* rejected Jesus by killing the Christ. In light of Jewish rejection of the gospel, we must take note that, in Matthew 28, Jesus did not tell His disciples to shake the dust off their feet and leave Jerusalem. On the contrary, He sent them back. In fact, He sent them specifically to Jerusalem. And the result was that Jewish people, by the thousands, flocked to hear Jesus' message.

While shaking the dust off of our feet may be a necessary response in some settings, we must seek divine guidance to know when, where, and for how long such a response is appropriate. And we would be wise not to enter into that decision easily or quickly and certainly not forever.

Jesus, as the spiritual and administrative leader of His disciples, drew definite and clear parameters. But He then left the decision of when to leave to the Spirit-led judgment of those He had sent out. The decision to stay or to leave was made by those "on site" within the parameters clearly set by Jesus and based on discernment that would come only by faith, prayer, and fasting.

So, who decides when enough is enough? When is it time to make the decision to leave a difficult place? The Bible and Jesus give us the parameters. Biblically, the dust is shaken off our feet when either Christ's people or His gospel is rejected. This decision to leave is tactical; it is not a permanent decree for an entire people group for all time. Perhaps, after a community has been left, it can be reengaged in a year, in a decade, or whenever or however the Spirit leads. Shaking the dust off our feet is a public protest among those who have rejected Jesus; it is a symbolic gesture directed toward hard hearts, particularly the hard hearts of people who are already acquainted with the Scriptures.

Prayers based on Scripture passages such as 1 Corinthians 16:9, 2 Corinthians 2:12–13, and 2 Thessalonians 3:1–2 are appropriate for use by those working among the dangerously unreached and unresponsive, including communities that have already rejected the gospel. If Christ's gospel has not clearly been shared, then discernment and staying power are required.

Jesus, indeed, called harvesters to the harvest in Matthew 9:35–38. But He did so in light of the cross and He was clear about the nature of His call. He sent His disciples out as "sheep among wolves" (Matt. 10). Jesus would want us to understand that spiritual harvest and persecution go hand in hand. As we have already noted, persecution is the New Testament norm, not the exception, in environments of rejection and in environments of harvest. Harvest without persecution may be what we desire, but it is not what we encounter in the New Testament witness.

The apostle Paul serves as the model for today's sent out ones. While his life story is certainly filled with "house church planting success," his struggles and heartaches are equally important. Paul had to escape from Damascus (Acts 9:23). He disagreed intensely with Barnabas (Acts 15:37–39). He was charged with treason (Acts 18:13). He was imprisoned in Philippi. He was stripped naked and beaten (Acts 16:16ff.). He was arrested in Jerusalem (Acts 21:27). And he was imprisoned twice in Rome (Phil. 1:19–21).

If the apostle Paul were serving today, and if he encountered similar experiences, many mission-sending agencies would tell him early on to shake the dust off his feet, to stay only in the non-persecuting, harvest areas, or even to come home, because he had done enough.

We praise God that Paul did not receive that instruction! We praise God for Paul's willingness to stay even when the harvest seemed too small to measure. In staying, Paul remained faithful to God's call. In staying, Paul sacrificed his life. In his obedience, Paul honored God's call and, in doing that, his willing sacrifice broke the hearts of the churches he helped to plant and his sending churches back home!

One should always seek godly counsel. A decision about when to enter or exit a people group is a "family decision," done within the Body of Christ. Only God could tell Paul, and those traveling with him, when to stay and when to leave. Only God can tell us the same thing today.

Keeping It Real

- Where in your world are discussions concerning persecution and ill-treatment of believers part of your weekly worship cycle?
- What could cause you to quit the ministry given you by God; the death of a spouse, child, or a parent?
- To what are we entitled as Western Christians? Sunday morning messages from a pulpit to always be heard? Are we entitled to die peacefully in our sleep at a comfortable old age?
- Has Christ promised ought but a cross?
- Why is there such a hemorrhage of evangelical church members moving from church to church to church? Why are Western denominations in a 3 to 5 percent decline?
- Where would we be if God has shaken the dust off His feet in regard to our disobedience?

Part II
_____

The Birth of Faith in Persecution Environments

9

The Persecutors

Of all the obstacles noted in chapter five, the final word about persecution is perhaps the most disturbing. As we strive to understand more fully this world filled with wolves, a profile of the persecutors is instructive.

Persecution of believers is distinctly different in various settings. For the purposes of definition, there are three major types of persecutors. These three types of persecutors can be found throughout the history of Christianity and all three types are present in opposition to Jesus today. As we work down through the list, we find persecution becoming more effective with each type and setting of persecutor described. Please note that the lines between these three types of persecution are fluid; often the categories overlap.

Historically, the most common persecutor of believers is the State. In this situation, persecution is led or sanctioned by the government. *We*

refer to it here as top-down persecution. Persecution occurs when the State perceives the church (or individual believers) as a threat to order, control, or its own existence. When this kind of persecution is dominant, it originates from outside the family. In fact, in this scenario of persecution, the family and the community will, in many cases, provide a measure of protection for believers, especially if they are family members. The persecution comes from "the outside."

In this setting, there is good news and bad news. The good news is, if there is little perceived threat toward the government, there can be literally decades for people to hear about Jesus, to understand, to believe, to be baptized, and to be gathered into churches and even denominations. In this situation, a family member or neighbor will not likely report a believer to the authorities. If the government is looking for a believer, even his or her unbelieving parents will hide the believer from the government. If a believer is arrested, parents will likely pay a bribe or a fee to get the believer out of jail (even if the believer argues against that action). In this first category, persecution is a concern of the government, and even non-believing individuals will not generally participate in the oppression of believers.

In this first type of persecution, the government might demand utter loyalty, and it might conclude that calling Jesus "Lord" is an affront to the authority, the lordship, of the State. It is threatening to the State to say, "Jesus is Lord," when Caesar is lord and already fills such a position. The State might conclude that believers, because of their commitment to Jesus, will be unable or unwilling to give total allegiance to their country. Perhaps an emperor or a king will be unwilling to allow citizens to give devotion to another ruler (in this case, a ruler named Jesus). Whatever the specific motivation, the State chooses to persecute believers, and it does whatever is necessary to exert control over those who are submitting to an alternative authority.

Interestingly, this type of persecution is highly avoidable. As long as the church is not perceived as a direct threat to the government, the persecution will be minimal. In our interviews, we learned of situations where groups of believers chose to cooperate with oppressive governments and lessen—for a time—the persecution they were experiencing (or the persecution they believed they would potentially experience).

We also heard of situations where the exact opposite decision was made; some believers actually chose to be bolder with their witness even though they knew that such behavior could increase persecution from the government. In the former USSR a denominational leader was miraculously allowed to study at a seminary in Western Europe. Returning three years later to his home country he brought a troubling and challenging report. He claimed that in his three years in seminary he had learned but one biblical point of view helpful to their church in persecution. He proclaimed to his fellow pastors that they were free in Christ and should boldly increase the church planting efforts of the church as they had erroneously lived in fear for too long. Seventy plus pastors prayed and fasted for one year. After one year they carefully crafted a letter to the State saying they respected and prayed for the government but they must serve God rather than man and therefore were committed to a rapid expanse in the evangelism through existing churches. Many pastors refused to sign such a bold letter. After this missive was sent into the proper government authority, scores of pastors waited for the knock on the door which signified their arrest and imprisonment.

Not one pastor was arrested. No one went to jail. Their fear of persecution by the State led them to restrict, to persecute themselves. Often the fear of persecution is far greater than persecution itself!

Yet the general truth remains, the government's perception of the threat from the growth of believers and the church is directly tied to the intensity of the persecution.

The bad news is that when the State is threatened, it can kill the people it perceives to be a threat, and people can be killed by the millions. King Herod, disturbed by the news of the birth of the "King of the Jews," did what the Herods of history have always done. He slaughtered hundreds, if not thousands, of innocent babies to protect his Roman kingdom, his military, his government, his family, and his way of life. That tragic pattern has been repeated throughout history.

By the time this kind of persecution happens, the church has often acquired significant investments in property: buildings, seminaries, Bible colleges, and denominational headquarters. The State is adept at using such properties as tools for holding the Body of Christ hostage to its own blessings. In many places in the former USSR pastors had to report to their "religious handler" weekly. As persecution progressed, with the State adept at making the clergy reluctant copartners in the persecutions of the pastor's ministry, they would call the pastor in for his weekly "debrief." The State's representative might say something like, "Pastor, that's a nice house you have. It would be a shame for you to lose it." Or, "Pastor, it's gratifying to see how nice your church building has become and how large is your seminary. It would be a shame to have them closed, would it not?"

In some former USSR countries, such pressure was so effective in holding the clergy hostage to their own blessings/possessions, government records show that 90 percent of the clergy cooperated with the State in persecuting their own flock of believers.

In the 1960s, the Chinese government wrote in a secret "white paper" concerning faith in China: "The church in China has grown too large and too deep; we cannot kill it. We have determined to give the church properties, buildings, seminaries, and denominational headquarters so as to make the church rich. Once we do that, we will be more successful in controlling the church." I saw an English translation of this white paper, given by a believer inside the government to a friend.

This is a prophetic and hard word for the church in the West today!

We have done to ourselves what the State would attempt to do if we were, indeed, a threat to the government. Self-persecution is normally subtler and more effective than what can be imposed from the outside!

The second type of persecution once again involves the State. In this case, however, an "ideological partner" joins the State. Often, surprisingly, this ideological partner is a religious institution that cooperates with the government. This ideological partner can be a mosque, temple, synagogue or, sadly, a historical "Christian" church.

One of the tragedies of Christian history is that Christian institutions are significant persecutors of believers. Historically, the church is the fourth largest persecutor of the church! On the one hand, this makes absolutely no sense. On the other hand, history is filled with disturbing stories, and this is one of those stories. A religious group—especially one that is seeking the favor of the government or working to ensure its own survival or is attempting to protect its own properties, buildings, and possessions—will partner with the government to persecute believers who are part of a different group or movement. At first, there might be simple agreement or acquiescence toward the government's persecution. Later, however, there may be greater complicity and cooperation. This ideological partner may even lead in the persecution of believers.

Sometimes, working with an ideological partner is simply a tactical decision on the part of the government. The desire is to turn one group against another and, thereby, to exact a greater measure of control over both groups. Historically in China, leaders and members within the official "Three Self" church were encouraged to betray believers within house church movements. With varying degrees of success, the government attempts to co-opt an ideological partner to maintain control. This ideological partner is usually an historical religious, sometimes Christian, entity.

This ideological partner gives the State eyes and ears on the ground. It also gives both persecutors total deniability.

To understand this point, imagine this scene: Jesus has been crucified. A human rights agency has gone to interview Pilate concerning his involvement in the death of Jesus. Pilate would likely react with righteous anger and exclaim, "I wanted to set Jesus free. I found no fault in the man. I so disliked what the Jews did that I washed my hands of the entire matter. If it weren't for the Jewish leaders, Jesus would be alive today."

If the same human rights group were to seek out the Jewish leadership concerning their culpability in the death of Jesus, they would hear a very different story. The Jewish leaders might say, "Look at our photos. Notice the hands which are nailing Jesus to the cross? Those are Roman hands. Look at this photo. Do you see those men? Those are Roman soldiers crucifying Jesus. If it weren't for the Romans, Jesus would be alive today."

Such a situation is common in this second example of persecution. Looking at it from the outside, it is difficult to assign responsibility or fix blame. In fact, it might be concluded that no one is to blame. The State and its ideological partner have their denials and excuses ready. They can always point to someone else and claim personal innocence. The fault typically lies with "the other party." Governments such as Saudi Arabia and India can keep their relationship within the international community intact and even sign documents on human rights and freedom of religion. Their ideological partners keep their prestigious relationship with the government intact while increasing their properties, buildings, and possessions.

The third type of persecutor involves both the State and an ideological partner. In this case, however, a third human entity is the primary persecutor: the extended family and the basic structures of society. In the first type of persecution, we noted that the family would likely provide a measure of protection; a family member or neighbor would not typically report a believer to authorities. In *top-down persecution*, a believer's parents would even attempt to get their family member out of jail.

In this third type of persecution, however, *one's persecutor is at the breakfast table and sleeps in the next room.*

In *top-down persecution*, there might be decades to hear, to understand, to believe, and to be baptized in Jesus. But in this third kind of persecution, that length of time will not be possible. In fact, family members and neighbors will harm their own children and blood relatives while reporting believers to the authorities immediately. They often lead the persecution themselves. *We call this kind of persecution bottom-up persecution.*

This is the most effective and devastating of all the forms of persecution.

In this third kind of persecution, the State can be involved, and the participation of an ideological partner is often essential. But what makes this particular type of persecution so devastating and insidious is the involvement of those who are in close relationship with the believer.

This type of persecution is profoundly effective. Typically, in this kind of setting, even someone who is simply asking questions about the Christian faith is reported to authorities or simply dealt with severely by family members. A believer in this setting will typically be isolated and will normally be completely aware of what is likely to happen next. The fear of consequences can be utterly crushing. That fear itself can inhibit the asking of spiritual questions and the searching for spiritual answers. In *bottom-up persecution*, persecutors prevent spiritual birth before it ever has an opportunity to happen.

All three types of persecution are difficult to deal with, but it is this last type which is especially devastating. Traditionally, Western approaches to evangelism lead to conversions one person at a time. If this occurs within the first type of "top-down persecution," the individual believer's family will likely protect him or her. In this scenario, it will be possible for even years to pass and it will be possible for spiritual growth to happen. In this setting, the believer might even come to a place where he or she is able to share the faith with another person. Over time new believers can be gathered together into a church. This kind of numerical and spiritual growth is something that we know and understand. And this kind of incremental growth can happen even in a setting of persecution, provided that the persecution is top-down.

In the third type of persecution, however, this kind of outcome is not possible. In this third type of persecution, the family provides no protection. Family members, in fact, are the primary leaders in the persecution. It is family members who will beat those who are professing faith in Jesus. It is the grandparents who will admit those new believers to institutions for the mentally ill, while stealing the children of the believers away because their parents are no longer fit to raise their own children. When young women profess faith in Christ and then refuse to recant, it is the family who will marry the daughter to a conservative religious leader—someone often thirty years her senior. Often, this young woman will be a second wife in a house guarded by her new mother-in-law. From the outside, that situation may not look like prison. But in persecution, prisons come in all shapes and sizes.

In this bottom-up persecution setting, there will be no time for spiritual growth and certainly little opportunity or desire to share the faith with others. Evangelism and conversion within bottom-up persecution simply cannot be one person at a time. Instead, evangelism and conversion must model the biblical "household conversion" stories of Cornelius and his household in Acts 10 and the Philippian jailer and his family in Acts 16. Within the context of a *family* of believers, time could pass and spiritual growth could happen. There is absolutely no suggestion that this would be an easy or simple process; *yet we are suggesting that this is the biblical pattern for conversion,* especially in the most profoundly oppressive settings.

Church planting movements are happening all around the world today. And, surprisingly, most church planting movements are happening today *within settings of persecution.* Historically, most church planting movements emerge within settings of persecution that are primarily within the first type of top-down persecution. The reasons for this seem clear. In the first type of persecution, there is a level of personal and familial protection; the persecution comes from outside the family and community. At least in the early stages of faith, there is time for spiritual growth in this setting. Surprisingly, movements are also beginning to emerge from within bottom-up persecution today, and this is increasingly possible as families and communities come to faith in Jesus *as families and communities.*

Here's the amazing biblical insight. One reaps as they sow. If we sow a one-by-one witness we shall reap a one-by-one harvest. If we invest our witness to families, families then have the opportunity to come to Jesus ***together!*** Believers in persecution are teaching us deep truths—biblical truths. Within all forms and settings of persecution, the focus is on families (teams) reaching families. As families give their hearts to Jesus, they are baptized, and a church is then birthed inside their homes.

Regardless of the type of persecution, it is historically accurate to say that the persecutors attempt to exert control over the persecuted. It is also natural for the persecutors to believe they have the power to determine how believers will live and how bold they will be with their faith. One of the central lessons of our interviews, however, taught us that it is the persecuted—not the persecutors—who determine how they will live and how bold they will be with their faith. The persecutors determine the consequences for bold sharing of the faith, but believers in persecution told us plainly they are free to share their faith in any setting, regardless of the consequences!

The persecutors can determine the severity of the persecution. Yet it is the believer alone who can decide to love, to live for, and to share his or her faith with others.

We are inclined to look at oppressive situations and conclude believers in those settings are simply not free to share their faith. But believers in persecution around the world have a different view of things. They believe they are always free to share, even if the consequences are devastating. The persecutors will, in fact, determine the negative consequences of witness, but the persecutors never determine the believers' freedom to share nor the harvest which will follow. Believers will simply not give their persecutors that power!

This is a profoundly important lesson. Even the language that we use reveals our view of things. We might say that someone is "free to share his or her faith," or we might say that people in a certain country are "not free to share Jesus." *Globally, believers within persecution have taught us that every believer is free to witness, regardless of the setting.* There might, in fact, be painful consequences for a believer sharing his or her faith, but the freedom to share is a privilege granted by God and that freedom is always there.

Witness is ultimately not about freedom; it is about obedience. Witness is, in every case, built on the courage to suffer the consequences of exercising our God-given freedom to witness. Too often have the persecutors been given center stage, the media attention they do not deserve. It's time to focus on Jesus and witness rather than the persecutors and their nefarious methods of limiting witness and harming the children of God.

Let's Locate Our Persecutors

- In your setting today, where is the persecutor(s) located? Are you in a "top-down" environment or a "bottom-up"?
- How are we loving those perceived as hostile to the kingdom of God?
- Explore the statement "Thank God we live in a country where we are free to worship," against the almost never heard prayer, "Thank God we live in a country where we are free to witness."
- Are you focusing on reaching families or individuals?

10

God's Spirit in Present Active Tense Today

Just before ascending into heaven, Jesus spoke to His followers one final time. With the words of the Great Commission in the background, Jesus told His followers to wait in Jerusalem for the gift His Father had promised (Acts 1:4). Jesus had previously told them about this gift, the coming of the Holy Spirit (Acts 1:4–5). According to Jesus, this gift of the Spirit would empower bold witness. "But you will receive power when the Holy Spirit comes on you," Jesus explained, "and you will be my witnesses in Jerusalem, and in all Judea and Samaria, and to the ends of the earth" (Acts 1:8).

Jesus' followers obeyed His instructions. They returned to Jerusalem and waited. About a week or so later, on the day of Pentecost, the Holy Spirit came in power. We read about that dramatic event in Acts 2. The immediate result of the Spirit's arrival was bold and effective witness. In what becomes a repeated theme in the early chapters of the book of Acts, there was a huge response to the proclamation of the gospel. After Peter addressed the crowd and invited them to receive Jesus, about three thousand people accepted his message and were baptized (Acts 2:41).

Today, we refer to this historical event as Pentecost. Pentecost was already a Jewish feast that was connected both to the celebration of the annual harvest and to the historical giving of the Law to Moses. But now, within a Christian context, Pentecost takes on a new meaning: the Holy Spirit has come in power to equip Jesus' followers to embark on the task of mission. The power that Jesus talked about in Acts 1:8 had come, and His followers were equipped for the work of witness. With the coming of the Spirit in power, Jesus' followers were empowered for mission.

What happened next is dramatic. Huge numbers of people responded to the preaching of the apostles. These new believers were drawn together into community, resulting in a prolific number of house churches. Within this new Spirit-empowered community, believers worshipped and brought all things in common for use within the community. They shared both meals and the Lord's Supper together. Within this new community, they learned about the faith and they matured as believers. And out of this newly gathered community came growth—dramatic, numerical growth. New believers were added to the group daily. This growth was a gift granted by God and empowered by the Holy Spirit.

This Pentecost event described in Acts 2 could be described as a one-time, historical happening. At the same time, Pentecost also represents an occasion when the Holy Spirit works among a people group to gather scattered believers into sustaining and reproducing communities of faith. In an historical sense, the Pentecost event described in Acts 2 will never happen again. In another sense, however, a Pentecost-like event will often be necessary in order for the birth and growth of believing communities in any unengaged and unreached setting, especially those defined by persecution. In fact, only a Pentecost-like event would make that kind of spiritual birth and growth possible.

From our perspective, it is perhaps natural to say, "Well, Pentecost has already happened. We can read about that event in Acts 2. That's history." When we study Acts 2, we understand clearly that we are encountering something that happened a long time ago. However, in a very real sense, much of our world lives today in pre-Pentecost settings, in situations very much like the situation leading up to Acts 2. If sustaining and reproducing communities of faith are to be formed within this unreached world, an event like Pentecost will need to happen.

Because that's true, the Acts 2 Pentecost story serves as a model that can help us understand both the overall history of the Christian movement and the world of the dangerously unreached today. In this section of the book, we will use Pentecost *as an analogy*. We will attempt to describe the three stages of salvation history as the kingdom of God emerges and grows, and then (in some cases) ebbs and wanes. As the early church borrowed the word *Pentecost* from the Jewish tradition, we borrow it anew to further the kingdom of God and for illustrative purposes.

The Pre-Pentecost World

It can be argued that all events in the Bible, from Genesis 1 through Acts 1 are located in history as taken place before Pentecost and the birth of scores of house churches. Therefore all of this biblical history was pre-Pentecost, before the coming of the Holy Spirit in Acts 2. Pre-Pentecost is the norm for millions of lost souls today. They have never heard of the first Pentecost in Acts 2 and they certainly have never experienced such an outpouring of God's Spirit themselves.

In the world of the unengaged and the unreached, there are few known believers. There are few, if any, spiritual resources among such a people group. Bibles (oral or literate) are not present, there are few (or no) indigenous songs within this setting, and even basic spiritual disciplines are unfamiliar and perhaps nonexistent. Muslims often ask us: How do you pray? Do men and women worship together? Who takes care of your family if you are placed in prison? Who prays for you? Are there enough believers so that they can go to prison together?

The challenge within this setting is to move from an environment where there are no believers to a setting where there is the first believing family. The initial step is to move from zero to one (or a few), from no believing families to the first believing family. Once the Holy Spirit births this, the challenge is then to multiply by evangelizing additional believing families through word and deed. This is simply a description of the birth of faith, and the struggle is to understand how faith is born in this beginning moment and pre-Pentecost environment.

In these early stages, any new believers would obviously be first-generation believers. By definition, these new believers would be, perhaps, the first believers in their extended family, the first believers in their city, the first believers among their people group. As faith is born, in that beginning moment, there would be one believing family. Eventually, there might be a few more who believe. And, later, at some point, there might be a small group of believers, usually made up of an extended family or a slice of integrated society.

Early on, often because we mistakenly evangelize the unengaged and unreached one-by-one rather than by families, believers within this context would be scattered, alone, and afraid. Depending on the type of persecution setting, these few new believers might or might not have the protection of non-believing family members and neighbors. In some contexts, their new faith would be completely secret. While their families might not know that they are believers, Westerners living among them would likely know their faith as these new believers seek out the Westerner as someone safe to tell their closely held spiritual secret. In other contexts, family members might know of their new-found faith. In either case, there would be no "group" yet; certainly, there would be no church in their home. Sadly, in all likelihood, these few believers would be relatively one-dimensional in age, gender, and ethnicity. And, as we have discovered consistently in our interviews, these first few believers, in all likelihood, would be single. In Islam such first-generation believers, sadly, can often be described as men, under twenty-two years of age, single, without a job or a wife. Here men are an unreached people group. Horribly, women are both unengaged and unreached.

In a sense, this situation is similar to the biblical scene before Acts 2. This is a pre-Pentecost setting. What is most important is that Pentecost has not happened yet. In many settings Pentecost cannot even be imagined. Another borrowed word for such a setting could be the Old Testament.

The home environment for the unengaged and unreached today is very much like that. In much of the world, there is no gathered group. In much of the world, even where a few believers are present, there is no church. In much of the world, there is no reproducing community of believers. Within this setting, a particular person who believes in Jesus will be the first one, and perhaps a few more will be added one at a time.

For our purposes, it is interesting (and important) to pause here to consider this moment of beginning. How, for example, was this small group of Jesus' followers in Acts 2 able to manage the addition of about three thousand new believers in one day? Somehow, according to the story in Acts, they were ready and able to do just that, and things seemed to work out beautifully. Obviously Jesus and His disciples had prepared the way; plowed the ground and sowed thousands of barrels of seed in anticipation for the coming of the Holy Spirit.

Yet, in a pre-Pentecost setting (which is the setting for the world of the unreached today), how would an overseas worker even know where to begin? When there are no traditional forms and where there is no common vocabulary, where would a worker even start? We might assume that the overseas worker would simply start by sharing the story of Jesus, but even that simple first step surfaces a world of questions.

Kevin Greeson, author of *The Camel: How Muslims Are Coming to Faith in Christ*, identifies four initial questions that surface at this point of beginning. These are the questions which must be answered for believers to be prepared to share their faith with others. They are:

- What do I say?
- To whom do I say it? (age, gender, societal standing, singles, or families?)
- Who will hold me accountable in regard to how often I witness for my faith?
- What in the world do I do if someone says "yes" to Jesus?[8]

This final question, especially, calls to mind the situation in Acts 2. Evidently, Jesus' followers were prepared for the response that happened after the gospel was shared and faith exploded.

Early on, however, unless the gospel is wisely sown among families, the response will likely be one person at a time. Given a response, what will matter most at this point? What will these new believers need to know? What do they need to learn from Western workers who have likely spent most of their lives in a religious environment much different from a pre-Pentecost one? Where do they start?

First, these new believers will need to know what the Bible says. Often it is likely that these new believers will be unable to read or write, so this sharing will necessarily be oral. In answer to questions, Bible stories will need to be told. The Bible will need to be shared orally, and an oral Bible will need to be absorbed. Generally, a Westerner needs to hear a story or piece of information seven times to "own" it. Oral communicators need to hear information only once to absorb it! Our model here is Jesus as He read from a text, as recorded in the Gospels, one time. The rest of His ministry He was able to re-create God's Old Testament by memory.

Second, these first believers will need to understand who Jesus is. Again, Bible stories will be crucial in answering this need. When asked a question, the believer will tell the listener a story. When asked a question about the first story, the believer will tell the listener a second story! It is important to "map" a nonbeliever's biblical or spiritual understanding. Do they know the origin of the world? Have they enough of the Ten Commandments written on their hearts for an awareness of sin? Can they understand the stories of Jesus in the context of their spiritual history?

Third, these first believers will need to see a model of faithful living. They will likely look to the one who has told them about Jesus to find an incarnational example of Christian living. The one who shares the faith will also need to say to the new believer, *"Look at me! This is what a follower of Jesus looks like! If you look at my life, you will see what it looks like to follow Jesus. I will model for you how a follower of Jesus lives and how a follower of Jesus dies."*

It is no coincidence that this was exactly the approach of the apostle Paul. Instructing new believers, Paul first recited scriptural accounts of God's activity. Second, he kept his focus on the person and work of Jesus. And, third, he held up his own life as an example of Christian living. His method was consistent: Paul told stories about Jesus, he explained exactly who Jesus is, and he held up his own life as an example. In fulfilling that final need, Paul essentially said, "Imitate me. Do what you see me doing. If you imitate me, you will be imitating Christ."

The theological emphasis in this pre-Pentecost environment will invariably focus on the first coming of Jesus. At this point especially, it is essential for a new believer to understand both why Jesus came and what He came to accomplish. Other things are important, of course, but nothing will be more important than grasping this core aspect of the Christian story.

This pre-Pentecost setting accurately describes the situation before Acts 2. Importantly, it also describes the world of the unreached today. Within particular people groups today, there may be no believers at all or perhaps only a handful. There is not yet a gathered community of faith. This is a beginning time. The situation reminds us of that small group of Jesus' followers in that season of waiting before the day of Pentecost.

In real terms, what we are asking workers to attempt today is to sow the gospel in such a way that entire people groups can come out of their Old Testament, pre-Pentecost environments, experience a Pentecost-like experience, and emerge into a house church movement for themselves much like the one first recorded in Acts 2.[9]

The Pentecost World

According to the biblical account, the Holy Spirit gathered the scattered believers into a sustaining and reproducing community. Believers who had been alone and afraid almost instantaneously became a group of bold thousands. And that initial growth was not an end in itself; the growth, in fact, continued and became exponential. The key focus of the group was the telling of the gospel story and the expansion of the faith community as they cared for one another. Today, we would call this evangelism, if we understood the term as telling Jesus' story as the community fed the hungry, cared for the widows and orphans, healed the sick, in essence modeled everything Jesus said and did. In the Acts 2 story, this growing group was multiethnic and house-church based. The gospel message was typically passed on orally and leadership within the group emerged from local house churches, which were fluid, and adaptable.

When church planting movements emerge today from within contexts of the unreached, these same Pentecost realities from Acts 2 are present. Quickly moving from a few believers to thousands, these church planting movements focus largely on the Gospels and Acts; what matters most is the telling of the gospel story. Initial growth continues and becomes exponential. The movement is typically multiethnic. The message is passed on orally because it is impossible to teach people to read quickly enough to keep up with the harvest through the Holy Spirit. Leadership within the group is fluid and adaptable. Leadership is homegrown with high trust placed in these lay leaders who exhibit the Fruit of the Spirit. Most of the believers baptized in this Pentecost-like experience will also be first-generation believers. It is very common in Pentecost-like settings for entire extended families to be baptized together, and then immediately and naturally hosting a house church. We would consistently suggest that evangelism and discipleship are interchangeable terms. Healthy faith is always doing both together, inseparable, at the same time. Can it be the emphasis on discipleship in Western churches is a camouflage for refusing to evangelize?

Some further observations are instructive. While believers around the world long for the written Word of God, in a church planting movement, there is little time for literacy training or translation of Scripture. The written Word and the ability to read it are of absolute importance, but while those goals are being sought (through Bible translation and literacy training), the stories of the Bible are communicated orally. Taking the time to translate Scripture or taking the time to provide literacy training is a luxury that these rapidly growing movements cannot afford. Those without Jesus should not be forced to become literate in order to be welcomed into God's kingdom. The need to share the gospel is immediate, and so it is shared in the only way that it can be shared: orally. The point must be repeated; a literate Bible is indispensable. Yet those carrying the gospel to the nations must not wait ten to twenty years for the first printed Bible in an unengaged and unreached environment before broadly sowing the Good News and seeing a Pentecost-like movement emerge.

We found the church in China, in particular, hungry for the written Word of God; at the same time, the church in China was not paralyzed by the absence of the written Word of God. Earlier in their movements, copies of the Bible were extremely rare, but Bible stories were known and repeated and memorized. In this time of beginning, there is a sense of urgency. Waiting for ten years (or more) for an initial Bible translation is simply not an option. By its nature and by necessity, the incipient movement is oral.

In the same way, there is not sufficient time, nor necessity, to wait for leaders to be formally trained, using Western, literate methodologies. It is perhaps instructive that Jesus did not employ an institutional training model. In our culture, it might take seven to ten years to prepare an evangelist, church planter, and pastor for service. Without trained leaders, however, what might happen in those intervening seven years? Within church planting movements, it is impossible to wait for formal, literate training to happen; leaders simply rise from within the gathered community. These leaders receive their training *as they serve* or they receive their training when they are arrested and imprisoned for the sharing of their faith. They are trained! Yet they are trained inside the local church and for the movements of God.

Furthermore, buildings are not necessary; in fact, usually buildings are seen as a hindrance. Constructing buildings requires too much time and money. Buildings are dangerous because they allow the persecutors to locate most of the believers at a set place and at a set time. In a sense, buildings become a kind of "one-stop shopping" for those opposed to Jesus, His gospel, and His followers. The question demands consideration: Was the construction of church buildings, separate from house churches, the norm in the New Testament? In the New Testament, the construction of buildings is not even mentioned.

For that reason, these church planting movements are usually "house movements." In many places the size of the house determines the size of the church. Or the level of persecution determines the size of the house church. As a group grows, it is constantly dividing into new, smaller groups. During our time of interviews in China, house-church leaders explained that groups of more than thirty people, or groups that gathered together for more than three days at a time, attracted too much attention from the authorities. That kind of awareness shapes the typical makeup of house churches. Normally, especially where persecution is intense, house churches involve fewer than thirty believers, and gatherings are invariably shorter than three days. Especially in the early stages, these "house movements" are remarkably adaptable and fluid concerning what day of the week they meet, where they meet, and what time they meet.

What we haven't really talked about yet is the spiritual dimension of this Pentecost-like event. Though we want to be excellent partners with God, it is the activity of the Holy Spirit who empowers this dramatic growth. In a short time, scattered believers are drawn together. This drawing together is something that God Himself does. Responding to His activity, these now-gathered believers become a sustaining community committed to growth and reproduction. This is precisely the process that we see happening in Acts 2. And this same process happens within the world of the unreached today when Pentecost-like movements break out. God desires for such movements for every unengaged and unreached people group globally. Does He not also desire such a movement in the West?

The Post-Pentecost World

This final movement in the story cannot easily be seen in the world of the unreached; perhaps it simply has not happened there yet. However, this part of the story can easily be seen in our own history. To put it one way, Pentecost was a long time ago. We understand what happened in those early days when scattered and fearful believers were transformed by the power of the Holy Spirit. But what happened as time passed?

Today, at least in the West, our world might be described as a post-Pentecost world. What does the church look like more than two thousand years after the Pentecost event described in Acts 2? Perhaps the following description is overstated, but the overstatement might be necessary to get our attention.

While the gathered group in the days of Pentecost emphasized the telling of the story, the church in our post-Pentecost world focuses on maintaining the organization.

Many church leaders today care most about managing what is already in place rather than reaching new people. New believers typically come from within the church population; this kind of growth is sometimes referred to as biological growth.

Buildings, staff, and denominational identity are extremely important in much of the post-Pentecost world, and significant resources are committed to building new buildings, maintaining those buildings, and servicing debt required to build those buildings. The majority of a church's funds are spent on the ninety-nine sheep already found, while much less is spent in an effort to reach that one lost sheep. Training is often based on the transfer of information and may have little to do with character formation.

Many of the churches in this post-Pentecost setting are monoethnic. If mixed races are found within a church building they are often from the same socioeconomic background.

Ministries and programs, in almost every case, are dependent on literacy. Most believers in the post-Pentecost world, of course, live in literate settings. At the same time, it is crucial to keep in mind that more than 83 percent of the world's unreached people cannot functionally read or write.

While the gathered community moving into a Pentecost moment is consumed with understanding and proclaiming the first coming of Jesus, the church in the post-Pentecost world often focuses more on the second coming of Jesus. Perhaps it makes perfect sense within this context, but teaching and preaching is often focused on the part of Scripture from Romans to Revelation. Since this is a "church context," the focus is on "life in the church."

A very high percentage of those baptized in the post-Pentecost church were born to those in the church. There are few first-generation believers.

No judgment or criticism is intended here! We want to be both kind and careful since we are talking about the Bride of Christ. These historical developments are not all necessarily negative. These developments do, however, represent a radically different perspective from that of pre-Pentecost and Pentecost. If we pay attention, these developments and differences can provide profound missiological and evangelistic insights.

For example, how does a believer coming from a post-Pentecost setting move into a pre-Pentecost world and communicate the grace of Jesus? Most overseas personnel have been raised and trained in a post-Pentecost world; how can these people step into a very different world and share the gospel? In that pre-Pentecost world, the known and familiar forms and traditions are no longer present. Traditionally, and sometimes tragically, believers have simply attempted to take the forms of a post-Pentecost church and implement (and sometimes translate) them in a pre-Pentecost setting. This is not an effective and appropriate way to proceed.

In our experience, moving from a post-Pentecost to a pre-Pentecost world felt like getting on an airplane in a New Testament world and landing in an Old Testament world! Little in the post-Pentecost world prepares us to go to pre-Pentecost. Post-Pentecost and its churches focus on the role and training of pastors. Pre-Pentecost begs for evangelists and church planters. Most seminaries in the post-Pentecost world train its students for the pastorate or teaching ministries. Few are those theological institutions that focus on the unengaged, unreached, and pre-Pentecost.

This Pentecost construct speaks powerfully to several concerns that are at the heart of this book. First, what does this Pentecost model say about the role of the overseas worker? Second, how does this model help us understand persecution and martyrdom?

Regarding the role of overseas workers, the skill set needed will change and relationships will change in different stages of the movement. In a pre-Pentecost world, the worker is responsible for broadly sowing the gospel seed. In this setting, there are no believers or perhaps only a few. The believers who are present are probably scattered, alone, and afraid. They have only recently come out of lostness. They are in need of companionship and encouragement. They are first-generation believers. They need their families to become followers of Jesus.

What is most needed in a pre-Pentecost world is an incarnational witness. What these new believers need to know is what the Bible says and who Jesus is. They need a model that is willing to say, "Watch my life and I will show you how a follower of Jesus lives and how a follower of Jesus dies." Those basic needs dictate the role of the worker. It is this simple. A worker in pre-Pentecost may be more defined by what they leave behind in post-Pentecost than by what they take with them to pre-Pentecost. In pre-Pentecost, entry strategies are of vast importance as we decide where to go next.

As a Pentecost-like event happens, and as house churches begin to multiply, the role of the worker is to discern the right time to leave. Here, exit strategies must gain more predominance. When Pentecost comes, nothing would be more important than an appropriate exit strategy. At that point, the worker would ideally be planning to begin serving in another pre-Pentecost setting. *Generally if a worker stays long enough in a Pentecost-like movement for denominational identities to emerge, millions of people will remain without any access to Jesus.*

Finally, as the worker finds himself or herself in post-Pentecost settings, the sent out one would take on the role of helping their historical church embrace the world of the unengaged and unreached, especially in their own backyards within the Western world. This has not been a traditional worker role, but it is an essential one as the church struggles to transcend the captivity of institution, tradition, and culture.

The role of the sent out one changes significantly through the different movements of this Pentecost analogy. Candidly, one of the most common missiological mistakes made by overseas workers is to prepackage everything that has been gathered in a post-Pentecost church world for thousands of years and then simply to superimpose it in a pre-Pentecost environment. *Tragically, this often results in new believers experiencing all the divisions of the Body of Christ before they ever experience being one in Jesus.*

The well-trained and clearly focused overseas worker will often be asked to interact within all three stages of salvation history from pre-Pentecost through post-Pentecost. They know that each stage of this spiritual history requires a different spiritual toolset. With increasing language and cultural acquisition, they are comfortable ministering within all three diverse and different stages of the Pentecost story.

In the context of this discussion, it is crucial that we understand "the sent out ones." The task that stands before us is to give billions of people access to Jesus. This requires that we deliberately leave our post-Pentecost nests, go to a pre-Pentecost world, and exit quickly from any Pentecost-like outpouring of the Holy Spirit. This task also requires that many overseas workers exit historical and traditional mission fields for the sake of those in pre-Pentecost. This might be the largest missiological challenge still to be faced. We must also remember that Pentecost is clearly the work of the Holy Spirit and it requires a clear exit strategy. Overseas workers can wisely partner with God in assisting new, emerging believers to experience exponential growth similar to what happened within the first Pentecost. At the same time, Pentecost-like movements remain the purview of the Holy Spirit. What's more, renewal even in the post-Pentecost church can be experienced as believers obediently embrace those without Jesus in pre-Pentecost settings, across the planet or across the street.

Consider now the impact of persecution and martyrdom in these different movements of the story. In the pre-Pentecost world, persecution can be deadly, not just to individuals, but to any emerging movements. Church history tells us "the blood of the martyrs is the seed of the church." But this turns out not to be true in a pre-Pentecost setting. *In a pre-Pentecost setting, in fact, the blood of the martyrs can be . . . the death of the church!* It is crucial to remember, in this setting, there are very few believers; these few believers are scattered and alone. What these first believers need most is a window of safety. Persecution may come. In fact, Jesus assures us that it will come! But if persecution comes too quickly, there will be no time for spiritual growth or reproduction of the faith.

As an instructive parallel, consider Jesus' disciples and followers. Before Jesus' death on the cross, His followers did not suffer imprisonment. Other than John the Baptist, Jesus' followers (before Jesus' death on the cross) did not die because of their relationship with Him. Any follower of Jesus who died before the resurrection died of natural causes! Certainly, their message was not warmly received in every case and, yes, they were sometimes rejected when they shared, but their time with Jesus was a season of shaping and safety. There was an opportunity for growth and learning. *Consider carefully what Jesus did! With heavenly skill, He created a safe place, a bubble in history. He provided three years in which thousands around Him could hear, understand, believe, be baptized, and be gathered together in house churches before serious persecution arrived.*

This, indeed, is the role of overseas workers in pre-Pentecost. They are to create a bubble in history, a safe place for people to believe in Jesus and become part of the Body of Christ. When serious persecution arises in pre-Pentecost (much too often because of the untrained, outside, overseas worker), this persecution is effective in killing everything begun by the Holy Spirit. The result can be devastating.

After Pentecost, this changed dramatically. Suddenly, Jesus' followers began to experience everything He had promised in Matthew 10. Even more, they began to experience everything Jesus had experienced. They were arrested and threatened; some of them even lost their lives. Indeed, the blood of *these* martyrs (in this Pentecost setting) did become the seed of the church—where the church was in existence and reproducing. Often, the result of persecution in the original Pentecost setting was explosive growth. Persecution authenticated their faith and allowed the followers of Jesus to share in His sufferings.

The same thing will be true in Pentecost-like settings today. Several times already, we have made the point that persecution is normal and expected. That is true within a setting of Pentecost. In a pre-Pentecost setting, however, the death of those believers will quite possibly decimate the incipient movement. On the other hand, in a Pentecost setting, the death of believers can serve as fuel for an unstoppable movement.

This is not to say that God cannot use the suffering of believers in pre-Pentecost settings; He can certainly use their suffering for His purposes. Yet the evidence of decades of study seems to suggest that persecution within pre-Pentecost settings is deadly, especially if it is a result of secondary issues. But within the context of Pentecost, persecution typically leads to even greater growth. This is what we see happening in the book of Acts and this is what we see happening all around the world today.

Persecution, it seems, is rare in a post-Pentecost setting. Perhaps the church does not face significant persecution as it becomes less and less a threat to lostness. On the other hand, when persecution does come within a post-Pentecost church setting, such persecution almost always divides the church. Not surprisingly, it becomes easier and easier to compromise the faith when buildings and property are at risk. Those problems would never be faced in pre-Pentecost or Pentecost settings. Often pastors say to us, "persecution is coming to the church in America." When asked to explain the origin of this expected persecution, the response is often revolving around conservative evangelical stances on abortion and homosexuality. Please hear me carefully; these are important issues. But the U.S. churches' stance opposing these activities and lifestyles is the same as conservative Islam, the same as Saudi Arabia! Is this how we are to be defined for our lifetime? Social issues are important. Yet what we are "measuring" through our interviews is a persecution which comes directly related to making Jesus known to those who have little or no opportunity to hear otherwise. It is a persecution which soars when the gospel is incarnated in Satan's backyard.

In every movement of the story and in every part of this analogy, whether we find ourselves in a pre-Pentecost, Pentecost, or post-Pentecost setting, *the needs of the lost carry more weight than the needs of the witnesser.* This selfless approach to ministry is not our normal way of living or serving. We tend to think mostly about ourselves. Institutions tend to care most about institutional survival. If, however, the needs of the unengaged and unreached matter most, the church and its people are compelled to rethink what matters most and what sacrifices will be required! It will redefine our training, where we go, and how long we stay.

Using Pentecost as a model is more than a theoretical exercise. During our time in Somalia, we heard of a significant number of Somalis who were ready to declare their faith in Jesus. As exciting as that was, we actually heard Western workers say, "Oh, no! What are we going to do now?" They could not imagine how they would care for large numbers of new believers coming from a pre-Pentecost environment using Western, post-Pentecost models of "doing church."

That response of concern was rooted in reality. Where would we find support for these new believers? At that point, there was no church and no cohesive faith community. Where would these Somali believers find shelter, food, employment, and education? What would become of their families and their children? Where would these new believers find community? What would happen if one tried to build a church building, start a seminary, or promote denominational agendas?

Of course, these Somali believers were not the first believers to face such hard questions. New believers in the book of Acts faced similar situations. As they followed Christ, they were excluded from the synagogue and cut off from community. Believing widows and orphans were disenfranchised. *But here is the difference: In the book of Acts, there was a believing community.* Because of Pentecost, the church had burst into existence. Yes, there was intense persecution, but the persecution happened in a Pentecost setting. In Acts, when believers lost homes and jobs and opportunities, they lost those things within a community that was able to provide basic human needs by bringing all things common. In Somalia, we encountered similar needs *without the presence of church*. After Acts 2 there were thousands of believers in hundreds of house churches.

Interestingly, in the book of Acts, a Pentecost-type event is repeated within different people groups. What happened for the Jews in Acts 2 was repeated for Samaritans in Acts 8. A similar event happened for Gentiles in Acts 10. It would seem that Pentecost is a church growth movement always made possible by the Holy Spirit Himself.

It is essential to discern whether a particular setting is a pre-Pentecost setting or if Pentecost has already happened. In a pre-Pentecost world, believers must be protected and given room to grow. After Pentecost, however, the Spirit-empowered believing community should be well equipped to care for its own. This Pentecost model is instructive as we try to sense what God is doing in different parts of His world, and it is especially helpful as we try to discern our role in joining in His work.

We never want to cheat new believers out of Pentecost, moving them directly from pre-Pentecost to post-Pentecost and taking them directly to the slice of religious history in which Westerners are most familiar and most comfortable.

Truly this would be a tragedy.

Even as we try to understand how it is that God brings new believers into His family, it is overwhelming to discover that God continues to do exactly what He has always done! In settings where the birth of the church might seem to us to be impossible, God, even today, is finding ways to reach people and draw them together in community. God never leaves Himself without a witness. Satan never leaves himself without a persecutor. It is time for us to talk about exactly how that is happening, how the spiritual battle is being shaped.

If I Hear the Word "Flexible" One More Time!"

- Where is your faith being lived out at this time in regard to the Pentecost model shared above?
- How do you prepare someone to go from post-Pentecost to pre-Pentecost using the Old and New Testament analogy?
- What should we take with us to pre-Pentecost?
- What should we leave behind?

11

Supernatural Conversions
through Western Eyes

Our interviews with believers in persecution revealed a number of faulty assumptions on our part. For example, before our interviews, we believed that we understood well the process of conversion for most people groups. We knew that people in unreached settings were coming to faith in Christ. Our assumption was that, in most cases, the role of the overseas worker was indispensable in the conversion experience. We had a high opinion of ourselves. Our interviews, however, revealed a very different picture.

Allow us to share with you a snapshot of history. This particular snapshot focuses on conversion. Because things in the world change so rapidly, we are not suggesting that this snapshot is accurate for every people group and for every time. What is most important, perhaps, is to discern the truths that appear in this snapshot and then to apply those truths more broadly from one culture to another.

In talking with more than 250 MBBs, we discovered that fewer than 10 percent of them had ever met a Western **worker** or "outside" believer before coming to faith in Jesus. To put it another way, *more than 90 percent of these followers of Jesus had come to faith without the help of an outsider or a believer from another culture.* Our earlier assumptions had elevated the role of the Western worker; our interviews humbled us in suggesting how small the worker's role actually was.

Encountering the same pattern so often, we were driven to find some meaningful explanations. Several key insights quickly came to the surface.

First, we realized (and we were compelled to admit) that believers in the West typically fear persecution; even more, they tend to avoid persecution at any cost. It dawned on us that God might be hesitant to put Western believers in the lives of new believers who would, in all likelihood, live with severe persecution daily. Perhaps believers from the West are not especially well suited to help believers deal with life in settings where persecution would be common. It would be likely that Western believers would instill fear in new believers in pre-Pentecost settings.

Second, we realized the rather obvious truth that God is not waiting on Western workers to reach the peoples of the world! God always takes the initiative. He is always seeking ways to reveal Himself in the darkest corners of the earth. When we began working with Muslims in 1991, there was one Western worker for approximately every 1.2 million Muslims. More recently, that statistic has changed. Today, given a greater emphasis on sharing the gospel in Muslim contexts, there is one Western worker for approximately every 750,000 Muslims. Even with that "improved" ratio, it is clear that there are simply not enough overseas workers to reach the Muslim populations of our world. To put it bluntly, if God were required to wait until Western workers "showed up" to help Muslims find Jesus, He would be waiting for a long time for us to become obedient. On the contrary, our interviews suggested that God has ways of reaching Muslims that are not dependent on Western workers!

Those rather basic observations led us to a fascinating and important question: If Muslims are coming to Jesus (and they are), and if these conversions are not currently enhanced by the presence of Western workers (and they are not), then how exactly are these conversions happening?

How, within this snapshot of history, are Muslims coming to Christ?

The question is crucial, and it was addressed in every one of our interviews. Typically, Western workers envision their role as somehow bringing God to a location where He has not yet been active. Though it sounds ridiculous to say, we tend to believe that we travel to another land and "bring God with us." But the wisdom garnered from the interviews turned that presumption upside down. It turns out that there is no place where God is not working. In every place, God is already calling people to Himself. In fact, it might even be suggested that we go out and witness *so that we might* discover where God is already at work!

When we discern God's activity and we join in His work, we have the high privilege of partnering with Him. But, evidently, God has ways of accomplishing His work with or without our participation. From our interviews, we gained insights about how Muslims were coming to Jesus. Obviously, God is not compelled to work in *only* these ways; these are simply the insights we gained through our interviews. These interviews depict how God is bringing Muslims to Himself, particularly where there are no Western workers.

The Conversion of MBBs

For Muslim Background Believers, there are three major components in the journey to faith in Jesus.

Dreams and Visions

First, there are dreams and visions which lead to a spiritual pilgrimage. In talking with hundreds of MBBs, we heard repeatedly of a period of time lasting from three to five years when dreams and visions were present and life-shaping in their pilgrimage to Jesus. These dreams and visions typically sent the Muslim on a spiritual journey. It was very common for them to hear a voice without a body speaking to them. It was very common for them to see a bright light, dream about the Bible, or hear the voice of the angel Gabriel. It was not uncommon for them to dream of Jesus. These dreams and visions were sign-posts and attention-getters.

In most cases, dreams and visions are not considered to be miraculous events for Muslims; they are, in fact, quite common. What is miraculous is the manner in which God breaks into these dreams and visions and changes the content of the dreams. Over time, the Holy Spirit shapes these visitations and leads the seeker to begin a spiritual pilgrimage.

Dreams and visions are not salvific. The dreams allow God to get the recipient's attention and lead seekers to Jesus. Only Jesus has the power to change souls.

During this long period of time, the seeker might be experiencing other kinds of spiritual encounters. For example, there might be conversations with believers, a clandestine visit to an historical church, conversation with a pastor, listening to Christian radio or exposure to "*The JESUS Film.*" In fact, most MBBs report at least twenty to thirty different spiritual encounters prior to their decision to follow

Jesus. But, in almost every case, dreams and visions both fueled and informed their search.

Often, as mentioned above, the angel Gabriel is present in these dreams and visions. For MBBs, Gabriel's presence is extremely significant because Gabriel is believed to have given the Qur'an to Mohammed. Even more, the Qur'an also refers to Jesus as "the Word of God." When a Muslim, perhaps through a dream or vision, is invited (or instructed) to "find Jesus" or "find the good news," this Muslim is being set free to begin a spiritual quest. And later, when this Muslim encounters Jesus, who is called in John's Gospel "the Word of God," significant connections are made.

Strangely, when these dreams and visions begin, a Muslim will typically turn to the mosque for answers and explanations. This would be a natural place for a Muslim to turn for spiritual answers. The spiritual leaders from the mosque will normally be sought out for spiritual counsel. "What do these dreams mean?" would be a predictable first question. Interestingly, spiritual leaders in the mosque will typically affirm that the dreams and visions are from God, and they will often tell the seeker that the instructions in the dreams and visions should be followed. Strangely, once God begins to break into their consciousness through this means, Muslims begin to visit and pray in the mosque as never before. They may grow a long beard, change the way they dress, become a conservative practitioner of Islam.

Normally, the presence of the dreams and visions will also give rise to additional questions that will not always be easily answered in the mosque. For example, the seeker might be led to ask, "How can I know that God loves me?" The answer from the mosque might be, "Well, you can't know that."

Another question might be, "How can I be sure that I will go to paradise when I die?" Again, the answer of the mosque might very well be, "You cannot know that with certainty either."

Another question might be, "How can I know if my sins are forgiven?" Once again, this question will typically be greeted with uncertainty. "You cannot know that with certainty," the spiritual leader might say.

Often the seeker will be harshly commanded to stop asking such questions and to simply submit to Islam and obey the Qur'an. At some point, unanswerable questions like these will lead to frustration. And often, within three to six months, the seeker will leave the mosque and look for answers elsewhere. *In most cases, the seeker will never return to the mosque.*

At the beginning of this chapter, we wondered about the role of Western workers in this mysterious process of conversion. We had assumed (or perhaps we had wanted to believe) that the Western worker was indispensable. Through our interviews, however, we discovered it was these God-given dreams and visions that led most Muslims to begin their spiritual quest. Often, Western workers entered the story only after these seekers had already encountered Jesus. In simplest terms, these MBBs came to Jesus first, and then they came looking for Western workers to provide additional insight, understanding, baptism, resources, and community.

Separation from the mosque was another surprising insight that we gathered from our interviews. Sometime during this period of dreams and visions (which would normally last as long as three to five years), seekers reported that they would separate from the mosque and pursue their spiritual search in other ways. Coming to faith in Jesus, they would then typically not return to the mosque. At first, we suspected that these new believers would return to the mosque for security or even for evangelistic purposes, but we discovered that such returns were rare.

Encounters with the Bible

Second, as part of this spiritual quest, there were dramatic encounters with the Bible. Often these encounters were miraculous in nature. To be fair, simply finding a Bible in many of these settings would require a miracle. Bibles are simply not available. Even so, our interviews were filled with stories of dramatic encounters with Scripture. This is both good news and bad news.

First, let's look at the good news. In some cases, a Muslim might begin to dream about the Bible, but this Muslim will have no idea where to find such a book. In Central Asia one seeker, who had been attempting to find a Bible for months, went to the all-male market one day. There, a stranger simply appeared in this busy marketplace and handed a copy of the Bible to this seeker. The stranger said, "The Holy Spirit told me to give this to you." And then the stranger simply disappeared into the crowd. The seeker is stunned. He is now suddenly alone, holding a Bible.

In another case, a seeker, having been told in a dream to find a Bible, wandered through a bookstore filled with green Qur'ans. There he noticed a single blue-covered volume in the back of the shop. It turned out to be a copy of the Bible and he purchased it . . . in a bookstore dedicated solely to the sale of Qur'ans!

A young lady within Islam began to dream about the Bible. Wisely, she shared her dreams with her family at the breakfast table, asking them for advice as to the meaning of her dreams. After a number of weeks her father called his daughter into his office. From the bottom of his desk he pulled out a blue book, the Bible, and he gave it to her. No one in her family would have ever dreamed that her father would have possessed a copy of God's Word.

We heard stories like these stories over and over again. Motivated by dreams and visions, Muslim seekers find the Bible and typically read it voraciously. We discovered that more than 90 percent of all MBBs have had significant encounters with the Bible, and most of them read the Bible completely through three to five times before coming to faith in Christ. (We met one MBB who had read the Bible through twenty-two times in less than a year.) What that means, among other things, is that most MBBs have profound knowledge of Scripture *before* making their faith decision. This discovery was so prevalent that we feel comfortable in affirming this conclusion: *"Where there is no Bible, there is no salvation."*

The centrality of Scripture in this salvation process is both important and interesting. In some Western evangelical denominations, the average age for a person being baptized is eight or nine years old. It is fair to ask about the amount of Bible knowledge that such a young child might have. In contrast, a typical MBB has had much greater exposure to Scripture before conversion. When these seekers finally come to faith in Jesus, they have already spent significant time in God's Word. The dreams and visions have encouraged and even required that kind of encounter with the Bible. And that kind of encounter seems to be indispensable in the conversion process. Because Muslims have such a high regard for their own holy book, they are seeking for a copy of the Bible in their language with great hunger.

There is also bad news. As important as that part of the process is, however, it is problematic in a world that is largely oral. If this encounter with Scripture is indispensable in conversion, what happens to a seeker who cannot read? Clearly, we are compelled to see the importance of making the Bible available in oral forms for those who cannot read or write. If seekers are instructed by God to seek out the Bible, the Bible will need to be available in forms that are accessible and understandable.

Most Muslim men who come to faith in Jesus travel a more literate path. However, many Muslim women cannot read, so other kinds of Bible encounters will be needed. Interestingly, modern linguistic studies indicate that written words, in any format, constitute only 7 or 8 percent of communication. More than 90 percent of communication is nonverbal (revealed through body language, tone of voice, eye contact, and other oral means).

Jesus was a master of nonliterate communication. Even though His words and stories were powerful, literacy was never a requirement for understanding His message. Literacy was not a requirement for leadership training. We would be wise to follow Jesus' example of communication and sharing.

The interviews clearly demonstrated that Muslim women are having dreams and visions by the millions. Yet the illiteracy rate for women is almost double what it is for men. *We have utterly failed these Muslim women who are having dreams and visions and searching for Jesus by not providing them with access to the Word of God in oral forms.* We have utterly failed Muslim women by denying them the opportunity to be witnessed to by women from the Western world who believe in Jesus. When Western, literate, male workers share Jesus only with literate Muslim men—leaving Muslim women without any witness from believing Western women—the result is devastating. The obvious implication for Muslim women is that Christianity is just like Islam—it is only for literate men. This is a tragic failure on our part.

Encounters with In-Culture or Near-Culture Believers

In the process of conversion, dreams and visions are typically present. Significant (and often miraculous) encounters with the Bible are also crucial. Then, third, there are encounters with in-culture or near-culture believers. These encounters often take the form of "divine appointments" where someone simply appears on the scene to provide guidance, counsel, and instruction.

In Scripture, these kinds of encounters happen frequently. God makes it possible for Joseph to bear witness to Pharaoh. God brings Ananias into Saul's life at a crucial point when instruction and guidance are needed. The Ethiopian eunuch is a seeker with spiritual questions when God arranges a meeting with Philip. In much the same way, God graciously brings in-culture or near-culture believers into the lives of Muslim seekers to answer questions and to provide guidance.

Often, these encounters have a miraculous feel that can be appreciated only in retrospect.

Imagine for a moment the story of the Ethiopian eunuch. We are not told how he began his spiritual journey from Queen Candace's court. When his story began, he was on his way back home. He was being driven in his chariot, surrounded by a caravan of people. He had spent time at the heart of religious practice, and he was returning home without having found salvation.

As he rode, he read from the scroll of Isaiah. This scroll would have been hand-copied and it would have been very expensive. Typically, scrolls of Scripture would have remained in the temple and the synagogues. Typically, only the men of Israel would have handled them. Yet here was this Ethiopian—a foreigner, a man of color, and an emasculated man—with the scroll of God!

Before interviewing MBBs who had miraculously interacted with the Word of God, I had never considered this question: "How in the world would this Ethiopian eunuch come to possess a scroll of Isaiah?" When I finally did ask this question, I sensed God Himself responding: "Nik, if you will get My Word out where it can be accessed by seekers, then I will get it in the hands of those who need it the most. Nik, I have been doing this sort of thing for a long time!"

Evidently, God is able to put people and His Word together as He sees fit.

We started this chapter considering the role of the Western worker in the conversion process. Our interviews suggested, in the lives of Muslims, a minimal role in the conversion process itself. Even more, we discovered that when Western workers are present and actively involved in the conversion process of MBBs, the involvement of the Western worker changes the typical conversion dynamic. When Western workers are involved in leading Muslims to Jesus, for example, the dreams and visions almost completely disappear from the process. Surely, this is an indication that many Western workers do not feel that dreams and visions are needed (or perhaps they wonder if they are even possible!). Since Western workers "know how to lead people to Christ," they would not need to rely on spiritual realities such as dreams and visions. In a disturbing twist, the activity of the Holy Spirit can be "replaced" by the wisdom, experience, strategy, and presence of the Western worker. Understandably, most Western workers are very generous. They provide the seeker with a witness that quickly leads to salvation. They proceed to provide a Bible, baptism, a place to worship, and opportunities for discipleship. They might even offer a job, education, and perhaps the opportunity of finding a wife. This new believer might even be invited to move to the West.

If the outsider provides everything for the seeker, what is left for the Holy Spirit to provide?

Our interviews suggest that God is perfectly able to draw people to Himself, and our task is not to co-opt this process. Instead, we should carefully and prayerfully discern what God is doing and join Him. Instructively, in Acts 8, God brings Philip into the story at exactly the right moment, and then God takes him out of the story just as suddenly. In all likelihood, the Ethiopian man has already had years of dreams and visions. He is in the midst of his dramatic encounter with Scripture. And, precisely at that point, God arranges a meeting with a near-culture believer to provide guidance, instruction, and counsel.

How exactly are Muslims coming to faith in Christ? First, dreams and visions open the door to a spiritual pilgrimage. Second, there is a dramatic and extensive (and often miraculous) encounter with Scripture. Third, there is a meeting with an in-culture or near-culture believer who can explain the dreams they are having and the Scriptures they are reading.

Before our interviews, we assumed that Muslims would not come to faith without the help of a Western worker. God is not waiting on us, but He loves to use us in His work. However, our presence has not been as strategically important as we thought. Perhaps if we were more obedient in our going and if we were to go with less fear, then God would use us in a greater way in the conversion process of millions of Muslims.

Again, our interviews are simply a snapshot of a specific place in a specific period of time. It may be that God is doing different things in other places among other people. In any case, these snapshots help us understand what God is doing and how we might join Him more effectively in His work. These interviews are certainly not to be seen as the only truth for all time; even exhaustive interviews could never capture God's methodology. As the number of workers increases, as the Bible becomes more available in oral and written forms, and as more local believers emerge, the precise way that people come to know Jesus will probably change. The picture presented here is descriptive rather than prescriptive. We are simply talking about what God was doing in one snapshot of history. We are not limiting what God might be doing in other contexts or what He might choose to do next.

Our goal here is to be so in tune to the Holy Spirit that we join with God in what He is already about and seek to greatly multiply His efforts.

One further insight is needed. While it is true God does not wait on anyone to make Himself known, He partners with His believing children at great risk. While we have found followers of Jesus everywhere, even within the most spiritually dark corners globally, we seldom if ever find house churches (or churches of any type) started without humans partnering with God in the genesis of a new body. What a responsibility! It is true God calls the lost to Him. It seems to be equally true He depends on a human partner to start a church!

The Conversion of HBBs

Much to our surprise, the conversion experience of Hindu Background Believers was quite different from MBBs. The larger lesson here is that we need to discover what God is already doing with different groups. And it turns out that people in different groups are coming to faith in Jesus in very different ways.

Common elements in the conversion of a MBB include dreams and visions, an encounter with the Bible, and a meeting with an in-culture or near-culture believer. The typical conversion process for people in a Hindu culture was quite different.

The Hindu world is based on castes or levels in society. For decades, the traditional Western approach to evangelism in the Hindu world has focused on the lower castes, particularly the untouchables. The theory was that the lower castes would be more open to the gospel and that, once reached, these people would somehow then reach the higher castes in society. Unfortunately, this theory did not play out in reality. More recently, greater emphasis has been placed on reaching families within the higher castes, based on the hope that, once reached, the higher castes might be willing to reach the lower castes with the gospel.

Regardless of the focus group, however, the process that surfaced in our interviews of Hindus coming to Jesus was miraculously widespread. Please remember, this is a snapshot of one slice of history and not meant to be prescriptive.

In our interviews, we encountered some common steps. The first step involves a group of HBBs. These believers will go out in small groups as evangelists. They will travel to an area that shares a cultural affinity. This will constitute an in-culture or near-culture encounter. Arriving in this area, the evangelists will typically discover profound physical needs, and they will offer the gift of healing. In the name of Jesus, they will pray for healing, and literally hundreds of people will be healed of various diseases and ailments immediately. It appears to be a scene taken straight from the New Testament.

Having been healed, these people will then be invited to pray a prayer asking for God's salvation. They will be asked if they want to receive the Jesus who just healed them? Typically, after praying that prayer, they will also be baptized almost immediately. And because this process normally involves hundreds (and even thousands) of people, by the end of the day "church" has broken out. Physical healing has happened, a spiritual relationship with God has been established, and new believers have come together as the people of God.

The HBB evangelists will then travel to another area and repeat the same process.

This is a very different conversion model than what we encountered among MBBs. In contrast to our understanding of conversion for MBBs, note how little the Word of God plays a part in this "conversion" process. Two questions surfaced quickly as we listened to over seventy stories with these common threads. Without a biblical foundation (seventy-four "converts could not retell even one Bible story), what will these new believers do when persecution comes or when they are sick once more and not healed? Having literally millions of gods in their religious pantheon, are they simply placing Jesus in a place of honor among all their other gods?

One of the most interesting dynamics, in fact, shows up in areas where both Muslims and Hindus are present. Typically, Muslims in traditionally Hindu areas are most often found in the higher levels of society. And HBBs are sometimes willing to share the faith with them as well. Using their normal procedure, the Hindu Background evangelists will gather a group in a new area. (If it happens to be a Muslim area, they will first be surprised by how few people seem to be interested; in Hindu areas, a massive gathering is all but certain.) Another surprise comes quickly, though. The HBBs will begin to talk about physical sickness and the need for healing. Typically, the

Muslims are not especially interested in healing. Compared to low caste Hindus, the Muslims in these areas already possess houses, cars, and access to education and medical care. Therefore, their need for a healing experience from Jesus is lessened.

Instead of healing, they want help understanding the dreams and visions that they have been having! They are hungry for someone to explain to them the biblical passages they have been secretly reading. The Hindu believers, however, have little to offer in that regard. They know how to heal sick people, but they do not seem to have much to say about dreams and visions. They know how to lead Hindus to a salvific experience with Jesus. They know how to lead people to Christ within their own culture (Hindus), but have no clue how God might be working among near-culture peoples (Muslims) who have had little access to the gospel. Obviously, there is a startling disconnect. Often these HBBs will leave Muslim people and return to their own people, shaking the dust off their feet, disappointed by how "unspiritual" Muslims can be.

A similar dynamic can also play out in the other direction. MBBs might gather a group of Hindus for the purpose of sharing their faith in Jesus. These MBBs are first surprised by the huge group that gathers when they arrive. They begin immediately to talk about dreams and visions and about a profound interaction with the Bible. All the while, the gathered group will be confused. They have not had dreams and visions! They do not care much about a holy book called the Bible! Rather, they are eager to have their physical pain addressed. They are filled with parasites, demon possessed, suffering from skin diseases—all the ailments expected where medical care is extremely sparse. Again, there is a startling disconnect. These MBBs may quickly return to sharing their faith with Muslims only, shaking the dust off their feet, disappointed by the "unresponsiveness" of low caste Hindus.

Of course, these scenarios are broad generalizations, but they closely fit patterns that showed up often in our interviews. At the most obvious, basic level, the lesson is that *God uses different methodologies in different places to make Himself known.* At a deeper level, however, the lesson is that we must take the time to discern what God is doing so that we might join Him as He works. God always uses spiritual avenues open to the supernatural within a culture. He takes it and transforms it for His purpose. Our task is to learn from Him, then teach the Bible in ways which hopefully open up many spiritual avenues for salvation through Jesus alone.

Closer to our own experience, we can see how Western workers typically take a post-Pentecost mind-set and impose it upon a pre-Pentecost world. Western workers might want to talk about church structure while a seeker wants to know who Jesus is. Western workers might emphasize the second coming of Christ while a seeker is eager to understand why Jesus came the first time. Western workers might camp out in the letters of the apostle Paul when the Old Testament and the Gospels might actually be a fruitful place to spend time. Western workers might insist on a literate and educated clergy when most seekers and potential leaders are oral communicators. In general, Western workers focus on what they know and what they have experienced within their own home culture. Nothing could be more natural than that.

Unaware, and perhaps unintentionally, we transfer everything we know, everything we have experienced, and everything we have built in a post-Pentecost world (church buildings, Sunday schools, choirs, literacy, seminaries, and youth camps), and we assume that these are the only avenues for witness in every culture and in every time. We do this because it is through these events, channels, and structures that we found Jesus and grew in our faith, and we have difficulty imagining a scenario where others might come to believe in Jesus through some other approach.

It is fascinating, but MBBs and HBBs do the very same thing. MBBs might assume that every seeker has had dreams and visions. HBBs might assume that every seeker is eager to experience physical healing. Western workers might assume that the important questions are the same in every time and in every place. What matters most, however, is discerning the unique ways God might be using in a specific time and place. Such discernment takes time and it takes great humility. It also requires a willingness to listen carefully to others as they pursue God's call. This discernment almost always requires language learning and cultural acquisition. Until we take the time to discern what God is doing in another culture, we run the risk of substituting our own certainties and our own strategies for the activity of God.

This is especially true of church culture in the United States. Most pastors can easily explain how people who were born within the church family come to faith in Jesus. Those patterns are strong, predictable, and easily measured. When those same pastors, however, are asked, "How are people in the United States who have never been to church before coming to faith in Jesus?" explanations are universally hard to find.

Our surprising suggestion here is that the process of conversion for the radically unchurched in the United States will be very similar to the process of conversion experienced by Muslims, Hindus, and Buddhists. In fact, the process of conversion for these radically unchurched will be much more similar to conversions from other faith traditions. The process of conversion for the unchurched in America and for those who are raised in a church context may, in fact, have very little in common. Understanding well this process of conversion is perhaps the most important question facing the American church today.

We Must Consider These Questions

- How are people in my own country who do not come from a church background finding Jesus Christ as their Lord and Savior?
- How can we know what God is doing within our own culture and country and join Him in His work?

Part III

Reaching Grandma and the
Rest of the Family

12

Working Smarter, Not Harder

Understanding the process of conversion is a difficult challenge.
On the one hand, we are dealing with what can only be called
the miraculous; clearly, every story of salvation is steeped in miracle.
God's ways of finding us are far beyond our understanding and, in
conversion, we are considering the most intimate of spiritual encounters. How God does what God does is something that we clearly cannot grasp or describe.

On the other hand, by God's choice and determination, human
dynamics are involved even in the mysterious process of conversion.
In His grace, God has chosen to use human instruments, testimonies,
and relationships in His salvific work. God does what only God can
do, but He graciously chooses to use people in His work. That human
element is more easily grasped and described.

Understanding the mystery of conversion is complicated even further when we consider different cultural contexts. What we seem to

know about conversion in a modern American context, for example, will often not be applicable in a Muslim or Hindu or Buddhist context. Even further, we find a multitude of situations present within each particular context.

In light of our earlier conversation about the post-Pentecost world that defines most of American Christianity, we can identify in a broad way how Americans might come to faith in Christ. For example, someone who has grown up within that post-Pentecost American church setting would likely be familiar with the language of faith and might be able to take the necessary steps toward a conversion experience. At the same time, it is clear that an American who has not grown up within that context would have a more difficult time or, at least, a different experience navigating that path. Recent research suggests that, for Americans who are outside of a traditional church environment, typical entry points to faith are either a significant personal crisis (such as divorce, the loss of a child, or a tragic accident), or a close relationship with a believer. Those might be obvious insights, but it is instructive to think in these terms.

It is interesting to note that Muslims and Hindus who are coming to Christ in the West are coming to Christ in the same ways that they would come to Christ in their home countries. It is also interesting to speculate about the indicators that might suggest when a faith response is serious and lasting. For an American believer, what might indicate an authentic faith? Though there may be many ways to measure true faith, behaviors such as sharing their faith with others and an increasing spiritual hunger might be good indicators. Some faith communities might identify other indicators of a serious faith, but what is most significant, perhaps, is that there is a general agreement that there are such indicators. What is the difference between a "member" and a "true follower" of Jesus in the West?

In the context of this book, similar questions might be asked about MBBs and HBBs. For a Muslim Background Believer, for example, what are the indicators of a serious and authentic faith in Jesus? Our research has surfaced two crucial insights.

First, we know there is a serious faith in Jesus when a Muslim believer (typically a male believer) would take the step of appropriately sharing with his own family—especially with his father—about his faith in Jesus. As we will see later in this chapter, family dynamics play a huge role in the faith experience of MBBs, and a believer sharing his personal faith with his family indicates a profound level of seriousness.

The second indicator is baptism at the hands of another MBB within an MBB house church context. This might not even be the first baptism experience. MBBs are often baptized secretly by a Western worker, for example. But the MBB seeking out baptism by another MBB is a marked sign of a serious commitment.

For HBBs, the indicators are quite different. The first indicator of a serious commitment in the life of a HBB is when the HBB is willing to reject and remove the household altar and gods. A HBB comes from an environment that honors a multitude of gods, and these gods are worshipped at a family altar. Most Hindus are more than happy to include Jesus among their pantheon of gods. Clearly, faith in Jesus has become real and substantial when this altar is removed from the home and destroyed, making Jesus the only God of the house.

The second indicator is a willingness to deal with the difficult questions related to the eternal destiny of the believer's ancestors. While this, in particular, is an extremely sensitive issue, at a certain point a HBB recognizes the implications of the exclusive claims of Christ and how those claims relate to matters of eternity. As those claims are considered, the focus often shifts from concerns about the eternal destiny of ancestors to the impact of this new-found faith on future generations.

Most Americans do not know what it means to truly belong to community. We are typically individualistic in our worldview. In order to emphasize the point, let me offer an observation: *Communal peoples, which include most of the peoples of the earth, would rather go to hell with their families than go to heaven by themselves!* That worldview may be the result of a faulty understanding of the horror of an eternity without Jesus or a misunderstanding about the joy of being with Jesus for all eternity, but it is a common viewpoint, nonetheless.

That future focus is important. As exciting as it is to see new believers, what is desired even more is a faith that is being passed on to others. The ultimate hope is for faith in Jesus to spread to older and future generations. A first-generation believer is perhaps the first believer in a family or among a certain people group. Second-generation believers come into existence when that first believer's faith is passed on. In this chapter, we will examine some of the barriers that might keep that from happening.

First, however, it is important to acknowledge that there are several different ways to define "second generation." The most obvious definition suggests that second generation simply means someone who has received the faith from another person. In this definition, there is no distinction related to age. For example, if I am a first-generation believer and I share Jesus with a friend and my friend receives Jesus, then I represent the first generation and my friend represents the second generation. (If my friend, then, shares Jesus with another friend and if that friend receives Jesus, then this third convert represents the third generation of faith.) As the faith is passed on, more and more generations are added.

There is another way, however, to define second (and subsequent) generations—a definition that makes a distinction related to biological families. This second definition relates to the generations that are found in a family. According to this definition, when a first-generation believer shares Jesus with *his or her children* (or with younger people who would technically be in the next generation), that embraced faith would be said to be a second-generation faith. And as those children mature as believers and share their faith with the next chronological generation, that would be called a third-generation faith (and so on). Biologically, faith can go in both directions. Faith can be seen to travel from the son to the parents and grandparents as well as from the son to his children. Therefore, in a short period of time faith has truly gone into multiple generations biologically.

Both definitions describe the passing on of faith, but they are essentially describing two different dynamics. Because of our interviews, we are inclined to focus on the definition that emphasizes biological family generations. Over and over again, we sat in rooms where three or even four generations of a family were represented. As a grandmother told her story, we could see how her faith had been passed on to her son, who had then passed it on to his wife and children (and so on). What we heard described in those settings was what can only be called a genealogy of faith.

This passing on of the faith is, obviously, what we strive for. We desire to see the faith spread in our own family units, and we long to see this happen in other cultures where faith is being embraced. This very thing is clearly a central part of God's strategy.

Unfortunately, that does not always happen, which is why our focus in this chapter is on some of the barriers that work against faith moving to the second generation and succeeding generations. Our research plainly suggests God can make Himself known and call people to Himself in even the darkest corners of the earth. God is not waiting for us to show up before bringing people into salvation. Yet our findings also suggest a weighty responsibility on our part and a risk on His part. God has called us, His created beings, into a partnership with Him for the planting of churches.

Stated boldly, we find no evidence of churches being planted without human believers working in direct partnership with God. As believers, we are to be partners with God in church planting. That is God's choice. As believers, our choice is in determining whether we will partner with God wisely or unwisely.

In thinking about this divine-human partnership, we have identified some significant barriers and challenges. In our interviews, four main barriers came to the surface.

The First Barrier: An Addiction to Literacy

According to our interviews, approximately 90 percent of MBBs came to faith through literate means. In most cases, these were Muslim men who were able to read and write. While these men were able to access literate means to come to faith, they were unable to share their faith with other people in any other way. In other words, both their reception of the gospel and their sharing of the gospel would require literacy. As long as they were seeking to share faith with other literate people, this would potentially not cause a problem. The problem, however, comes from the fact that so many people rely completely on oral means of communication. How can the faith be passed on using literate means when most of the people who need to hear the gospel do not have access to those literate means?

In some of our earliest interviews, Ruth and I were talking with an MBB who had rather grandiose plans for his faith and witness. He spoke of using the theatre and music to present the good news to millions. After talking with the man for about three hours, I prepared to ask him my next question. I commended this brother for both his faith and his desire to share his faith on a global stage. Then I asked him quietly, "You have told us that you are married. How has your wife found faith in Jesus? How does she share in your ministry?" This brother looked at me as if I had asked the unthinkable. He virtually shouted, "Why would I share my faith with my wife? She is just an ignorant old village woman!"

In many of the people groups that are without Jesus, illiteracy can be as high as 45 percent for the men and 90 percent for the women! Men are often not interested in sharing their faith with non-readers, even the non-readers in their own homes.

In simplest terms, if these MBBs do not have oral tools to communicate the gospel, the faith will not be transferable to the next generation. They will need both the tools for sharing and the desire to share their faith with non-literate spouses, daughters, and other female family members.

We were interviewing approximately fifteen men, most over fifty years of age, who declared themselves to be the leaders of local house churches. Taking an oral snapshot of the room, we learned that only five of the men had told their wives they were believers in Jesus, only three of their wives had believed, and only one of the wives had been baptized. These were the leaders! When we queried them concerning their lack of initiative and disinterest in sharing their faith with their wives, they were not upset or concerned. With what bordered on unconcern (maybe boredom?), they said to us, "Our wives cannot come to Jesus because they are illiterate."

The lack of oral means of communicating the gospel is a significant barrier that can prevent faith from moving into the second generation. When a first-generation believer (literate) is unable or unwilling to share the gospel orally with the next (illiterate) generations, the multiplication of the faith stops with the first generation. Remembering the previous chapter, we often expect others to come to faith in the same way that we encountered Jesus. If we came to Jesus through literate means, then we usually expect others to come to Jesus through literate means. But if 90 percent of the women in a culture are illiterate, this clearly implies that the spread of the gospel will stop within that first generation.

From a Western perspective, it is commonplace to focus on literate means of communication, but much of the world has no access to those means. In fact, we notice a similar pattern in both the New Testament world and in modern church planting movements. *Historically and biblically, it appears that God always keeps His Word in oral forms in order to rapidly transmit truth. And He always keeps His Word in literate forms in order to preserve the truth.* Both the rapid spread of His Word and the preservation of His Word are equally crucial, but different aspects of that process seem to be more important in different moments of history. God in His wisdom has given us the greatest tool—His Word. And He has given us His Word in both oral and written forms. Using the Bible in both literate and oral forms doubles the effectiveness of ministry.

This much is obvious: at least in oral cultures, developing oral ways of communicating the faith is indispensable if the faith is to be passed on to subsequent generations.

The Second Barrier: Specific Issues Related to Males

During our time in the Horn of Africa, we noticed some intriguing patterns that were later confirmed in more formal research. In fact, in interviewing significant numbers of believers who had come to faith over the previous fifty years, we discovered that 83 percent of them had declared their faith in Jesus *only after the death of their father.* When we shared that statistic with Western workers in other similar religious cultures, they often assured us that their setting was different and that the Horn of Africa pattern would not be consistent within their places of ministry. However, when we were able to interview believers in other settings of persecution (particularly in top-down persecution), we found the same pattern in every location. In fact, in some places the percentages were even higher, and in several places, the statistic approached 100 percent. Among believers from one religion, an overwhelming number of believers declared their faith in Jesus only after the death of their father.

In many of these contexts, the Christian faith is typically labeled by the majority religion as being "anti-family." And, in fact, we have encountered extreme bitterness toward fathers in the lives of most "believers" in Jesus coming out of certain religious backgrounds. Even further, it might be fair to say that hatred of father was a prime motivation behind many of these majority peoples coming to faith in Christ. As strange as it sounds, becoming a Christian is a way of "getting back" at fathers who are either hated or feared. Obviously, this dynamic is a barrier to the faith spreading to a second generation.

If fear of the father is the dominant emotion, it is easy to understand why a potential believer would feel the need to wait until the death of the father before declaring faith in Jesus. If, on the other hand, hatred of the father is the dominant emotion, we can see that a declaration of faith in Jesus might be motivated by a desire to inflict pain on the father and the extended family. In either case, these motives are troubling and unhealthy—and these motives will obviously affect the passing of the faith on to others.

When new believers, out of this majority religion, are encouraged to share their faith with their families, and especially with their fathers, approximately 50 percent of them declare they are unwilling to do such a difficult thing. They will conclude, in fact, that it is more than difficult; they will call it "impossible."

"If loving my father is what Jesus requires of me," they might say, "then I do not want to have anything to do with this Jesus!" At the most basic level, it is easy to see how the broken relationships between young men and their fathers would profoundly inhibit the spread of the faith from one generation to the next. These candid interviews teach us not to be passive in evangelism. We are not to wait, especially, for young men who have huge father issues to come to us looking for faith and baptism. We are learning to take the gospel to the entire family, never separating the individual from his or her family. As Jesus did, we are also to look for men who have respect, age, and status within the community and who will naturally share their faith with their extended family. The more resistant, the more dysfunctional the culture, the older and more respected should be those we build relationships with in order to become a midwife to a rapid spread of the Good News. Historical Christian cultures will increasingly focus on reaching children in order to protect and preserve their denominational or theological base. To begin movements, befriending those thirty years and above with a godly, in-culture witness is the healthiest manner through which to see the kingdom of God start strong, grow deep and wide.

The Third Barrier: Issues Specifically Related to Females

In chapter eleven, we chronicled the way that a typical MBB comes to faith in Jesus. We talked about dreams and visions, about dramatic encounters with God's Word, and about meetings with in-culture or near-culture believers. We also made the point that Muslims *are* coming to faith in Christ. At this point, we need to step back and refine those observations.

Muslims are coming to faith in Christ, but the Muslims who are coming to faith in Christ are overwhelmingly men. There are very few Muslim women coming to Christ, though there are some significant exceptions. For decades, we have operated on the assumption that Muslim men who received Christ would automatically share Christ with their wives. The ultimate result, we surmised, would be that entire families would come to Christ. It turns out that our assumptions were in error.

In general, when male MBBs witness (and they do), they witness to their brothers, their uncles, and their male cousins, but not to their wives or to other women in the extended family. Rather than witnessing to their wives, these MBBs typically declare specifically that, because of the husband's faith, the entire household is automatically

a "Christian household." It is not uncommon for the MBB to baptize his wife and immediately take her to secret meetings of a house
church. Even though she has been baptized, she has no understanding
of who Jesus is and she has very little understanding of this decision
that has been made on her behalf. This model of "witness" (if it can
be called that) is grounded in the unquestioned cultural power and
authority of the male in the family structure. He makes determina-
tions about the faith for the entire family and he simply declares it to
be so.

The wife does have choices. She can betray him to the authorities,
divorce him, or stay with him. A long legacy of servitude within a
male-dominated culture has programmed her to accept the authority
of her husband even when it comes to matters that affect her spiritual
eternity. He has the right to declare faith for her.

For years in Somalia, we struggled to make sense of something we
had noticed in times when persecution increased the most dramatically. As we charted the martyrdom of believers, we stumbled on a
pattern. After several months of relative calm, there would be a brief
period when several believers would be put to death for their faith.
That period of martyrdom would then be followed by a season of
relative calm. Once again, that calm time would be interrupted by a
time when several more believers were put to death. We noticed the
pattern repeating itself for several years, and we were unable to make
any sense of it.

We were unable to make sense of it, that is, until we looked at this
increase in martyrdom in light of the situation of women as described
above. What was happening is that when one of these MBBs was
martyred, his wife would immediately return to the mosque and
she would almost as quickly turn in the names of the people who
were part of the network of believers she belonged to along with her
husband. This behavior, in turn, would lead to increased martyrdom
of those who were involved with her husband's group. In examining

this scenario, we could identify only one woman in this situation who "stayed with the faith" for more than forty-eight hours after her husband's death. When faith is simply declared for another person, it obviously has very little or no staying power.

Despite our presumption that both Muslim men and women have been coming to faith in Jesus, what we now understand is that, for the most part, Muslim men who meet Jesus share their faith with other Muslim men, while Muslim women largely remain without access to Jesus.

Several additional lessons have come to the surface. First, we came to understand that Muslim women would typically hear the gospel only from believing women or in the context of their family. In fact, it appears that the telling of biblical stories is a profoundly powerful way of communicating the gospel among Muslim women. We discovered that Muslim men, having heard the stories, typically keep the stories to themselves. Knowledge is power and it is not wise to give away power. In contrast, a Muslim woman who has heard a biblical story on a particular day will have shared it six to eight times before nightfall! Especially powerful is the sharing of these stories in large gatherings of Muslim women at weddings or parties.

A second lesson led us to see the wisdom in biblically and spiritually modeling for male MBBs how to *share* their faith with their wives instead of simply *declaring* faith for them. In this context, the biblical injunction for husbands to love their wives and to be willing to die for them (Eph. 5:25) is a powerful revelation. In fact, it is transforming! We had naively assumed that this kind of sharing would happen naturally and without specific modeling. Now we realize that our assumption was culturally unfounded. There is a marked difference between sharing the faith with someone and declaring the faith on behalf of someone. As another example of cultural myopia, I distinctly remember the day in Mogadishu when a long-term believer shouted at me, "Why didn't you Christians from America tell us that believers in Jesus do not divorce!" The making of untested cultural assumptions is deadly.

We also assumed these Muslim women who came to faith through the sharing of their believing husbands would then pass the faith on to their children. Instead, we find even though these women might have been baptized, they have very little understanding of exactly who Jesus is and, even more, they continue to raise their children as Muslims. Clearly, within this scenario, the faith is not moving to the second generation. The issues specifically related to women are a significant barrier to the growth of God's kingdom in tough places.

The standing of women in Islamic culture is a problematic and deeply troubling part of their story. Samuel Zwemer, in *Across the World of Islam*, paints a grim picture: "As a babe she is unwelcome; as a child untaught; as a wife unloved; as a mother unhonoured; in old age uncared for; and when her dark and dreary life is ended she is unmourned by those she has served."[10]

In regard to most women within Islam, let us look at some circumstantial evidence. In a court of law in a Muslim culture, it takes the testimony of three women to equal the testimony of one man. The illiteracy rate for women is often twice that of men. Seldom do women vote or drive. Most women cannot hold public office above a man. Women have few rights in a divorce, including parental rights. Most (90 percent) Muslim women have to pray at home and have little access to the mosque. While we must be very sensitive with our words here, it would seem that most Muslim men—and most Muslim women—believe that a woman's soul is not equal to a man's soul. Even more, it is possibly deep within the psyche of Islam that a woman's soul is not capable of "housing and holding the Holy Spirit." This may begin to explain why a Muslim husband typically holds spiritual authority for the entire household and why he typically witnesses only to the male members of his family.

When women workers interviewed Muslim women who were followers of Jesus about their faith, the deepest question was often: "How did you come to faith?" In most cases, the answer was simple and straightforward: "My husband became a follower of Jesus and he baptized me." We would try the same question differently. We would ask a "believing lady," "your neighbor has watched the relationship between you and your husband and she wants a husband like yours. How do you share Christ with this neighbor?" The answer came quickly and is almost universal as she replies, "I tell her to pray (good), pray that her husband believes and is baptized so she can be baptized also."

With words like these, the interview is over.

Most of our interviews with Muslim men who have followed Jesus lasted three or four hours. Interviews with Muslim women, for whom faith had been declared by their husbands, lasted about fifteen minutes. Typically, they had very little to share.

A specific missiological need is for women workers to live among Muslim women and to model for them the worth and dignity God affords to women. Believing women must learn and tell the biblical stories where women are central to the narrative. Western believing families must allow Muslims to access their homes, watching us as we model how believers love and raise their children, love and honor their wives. This is transforming—but will Western Christians and workers open their homes to those families with little witness and without Christian behavior. Lost people are messy, and most Christians do not want them around their children!

The Fourth Barrier: The Local CBB Church

Surprising for most Westerners, churches exist in places where we least expect to find them. In predominantly Muslim contexts, there are Christian churches that predate Islam. For the purposes of this discussion, we will refer to these communities as Christian Background Believers or CBB churches. These historical churches do what all churches do, though they tend to have very little interest in sharing Jesus with the majority population. In other words, there is a believing community present, but it is a believing community with little interest in evangelism with the majority population. They could be placed in the post-Pentecost classification. In almost every case, this church would be composed of a religious minority (Christian believers living in a Muslim-majority setting), and in most cases the church would be composed of a racial minority.

Despite what we might expect of churches, CBB churches in these kinds of settings are often unwilling to reach out evangelistically to the persecuting majority. Statistically, in settings of persecution, more than 95 percent of CBB churches simply reject the majority peoples in their midst. Predictably, this might include the absence of overt evangelism. Less predictably, this might also include a failure to welcome a believer who comes from the majority population and wants to unite with the church. Perhaps it is ironic to find the church itself standing in the way of the spread of the gospel; on the other hand, such has often been the role of the church throughout history.

Such a church, wherever located, has become a persecutor.

To make this explicit, imagine that there is a believing community in a predominantly Muslim area. Imagine a Muslim arriving at a church seeking faith in Christ. He is often told, "Go away; you have your own prophet." Or imagine that a Muslim man has (somehow) come to faith in Jesus, and he desires to become a part of this worshipping, historical community. In all likelihood, even if he desires uniting with this community, the CBB church will not allow it to happen, even refusing him baptism. Perhaps we can understand why. All the same, it is instructive to ask the question: What reasons are given for this lack of welcome and inclusion?

Our interviews revealed some of the answers which come from the leadership of these historical churches. Often with tears streaming down their face they will say:

- "These people are simply too lost. They are so lost that they cannot be saved. Ripken, in your country you have part-time pagans. Our country is filled with full-time pagans."

- "We simply don't want these people to be saved. Hell is what they deserve. You have no right to cheat hell out of those God has determined to go there."

- "Converts (or supposed converts) have fooled us in the past, and we will not allow these converts (or supposed converts) to fool us this time. They simply want to turn us in."

- "It is not cost effective to reach out to these people. The financial cost required is not worth the investment."

- "If we embrace believers from the majority culture, the persecutors will destroy our church building and confiscate our properties."

- "If we embrace believers who are from other racial groups, they will not only become part of our church, they will also become part of our families, and they will perhaps even marry our sons and daughters. We will not allow that to happen."

- "If we welcome these outside believers, they will eventually take our leadership positions in the church."

- "We will reach out to these believers only if we receive financial support from Westerners to do so, and when those finances are expended, we will no longer reach out to them."

These answers range from "predictable" to "startling" to "downright offensive," but they reveal the mind-set that is often found in CBB churches. The attitudes behind these comments reveal fear, racism, judgment, pride, and self-centeredness. Before judging these comments too harshly, however, we probably should look within our own hearts and grapple with similar attitudes that we might harbor. At the very least, we should strive to understand what it feels like to live out the faith as a religious and racial minority in a hostile environment.

It could be asked of Caucasian churches in the southern part of America, "How many churches have been planted among African-Americans in the past fifty years?" Yet even that is not an accurate way to represent the position of the CBB church in hostile settings. We would need to reverse the question and ask: "How many African-American churches have reached Caucasians with the gospel and planted churches among the predominantly white population in the past fifty years?"

This is not intended to excuse any of us from fulfilling the Great Commission, especially in the regions that represent our Judea and Samaria. Sadly, we are often willing to go to the ends of the earth while deliberately leaving alone those on our borders and in our neighborhoods. These are often the ones we love the least, and we leave them without the Gospel of Jesus Christ. Perhaps many of us are more like the CBB churches described in this chapter than we would want to admit.

In any case, we find that CBB churches often present a barrier that prevents the faith from moving to the second generation among the dangerously unreached. Along with the limitations related to orality and issues specifically related to males and females, this barrier works against the expansion of the faith.

Candidly Tackling the Big Four

- What oral tools are in your tool box for reaching those who are not literate or functionally illiterate? What tools can you suggest need developing?
- How much of the Bible can you reproduce upon request?

- Are we modelers of healthy marriages and homes which will attract those outside of the kingdom to Jesus?
- How many non-believing families have visited your home for a meal this past year?

13

More Barriers?

In simplest form, the question that we are asking is this: How can we, in environments defined by persecution, get to multigenerational, reproducing house churches? As individuals come to faith in Christ, how can that faith spread and grow? "Church" happens when faith includes the extended family both spiritually and biologically. The broader question must be: How can we get to a church planting movement? The point is not that we can, by force of will or human creativity, "make" that happen. Clearly, CPMs are fueled by the Holy Spirit. At the same time, we are convinced that human beings, empowered by God, can engage in healthy behaviors that will help "church" (and CPMs) happen. Please do not observe that CPMs denote a fixation with numbers. CPM language is a human attempt to observe the breadth and depth of what Almighty God is doing and desiring to be a good partner alongside the Holy Spirit.

How can we, as people chosen by God, become wise partners alongside the Holy Spirit? On the one hand, we might focus on positive steps that we can take. On the other hand, we might consider costly mistakes and errors that could be avoided. Clearly, well-meaning believers have made mistakes in the past that have inhibited the birth and growth of the church. We would be wise to learn from those mistakes, and we would be wise to avoid them in the future.

If we are wise, honest, and tough enough, we can have open conversations about the things that do not work. Candidly, Ruth and I are well versed in the making of mistakes. We are the poster children for mistakes and we have the scars to prove it. Hopefully, if you are able to learn from our mistakes, they can be avoided. At the very least, make sure that your mistakes are your own; do not repeat the ones that we have made!

So our questions for this chapter are these:

- How can we most quickly start reproducing house churches?
- In our lives and ministries, how can we contribute to CPMs?
- Are there behaviors and actions that we might want to avoid?
- Can we learn from mistakes that have been made?
- Can we identify some of the hindrances and barriers that stand in the way of a CPM?
- What will keep faith from moving to the next generation, and is there anything we can do about those hindrances?

In chapter twelve, we highlighted four major barriers that would tend to prevent faith from moving to a second generation. For purposes of illustration, imagine a group of one hundred MBBs. Statistically, of those one hundred MBBs, eighty will be men and twenty will be women. Let us also assume that these MBBs are genuine believers and that they have come to genuine faith in Jesus. And let us also assume that they sincerely desire to share their faith. Now, within that scenario, what might potentially keep multiple generations of family members from embracing Christ?

First, a significant number of these MBBs will not possess the tools to pass on their faith orally. Encountering the faith through literate means, some (and probably most) of these MBBs will be unable to share their faith in any other way. Out of the one hundred MBBs that we start with, a substantial number of them will be prevented or greatly inhibited from passing on their faith because of issues related to orality.

Second, several more of these believers will be severely hampered in their effort to share their faith because of the male issues that we identified. Some of these men have delayed their declaration of faith in Jesus due to crippling fear of their father, and perhaps that delay has damaged witness. Others have declared faith in Jesus specifically because of their hatred of father, and their witness now is so colored by that hatred that it has become unhealthy and damaging to others. There are many other possible scenarios, but, clearly, the witness of additional believers from our starting group of one hundred is further reduced and weakened because of these specific issues.

Third, there will be hindrances that come from issues specifically related to the women in our group. Though we are assuming that all one hundred of our MBBs are genuine believers, it is likely that a number of these women believers will not completely understand the faith, perhaps because their faith was simply declared by someone else. There may be genuine interest, but the Bible stories have not been heard or understood. Even further, perhaps there are not available settings for the stories to be shared. Again, there are many possible scenarios, but there are plenty of barriers that stand in the way of faith moving to the next generation through females.

Fourth, the CBB church, in its unwillingness to witness and help new believers to start house churches in their own language and culture, will present a significant barrier. It is a hard truth to swallow, but proximity does not make one a more skilled cross-cultural witness. Obedience does!

Many Western mission agencies pour millions of dollars in resources into "helping" local historical Christians reach their Muslim, Buddhist, or Hindu neighbors with the misplaced thought that proximity helps one go to Judea and Samaria. Wrong; it is only cheaper to go as they are closer. Again we must ask ourselves, how many Caucasians are planting churches among African-Americans and vice versa? Why would we expect this racial divide to play out differently in other cultures? If there is no spiritual community open to new believers, at least for encouragement, they will have little opportunity to grow and mature and be nurtured. Isolated and alone, the new believers will not be exposed to an ever expanding exposure to biblical truths, spiritual care, and fellowship. Once again, there might be a multitude of specific scenarios, but we can see how struggles in accessing local CBB congregations would further inhibit the spreading and deepening of the faith.

We identified these four barriers as the most significant ones. In light of these realities, how many of these one hundred MBBs are still sharing their faith in healthy and productive ways? Obviously, our initial number of one hundred who are carrying the faith into succeeding generations has been significantly reduced. As if that were not sobering enough, however, we are aware of a host of additional barriers that may stand in the way of faith moving to succeeding generations. After five or ten years, how many of these original MBBs will still be sharing their faith? Unless these MBBs are continuing to share their faith to a significant degree, it will be almost impossible to "get to church" (or to church planting movements).

Or, to put it another way, would it be possible to equip an MBB with the needed tools of orality? Is it possible that this believer has come to faith in Jesus without the destructive baggage related to his father or, at least, is it possible that he has been able to deal with those family issues in a healthy, God-honoring way? Is it possible to deliberately share one's faith with adult men who have positive relationships with their fathers with intentionality? Or, if this MBB is a woman, is it possible that she has somehow come to a faith that is healthy, personal, and self-chosen? Then, is it possible that there has been a community of faith (perhaps a CBB congregation) that has provided godly counsel that would appropriately lead to the planting of house churches in the MBB's language and culture? Sadly, all of that might, in fact, seem to be impossible! But that is the very thing that would open the door for faith to move to succeeding generations. And, even further, would it be possible for these MBBs, reduced from the initial one hundred, to overcome this next set of barriers?

Be advised and creatively aware, before one becomes too depressed; we are highlighting these barriers because it is the barriers themselves which suggest a bridge, the solution to the barrier.

We have identified thirteen additional barriers that can work against faith moving to the next generation. In answer to our question: "What is keeping us from getting to multigenerational house churches?" these thirteen issues (along with the four major barriers described above) might begin to answer our question. In fact, given our original starting group of one hundred MBBs, after five to ten years, it is alarming how few of the original one hundred MBBs will be actively living and sharing their faith. Obviously, if that is true, it will be extremely difficult to get to church.

Perhaps the best way to understand this discussion is, once again, to imagine that group of one hundred MBBs. If, in ten years, only three or four (certainly less than ten) of them are exhibiting a vibrant and reproducible faith, what has become of the other ninety-six or ninety-seven? These thirteen issues might provide us with an answer to that troubling question.

1. External extraction. Internationally, when severe persecution comes, about 50 percent of all believers in persecution will be extracted to other countries by well-meaning and soft-hearted Western workers. That minimum percentage holds true for MBBs, HBBs, and BBBs. Within contexts where Islam is dominant, that figure can be as high as 70 percent. (Obviously, if we lose seventy of God's one hundred MBBs to extraction, it is not hard to understand how we will eventually find only a few score of believers remaining in a situation of witness due to this one issue!)

As troubling as it is in terms of effective witness, extraction is extremely popular. Imagine that you have helped a Muslim man come to faith in Jesus. You have walked together, prayed together, and struggled together. It is not difficult to imagine the love that you share for one another. At the appropriate time, there is a faith response. In a way, you may erroneously believe that you are Paul to this man and he is Timothy to you. Because of his faith, this MBB begins to experience persecution. It is only natural that you would want to protect him, save him, and rescue him. And perhaps the easiest way to do that, you conclude, is extraction. As easy as that choice is to understand, we are compelled to admit that the apostle Paul never extracted Timothy from an environment of persecution.

There are hard, biblical questions that we must ask. How do we know when to leave Joseph in Pharaoh's prison? If "our" Joseph is unjustly imprisoned in a dictator's jail, what is our usual response? Typically, we write e-mails and we make phone calls to government officials demanding Joseph's release. And the basis of our appeal is Western human and civil rights.

Even so, what happens if we gain Joseph's release before he interprets Pharaoh's dream? In the case of Joseph, both Egyptians and Jews die of starvation. In the same way, it was imperative for the kingdom that Paul and Silas were found in an inner prison in Philippi for the salvation of the jailor's family.

Rescue and church planting are not the same thing. In fact, often they are diametrically opposed to each other. The deeper issue is these are not "our" believers, not "our" churches. They are God's and He still holds the rights to seeking the one lost sheep at the expense of the ninety and nine. They are His, not ours!

Through extraction, a physical life might, in fact, be saved. At the same time, however, witness and evangelism may be prevented. Evangelism is impossible when evangelists are extracted.

From a Western point of view, it is hard to criticize the decision to extract a persecuted brother or sister. The realities are heartbreaking. In large measure, for Western workers, extraction is the default response to those realities. It is instructive, however, to look at Jesus' life and ministry. Jesus was strategically extracted to Egypt for a season by God's command to Joseph. This was a strategic extraction with Jesus' family placed close to the events surrounding their people group. Later, Jesus, too, saw people come to faith. He prepared His followers to pay a high price for faith in Him, but never once did Jesus extract anyone. Instructing them to shake the dust from their feet, due to rejection of the coming kingdom of God, He simply sent His followers on to the next village, encouraging them to stay as close as possible to their own people and to other people groups in reach of their witness. In Matthew 10:23 Jesus explained, "When you are persecuted in one place, flee to another." Strategic extraction such as this is not what Western workers are typically practicing today.

Extraction seems to make human sense. At the same time, extraction can kill witness and it is a significant barrier that stands in the way of faith moving to the next generation.

2. Marriage to a majority woman. In many cases, when a young believer reaches approximately thirty years of age, a marriage is arranged for him. When a Muslim son is suspected of having faith in Jesus (or when his faith might be clearly known), his family will work toward a marriage that might draw him back into Islam. Marriage to a majority woman, a first cousin on his mother's side of the family, is the marriage of choice. Typically, the father of the believer (or suspected believer) will meet with the prospective wife and explain his and his wife's expectation for her.

First, it is her responsibility to draw the believer (or suspected believer) back to Islam. Second, if she is unable to do that, it is her responsibility to protect her future children from her husband's Christian faith and to keep the children firmly grounded in Islam. In such a situation, the faith of the believer will be severely compromised and his witness will be greatly diminished.

3. *Remaining single.* In many cultures, especially in pre-Pentecost ones, a single man will have a diminished witness. Perhaps the believer will resist an arranged marriage, and perhaps, understandably, this believer will desire to marry a believer. Because of the shortage of believing women, this desire, of course, will prove to be a difficult challenge. In fact, unable to find a suitable believing wife, the believer might decide to remain single. Right or wrong, this choice often diminishes witness. Not only is a single voice less valued in many cultures, the believer will also be unable, or unwilling, to reproduce the faith within his own nuclear family.

4. *Loss of voice and witness.* For a variety of reasons, many believers simply choose to remain silent about their relationship with Jesus. This disease, epidemic in the West, is an obvious barrier to faith spreading to the next generation. With or without the presence of persecution, we understand well how easily this choice can be made, and we intuitively understand how this choice prevents witness. Many Western workers find it challenging to insist that a new believer in an environment of persecution be a consistent witness because we often come from non-witnessing environments ourselves. "Keeping Jesus to oneself" in any culture, especially in Islamic countries, is the easiest means to avoid persecution. The consequence of this "loss of voice" is both clear and tragic.

5. *The presence of "fringe" people in the early stages of the movement.* For some reason, fringe people are attracted to the Christian faith. On the one hand, every person is included in Christ's invitation and, clearly, there is a place for fringe people. On the other hand, the presence of fringe people in a movement—especially early on—can greatly inhibit growth. Fringe people are already living at the edges of culture, and they are typically seeking to move even further away. And while they may be attracted to the faith, they may not be the most productive initial messengers of witness. Fringe people dress differently, act differently, and they are anticultural. Fringe people need Jesus. Yet fringe people seldom carry the Good News back to the culture they escaped from long before.

6. *Compulsive fleeing and internal extraction.* When confronted with the charge of being a believer, an MBB may flee to live with a relative in another town. When the rumor about his or her faith reaches that new town, the MBB may flee to yet another place. This is a self-chosen and self-imposed extraction. In reality, the MBB may believe that he or she is fleeing persecution when, in fact, he or she may actually be fleeing witness. The ultimate result is that witness is prevented, with the new believer geographically distanced from the center of his or her culture. The believer may even compulsively flee to another country.

7. *Expatriate hiring practices.* Wanting to be helpful and wanting to help meet the financial needs of believers in persecution, expatriates often provide employment for those who have come to faith. In many cases, these new believers are highly qualified for these positions. Often, however, the result of these hiring practices includes diminished witness. Employment at the hands of expatriates distances believers from in-culture or near-culture relationships, and it makes witness less likely.

Further, in the midst of persecution, hiring local believers can make them targets for elimination. In addition, such employment practices assure that local believers are overly dependent upon outsider money. The persecutors themselves desire for local believers to be financially dependent on Western workers. At the opportune moment, persecutors simply expel the Western workers and a large percentage of local believers are left destitute. Also, if this local believer is quite skilled at his job, it is often the practice of the Western agency to give him or her a better job in another country. How can local churches be planted when we export the apostle Paul to another continent?

There is no evidence in the New Testament where local believers were financially supported by outsiders. In fact, the opposite appears to be true. The first offering gathered in the New Testament was sacrificially given through the "mission" churches back to the mother church in Jerusalem for famine relief. Westerners have reversed this sacrificial type of local giving.

Perhaps Western workers should hire local believers in the same percentage that local believers exist in the local culture. So if 1 percent of the population follows Jesus, then 1 percent of the employees should be believers.

8. Education outside of culture. In a similar way, the effort to provide believers with education physically outside of their culture can have a detrimental impact on witness. Of those who travel outside of culture for education, 80 percent never return to their home country. With an entirely different motive, education can serve as simply a different version of extraction. Absent from the culture, the believer can never be effective in witness. This factor is not simply limited to believers in Jesus. It is equally true in the secular realm. Whether one is a doctor, a lawyer, or an agriculturalist, being educated outside of one's country of origin results in 70 to 80 percent not returning.

Demographic realities highlight even more challenges. Moving believers from the rural parts of Africa, for instance, into the seminaries of the cities sets the stage for most of those trained never to return home to their village or people of origin. It seems that every time we encounter a church planting challenge, we are neglecting some biblical pattern or story. It is true that Jesus lived with and trained the Twelve for three years. During that time, however, Jesus never removed them from their culture of origin. He did not take insiders and make them outsiders.

9. *Marriage to an expatriate.* If the material in this book were being taught to one hundred believing men from Muslim countries—believers who were financially and educationally upwardly mobile—more than 60 percent of them would be married to foreign women. There is no intention here to impugn or question biracial marriages! This insight is simply offered as an observation as to why we are not obtaining the goal of reproducing churches. Such couples are often able to offer valuable ministry in the husband's country of origin. Yet, usually, when the couple's children reach school age, they will typically leave their country for their wives' country of origin, seldom to return.

We are confident that many of these couples will continue to minister in new places. But we are also confident that their potential for ministry in the MBB's country of origin will have been severely reduced. Obviously, absence from the culture diminishes witness.

Let's take a moment to pause and reflect on these last three barriers. As we discuss this material with local believers in environments of persecution, their thoughts often run in this direction: "Oh, now we know what this workshop is about. Dr. Nik has a job and he wants us to stay in poverty. Dr. Nik has multiple degrees, but he wants us to remain uneducated. Dr. Nik has a wife, but he wants us to remain alone since there are no local women to marry who believe in Jesus. We know what this is about: Dr. Nik is a racist."

These last three barriers are not based on racism. They are merely observations and descriptions of why we are failing to get to reproducing churches in environments of persecution. If the central core of the most promising believers are hired away by expatriates, if they are sent out of the country for education never to return, and if they actually leave their countries due to marrying a Western, foreign, female believer, then the ability of the Holy Spirit to reproduce faith in that country using those believers is severely reduced.

10. "Pseudo-martyrdom." This is the kind of martyrdom that we discussed earlier. This is martyrdom for reasons "other than for who Jesus is." As unfortunate as it is, it makes witness impossible. This is a martyrdom precipitated by specific employment (perhaps working for a Western believer), or when local believers are found worshipping with outsiders. It is a martyrdom that results from openly possessing a literate Bible or being paid by outsiders to evangelize insiders. This would be martyrdom for another person rather than for Jesus.

11. Betrayal of faith. The biblical example of this focuses on the presence of Judas within the community of faith. (See the next chapter for a detailed explanation of this dynamic and its devastating consequences for the growth and transmission of faith.) If Jesus had a Judas in His mix of twelve disciples, we will likely not be able to avoid having a Judas either. Simply put, it is not the intention of Judas to start a church planting movement.

12. Grandparents. When Ahmed comes to Jesus, persecution arises from his family. When he marries Aisha, who is also a believer, persecution increases. Yet it is often possible for believers to live in relative peace with unbelieving family members . . . until children enter the picture. In most Muslim contexts (if not all?), it is legal for grandparents to take custody of grandchildren who are being raised by a believing couple. Believing parents seldom have any legal recourse. There is no easy answer to this horrific reality other than to strive to win grandparents to faith. Remember, each barrier has its bridge.

13. Globalization and a desire for a better life. Aware of opportunities around the world, believers dream about a better life. Often, the pull of financial and physical blessings is as devastating to witness as persecution is. Sadly, Western workers often arrive in overseas settings and, perhaps unintentionally, hold before seekers the possibility that faith in Jesus will result in financial and physical well-being. When those things become important, church planting movements are obviously compromised. What is most deadly is when we transfer these ungodly expectations to first generation believers or to anyone standing for the faith in the midst of persecution.

As persecution in the Union of Soviet Socialist Republics was drawing to a close, fully 45 percent of the Russian pastors immigrated to the West. In Hong Kong, as China prepared to take control in 1997, nearly 75 percent of the pastors serving in Hong Kong left for other places. Currently, more than 20 percent of all Arab Christians are leaving their cultural contexts and emigrating to the West each year (this has soared with the so-called Arab Spring). This exodus has profound implications for the spread of the faith. At the very least, believers should prayerfully consider staying in their birth country for the sake of witness.

The ability of the Bride of Christ to multiply in succeeding generations may well depend upon a candid conversation concerning these thirteen not so minor issues.

Because of our failure to creatively address these issues, our group of one hundred MBBs, in a period of five to ten years, has in all likelihood been reduced to three or four people who remain where they started and who are deeply committed to witness.

It is no wonder that "getting to church" is a challenge! It is no wonder that the faith has a difficult time making its way to the next generation. The barriers are substantial and many. Still, the truth bears repeating once again. God has determined that those who receive salvation in Jesus Christ are to be His partners in the global spread of the gospel. This is His decision. This is His method. Our decision is whether or not we will partner wisely and obediently with Him in

His work. Now that you know the barriers, create bridges. "To whom much was given, of him much will be required" (Luke 12:48 ESV).

Let's Make This Easy

- Please discuss these thirteen barriers and suggest a creative bridge to overcome each of them.

14

An Historical Case Study: Persecution and Its Aftermath

In general, the more the faith community is defined by paid clergy, buildings, property, and denominational connections, the easier it is for persecutors to control and persecute the faith. Examining the situations and the outcomes of the Union of Soviet Socialist Republics (1917–1986) and China (1948–1983) illustrates this point clearly.

A cursory look at the religious histories of these two countries during the twentieth century reveals two countries marked both by strong faith and intense persecution. Beyond those common characteristics, however, the USSR and China have little in common. Despite a strong faith, the USSR experienced little numerical growth in believers during the middle part of the twentieth century. There was also little growth in the number of churches during the same period.

The story of China is very different. Again, there was initially a strong faith. There was also severe and intense persecution. The growth that came at that point was stunning. There were approximately 400,000 to 700,000 believers in China in 1948. By 1983, even with severe persecution, the number of believers had increased to more than ten million. And today, the estimate is approaching one hundred million believers in China, though one hears numbers ranging from seventy million upwards of two hundred million. In addition to that kind of growth, there are today thousands and thousands of growing and reproducing house churches.

How might we explain these different results? A simple list of the characteristics of the two countries is revealing.

- At the beginning of a time of intense persecution, church life in the USSR was largely led by ordained, literate clergy. The power and standing of the laity in the leadership of the church was minimal. Literate methods of doing church were the norm.
- As that time of persecution intensified, church life in the USSR was primarily based in church buildings. Gatherings typically happened at a facility known for religious functions. When believers were forced into small groups—house churches—they gathered in those settings only as long as it took for them to get back into "real churches."
- The church in the USSR was strongly anchored to a denominational base. There was a mind-set that relied on a "central headquarters," with a well-defined administrative hierarchy. When persecution intensified, the denominations tended to unify. But as soon as persecution lessened, believers generally returned to their own denominational roots.
- The church in the USSR was also largely focused on the church building itself and on maintaining the life of the local community.

- The theological stance of the church in the USSR was often anchored in Romans 13 and stressed complete obedience to the State. It was a common experience for the State to demand the church obey it, per Romans 13.

In addition, the church community was at least perceived as being literate and there were frequent ongoing contacts (and relationships) with churches in the West. Furthermore, when persecution came, it was diabolically piecemeal. Initially, it seemed easy for the church to cooperate with the authorities. Concessions were made piece by piece. At first, authorities simply wanted to know what was happening in churches. Eventually, more and more control was demanded. And, because of the reliance on buildings and property, it was simple for the government to exact control and spy upon the church. The fear of losing property was strong motivation to cooperate with the government. Even more, because of the elevation of clergy, imprisonment of church leaders was a devastating problem for the churches of the USSR. When church leaders were imprisoned, the church found itself with an alarming leadership vacuum.

The situation in China was completely different, and the result was completely different. As in the USSR, there was a strong faith and there was severe and intense persecution. Almost overnight, the Christian faith was declared illegal. Foreign workers were expelled and martyred. Pastors were martyred and imprisoned, and church buildings were burned and turned into brothels and beer halls. By the end of 1948, the church was fully aware that the State would not rest until every believer in China had been killed . . . or had recanted the faith.

In contrast to the situation in the USSR, however, church life in China was completely different.

- At the beginning of that time of intense persecution, church life in China was quickly borne by the laity. Literate and school-trained pastors were involved in ministry, of course, but churches in China emphasized the training of lay leaders who were always equal in their pastoral roles to those who had experienced the opportunity of literate, school-based training. When pastors were imprisoned, other pastors and lay leaders were prepared to serve.

- The church in China, when intense persecution began, was quickly based in home groups. These home groups were often called "secret" groups, but they were actually well known and not secret at all. It was impossible to hide anywhere from ten to seventy million believers as the years progressed! It was also impossible to jail millions of believers. These house churches were able to survive and thrive not because they were hidden, but because there were simply so many of them!

- The church in China at that time was purely Chinese. There were few denominational or international connections. Chinese believers reported: "All that we had in China from 1948 was the Bible and the Holy Spirit." Evidently, that was plenty!

- For the most part, the church in China was focused not on the church institution or the church building, but on evangelism. Even at the highest ecclesiastical levels, leaders never gave up their first love of sharing Jesus with those who did not know His grace and love.

- While conversant with Romans 13, the house churches of China were willing to hold Romans 13 in creative, theological tension with other words of Scripture. The church in China knew well Jesus' important teaching: "Give to Caesar what is Caesar's, and to God what is God's" (Luke 20:25). Believers in China lived out what Peter and John understood in their time of persecution: "Judge for yourselves whether it is right in God's sight to obey you rather than God. For we cannot help speaking about what we have seen and heard" (Acts 4:19–20). The Chinese church was well aware that Satan quoted Scripture to Jesus and would not allow the government to use their own Bible against them.

- The church community in China was comfortable with orally transmitted truth and there was almost total isolation from outside groups. Believers in China loved the written Word of God but they were not so addicted to literacy that they failed to tell God's story "in season and out of season."

In China, the persecution that came was massive, total, and acute. Authorities quickly imprisoned pastors and, almost immediately, other leaders simply took their places. Leadership in China was based more on character transformation than on information transfer. Concessions were not made to the government. Because buildings were unimportant or nonexistent, church groups simply moved and met wherever they could. To be fair, China has had a history of small, underground groups for more than four thousand years. It was not difficult for Chinese believers to embrace the house church model.

The resulting growth was explosive and the government could not control it. Because of the emphasis on orality, it was not possible to control the spread of Scripture either, and when written Scriptures were seized, such a loss did not hinder the work of the church. Even when this happened, the stories continued to be told and shared because they had been committed to memory.

This is obviously a cursory (and incomplete) summary of decades of history, but significant lessons are clear. At the same time, these lessons have much to instruct our current discussion about the birth and growth of the church in hostile environments today. As simplistic as this sounds, some of these lessons are crucial. These lessons could mark the line between a continuing Pentecost-like movement and remaining in post-Pentecost.

While the leadership of seminary-trained clergy is helpful, a heavy reliance on lay-led clergy at all levels will serve the church well, especially in hostile environments. More important than formal education is intimacy with Jesus and personal character. Generally, literate clergy are trained outside of the local church. In persecution, as well as in most church planting movements, leaders are homegrown and home-trained. The character of their lives is open for everyone to see from birth until the grave.

Small groups meeting in house settings will often be able to thrive in intense persecution. Buildings and property can prove to be a costly burden and are used to control the faithful. Ultimately, buildings, once they have lost their usefulness to the persecutors, are closed or destroyed. In some settings in the United States, 60 percent of all church giving is dedicated to interest payments on building debt! Can it be that we covertly do to ourselves that which the persecutors attempted to accomplish in both the USSR and China?

Sometimes, acute and total persecution is easier to absorb and survive than piecemeal persecution. Understanding the ultimate intent of the persecutors, early and clearly, assists greatly in preparation for persecution. Covert persecution is almost always more effective than overt persecution. Overt persecution is often used when covert efforts are understood and fail to hamper the life of Christ's church.

A church movement which focuses on evangelism is better equipped both to deal with persecution and to grow in a setting of persecution. It is clear that the Holy Spirit wants us to out-grow and out-love our persecutors.

A commitment to orality allows the gospel story to be more easily transmitted from person to person. It is most difficult for the persecutors to take away the Bible when believing communities have absorbed it orally, committed it to memory, and are active in boldly sharing the good news.

Certainly the stories of the church in the USSR and China are more complicated than this brief overview would suggest. Perhaps the lessons of history are more complex. At the same time, it would be a mistake to miss these simple truths.

Applications are abundant, and they relate both to the church in America and to the church in more hostile environments in our world.

A Place to Land

- How are leaders chosen in your environment? Is the process based on their gifts or the Fruit of the Spirit?
- How does truth travel in your culture? What roles do literacy and orality play?
- What stood out the most to you as you read these brief comparisons between the church in the USSR and China?

15

How to Deal with Judas

Betrayal within the faith community is a special concern, and it is important enough to demand specific attention. Consider these scenarios as we grapple with the presence of Judas within the family of faith.

Expectations were high. After years of struggle and prayer, a house church was emerging among a resistant Muslim people group. Lives had been spent with this precious moment in view. Seeds had been sown and those seeds were now bearing fruit. Fervent prayers were being answered. Bold witness was being blessed. It was an exciting time.

A church was being born.

Almost immediately, it seemed, a Judas arose from within the group, exposing the inner circle of leaders. The small core of believers fled in disarray and fear. In an instant, the infant church seemed to disappear.

Now, years later, these believers still wait in hiding for the birth of the first house church among their people.

In another location, a trusted "believer" from a Muslim background watched as his country descended into civil war and anarchy. Chased from his homeland, he was forced to flee into the desert region of a neighboring country. Intense persecution pursued this man and his family over the next five years. Starving and isolated, this man and his family were miraculously found in that desert territory and rescued by Western believers working for a local relief organization. But, sadly, their rescue had come too late; the man's baby son died of starvation the following day.

Over time, life improved greatly for this leader of the emerging house church; he soon found himself with food, a job, and a rented home complete with a battery-operated television and a maid.

Months later, now with much to lose, this believer who had shown such potential and promise, much like the first Judas, became yet another Judas. To the dismay and fear of his believing colleagues, he returned to the local mosque, he denied his faith, and he delivered to the persecutors the names of all the believers he knew in the area and within his house group. Widespread panic ensued among these believers.

Fourteen years later, they have yet to recover their zeal for evangelism and their desire to live as church.

After two decades in yet another Muslim country, it appeared that a CPM was on the horizon. Significant sacrifices had been made to proclaim the gospel, and the gospel had been received. A new generation of leaders had emerged; these were established community leaders—older, married, and employed. Amazingly, many had shared their faith with their children, making it possible for the gospel to be planted in succeeding generations. Western believers were deeply encouraged and were leading these mature believers in increasingly deeper levels of leadership training.

But once again, sitting in the meeting was a Judas who was betraying the fellowship daily—before, during, and after the training. He was blogging about those in the room, naming both local and Western believers on a Muslim website.

How will these believers respond to this cyber Judas?

And how might we respond to the Judas who arises in our midst? In light of the biblical record and in light of Jesus' response to His own Judas, let us consider some truths about Judas and let us consider what our response might mean for the growth and health of the gospel.

1. We can expect to find Judas within our inner circle. The presence of Judas within Jesus' inner circle is a rather troubling part of the gospel story. Candidly, if Jesus Himself did not exclude Judas within His inner circle of twelve disciples, what chance do we have of avoiding a similar relational nightmare? *History would suggest that a Judas has immaculate timing. He often emerges at a critical moment, perhaps when a church is being planted or when significant growth seems possible.* At that moment, Judas tends to arise from within the body of first-generation believers in a people group, a major city, or a population center.

When Judas makes himself known, our typical response is to ask, "What did we do wrong?" But that may be the wrong question. In fact, Judas' presence is often a clear indication that the Holy Spirit is working, that our missiology is sound, and that widespread seed sowing has been effective. Much to our surprise, Judas may enter the picture not because we have done something wrong, but because we have done something right! Judas appears when there is growth. Judas is likely to be found when there is a new movement of God's Spirit. Ironically, the presence of Judas may be an indication of something *good*. If there is little growth and little challenge to the lord of darkness, then there is little need for Judas to expose himself or place himself at risk.

2. We can expect Judas to grow up within the movement and not to be imported from outside. Jesus did not inherit Judas from another movement. Apparently, Jesus saw potential in this would-be disciple; He invited him to become one of His closest followers. Yet the fact remains that Jesus did choose and call Judas to follow Him as one among an intimate group of twelve disciples. Jesus invited Judas in and He grew Judas Himself. Jesus did not recruit him away from another organization with larger offers of funding or better accredited theological education. Jesus did not naïvely accept Judas at face value after Judas had bounced from movement to movement. Judas was Jesus' responsibility, and Jesus owned that responsibility.

In multiple interviews, Chinese house church leaders related numerous arrests after importing Judas from the outside. The story—repeated often—sounds like this: someone would arrive from the outside, seek out the house church, speak the language of Zion, and drop a name or two from other house churches. Soon this new outsider would be granted access and "membership" in the larger Body of Christ. It would then take a short time for government authorities to arrive, knowing exactly who to threaten, question, and arrest because they had deliberately sent their Judas informant to infiltrate the local house church.

Since learning this difficult lesson, numerous house church leaders now refuse to offer immediate fellowship when someone they do not know seeks to join their local house church. These experienced house church leaders may suggest to the outsider, "There are two million non-believing Chinese in this area. Go start your own house church." This strategic denial of fellowship is simply a wise tool to gauge the depth and reality of the new person's faith. These house church leaders suggest that it is wiser to be arrested for sharing one's faith boldly and appropriately to lost people than to be persecuted because Judas was imported blindly and prematurely into the fold.

3. With God's help, we can choose to deal with Judas ourselves and choose not to export him to others. Jesus did not leave Judas for Peter or Paul to deal with. He wisely recognized the betrayer's presence and He used Judas's actions and failings to carry out the Father's will for His own life. Jesus announced to the larger group that there was a betrayer among them. Then He confronted Judas appropriately. He told him to do quickly whatever it was he was planning (in harmony with Jesus' timing), and He pronounced judgment over him saying that it would have been better if "he had not been born" (Matt. 26:24).

Jesus set an example for us to follow. Dealing with a disciple's failings is perhaps the most dangerous and difficult issue a mentor will ever face. Confronting and dealing appropriately (likely with a broken heart) with that person who had been mentored and invested in for years will often precipitate Judas's accusations and attacks in the presence of the opposition. His is a kiss, which signifies an act of betrayal.

This difficult task, though, is at the heart of biblical disciple making. Knowing and loving one's sheep never exempts us from making the hard call of confronting a brother or sister held dear for a season. Ultimately, when Judas arises and threatens the very existence of the emerging Body of Christ, there may be nothing left to do than to hand him over to the judgment of the Holy Spirit. If not an actual death sentence, this holy judgment places Judas outside of the intimate fellowship he has known. Often the very ones who bought him with the forty pieces of silver scorn him. He becomes a non-person. A broken heart should always precede giving a Judas over to the judgment of the Holy Spirit.

4. We can learn to recognize Judas quickly. Though Judas was intentionally and personally chosen by Jesus, Jesus was soon aware of the evil one present within His inner circle. It may be puzzling that Jesus initially called Judas or refused to dismiss him quickly, before his betrayal became so destructive. Perhaps Jesus was holding before Judas the possibility of repentance. Or perhaps Judas was allowed to stay as a fulfillment of prophecy. Regardless of His thinking, Jesus understood the old adage, "Keep your friends close and your enemies closer." By recognizing Judas's true nature, and by keeping him close, Jesus could better discern this betrayer's heart, intent, and methods. Consequently, Jesus was able to use Judas to fulfill His godly plans rather than being manipulated by Judas for earthly treasures.

Jesus and Judas were constantly together. They lived with the other eleven disciples in community. They shared a twenty-four-hour-a-day, seven-day-a-week relationship where the Shepherd and sheep knew each other thoroughly. Jesus knew His sheep so intimately that He addressed their thoughts before they became actions. Sadly, in the world of Western workers, "our sheep" can stumble, deny, walk away from spouses, deny their faith, and betray others, and it may literally be months before we are even aware of the missteps. Jesus, recognizing Judas and predicting his actions, initiated ministry. Typically, Judas is exposed early when discipleship is based on an intimate relationship more than on the superficial exchange of information.

5. *We can be aware that Judas often has money issues.* This can be called the "Jesus-plus syndrome," especially where Westerners and Western largesse is present. There is little unique about those first forty pieces of silver. Often interest is shown in a kingdom relationship when that relationship seems to entail receiving Jesus plus a job, an apartment, a spouse, an education, or even a ticket to a Western country. *The more prolific the expectations for these Jesus-plus additions, the more likely it will be that Judases will multiply far beyond the ratio of only one out of twelve!*

Judas can step forward when he is refused funding to pursue a Western degree program. Job loss due to poor performance can cause a betrayal. Not funding an immature seeker to attend an international consortium can become the opportunity for Judas to show his true colors.

One believer from a Muslim background stated it this way, "When a seeker after Jesus comes to me, I ask them, 'What is it that you want: a car, a house, a wife, or to go to America?' I tell them that I cannot even give them an aspirin. All I have is a cross. Do you want to pick up your cross and follow Jesus? That is all that I can offer you."

He then continued, "Everyone who followed Jesus in the New Testament *gave up* something. Everyone who comes to Jesus through a Westerner is trying to *get* something."

We need to consider such comments carefully and candidly. The truth remains that Judas is often dealing with Jesus-plus desires and expectations.

6. Finally, we can reveal Christ in our midst by the way that we deal with Judas. Clearly, Judas's betrayal is frightening and heartbreaking. Betrayal hurts. It is devastating. The activity of Judas ushers in a dangerous time spiritually and physically. Judas can determine whether the emerging church marches forward into greater faith toward the coming Pentecost or if believers hide for a decade as those who are scattered, alone, and afraid. *It is precisely when Judas shows up that believers are called to make that history-altering decision to focus on Jesus and the resurrection more so than on Judas and his betrayal.* Running and hiding for a few nights and days are to be expected. Widespread denial by all the other disciples is also common. At that moment, the reality of "counting the cost" becomes more real.

But, after those few nights and days, the more important question rises to the surface: Will we choose fear or faith?

Unpacking Judas

- Judas is more than a non-tither or someone who disagrees with the pastoral staff. He has the potential to kill what God has started. Discuss where you have encountered such a Judas.
- If you have never met a Judas, why not?
- How does one focus on Jesus in an environment rift with persecution where Judas betrays everyone?

16

Bring on the Water

Though we might want to avoid it, we are going to take a risk and talk about baptism in the next few chapters. *Specifically, we will be talking about how baptism affects witness in church planting among the dangerously unreached.* Most of the time, it is simply amazing how different ministry organizations partner to provide every man, woman, and child access to Jesus Christ. We help each other gain access among people groups. We help one another in translating and printing Bibles in hundreds of languages around the planet. We partner in the creation of secure platforms that allow us to model and minister together. We broadly sow the gospel among unreached people groups together. We act like brothers and sisters across denominational lines with great joy.

There is such a wonderful partnership among the various bodies of Christ . . . until it comes to the matter of baptism!

When that issue surfaces, our cooperation often disappears. When the topic of baptism surfaces, conflicts arise between Western agencies and church-sent groups. Still, for these next few chapters, let's talk about this sensitive and important issue. Perhaps we can simply pause, take a deep breath, and discern God's presence and peace even in a potentially volatile area.

The role of baptism and the resulting persecution in emerging churches and CPMs is an important consideration. Because of so much historical and theological baggage, it is also a difficult topic to consider. Those of us who live in post-Pentecost settings tend to have formal and well-developed understandings of baptism. One crucial point of discussion, for example, might be the proper form of baptism. Different faith communities take different positions on this question and they might disagree about whether the proper form of baptism is immersion, pouring, or sprinkling.

Another point of discussion might focus theologically on whether baptism is a symbol, a sign, or a sacrament. For the purposes of this book, it is not necessary or essential to reach agreement on those important questions. Suffice it to say that believers of all stripes have strong opinions and convictions about these important issues. *What matters most for our present discussion is to realize how new believers in contexts of persecution experience and understand baptism.*

Some of what follows might seem terribly obvious and simplistic. All the same, it is essential to grapple with baptism at its most basic and, by definition, biblical level. To skip over this conversation is to avoid something crucial and revealing. This conversation is perhaps most needed for those of us who have become overly familiar with baptism as a church-initiation ceremony or for those of us who use baptism to measure success in ministry and denominational identity. Whatever baptism is, it is not that! And perhaps it is believers in persecution who can remind us of this important truth.

In light of our discussion in the previous few chapters, it turns out that baptism is indispensable in getting to the point of establishing churches and in helping faith move to the next generation. In fact, baptism, in contexts of persecution, will either signal the birth of a new church or the inclusion of a new believer in an already-existing local body within his culture and language. This is no small claim, and this observation reminds us of how very shaping and powerful baptism is.

Several basic observations are important at the beginning.

First, in the first generation of faith and environments of persecution, baptism invariably follows conversion. This might seem to be an obvious point, but it is a point that simply must be made. Baptism follows conversion. It may be a baptism such as located in a Philippian jail or the home of Cornelius where the entire household was baptized. The point we want to make here is not the age of those baptized but the community who were baptized after receiving Jesus as Lord and Savior.

Second, cultural norms regarding the age of adulthood should be observed and honored when it comes to baptism. In all of our interviews, we came across only three individuals in the world of Islam who were baptized before the age of eighteen. (Two of these were sixteen-year-olds, and one was fifteen. All three were baptized by their fathers in family settings.) In a Muslim context, it would be inappropriate to baptize believers who are not already considered adults and thereby not responsible for their own life-changing decision.

In a host of Muslim cultures, a male is considered a man at the age of eighteen. A male is often married at the age of thirty, eligible to sit with the council of elders at the age of forty, and eligible to be an elder at the age of fifty. *Those cultural realities suggest that our evangelism among Muslim men should be focused on men thirty years old and beyond!* A female in a Muslim context is considered a woman when she reaches the age when she is able to bear children. Again, it would be inappropriate to offer baptism without taking into account cultural norms related to adulthood, which first-generation believers within persecution ascribe to themselves.

As obvious as this might sound, it might be a startling thought for those of us who live in an American context. It is not uncommon for us to see very young children baptized. A similar thing in the Islamic world would be inappropriate and unnecessarily offensive.

Third, baptism serves the cause of witness. Hindus, Buddhists, and Muslims will all directly associate baptism with salvation. The act of baptism itself will bear witness to faith in Jesus. In Islam in particular, baptism is seen as "the point of no return." A person being baptized is, in effect, saying, "I will die for my faith." Persecution soars at baptism and those baptized need to know clearly the cost of their decision to follow Jesus, especially through baptism.

Fourth, baptism in a Muslim context typically follows discipleship. In fact, baptism generally follows an extensive process of discipleship (perhaps a period of several years). Something very different often happens in Hindu settings. A Hindu coming to faith in Jesus might have experienced a dramatic event of healing. Asked to profess faith in this Jesus who is responsible for the healing, the Hindu believer will express faith in Jesus and be baptized almost immediately. If this Hindu is asked about Jesus, he or she (at that point) will have very little to say other than the fact that Jesus has made the healing possible. Even though baptism has already happened, discipleship has not happened yet. Yet their baptism is in community, not secret, not performed by cultural outsiders.

The experience for MBBs is generally quite different. Typically, the Muslim believer has experienced years of discipleship before ever considering baptism. Personal failure during this time of training is almost expected and is not a surprise at all. At a certain point, however, baptism is offered or sought, and that event signifies a point of no return. Extensive discipleship has already happened, and baptism happens at the end of that process.

Fifth, baptism is practiced in and among the host, believing community. When Western workers or outsiders are involved in baptisms, persecution tends to increase dramatically. The best model is for baptism to happen *within an in-culture community with as little outside involvement as possible.*

Sixth, *baptism is at its biblical best when an in-culture or near-culture believer baptizes another believer.* Again, minimal involvement of Western workers or other outsiders is ideal.

For most MBBs and other first-generation believers within persecution, there is very little interest in the theology of baptism (is it a symbol, a sign, or a sacrament?), and there is very little interest in the mode of baptism (should it be done by immersion, pouring, or sprinkling?). *What matters most is the deeper meaning of what is happening. This new believer will understand that he or she is being baptized into Christ, and being baptized into a new Body of believers. Baptism is a profound expression of belonging, and it is a clear picture of a new family. Especially within contexts of persecution and suffering, it is simply impossible to overstate the power of this image and the meaning that it conveys.*

One interesting question related to baptism has to do with timing. Specifically, when does baptism happen relative to conversion? Should baptism happen immediately, should it happen soon, or should it happen years later? Our interviews have highlighted significant variety on this matter. We have already mentioned the typical Hindu situation of almost immediate baptism. In contrast, we have noticed two factors that affect the timing of baptism in persecution contexts.

The first issue has to do with how many people are coming to faith in Jesus and how quickly this is happening. In situations where just a few people are coming to faith in Jesus, baptism is often delayed. During this waiting time, discipleship training happens. If, on the other hand, thousands are quickly coming to faith in Jesus, baptism happens much more quickly. It appears that a larger number of converts can provide a more protected setting for growth and maturity. It is common for entire families to be baptized together quickly as they accept the good news together. The numbers of people coming to faith together is one factor that affects the timing of baptism.

The other issue is related to the severity of persecution. If persecution is typically quick and severe, then baptism happens less quickly. If, on the other hand, persecution is less severe or if it seems that it will be slower in coming, then baptism is experienced more quickly. If large numbers are coming to Jesus, even if persecution is severe, then baptism comes rapidly.

Whatever we might take baptism to mean, believers in contexts of persecution and suffering see it primarily as a radical identification with Jesus and a profoundly important identification with the community of faith. Clearly, baptism is no small thing. As a public, freely chosen point of no return, the believer is enacting and embracing faith in a visible and open way.

Let's Take a Baptism Pause

- Discuss what your baptism meant to you at the time you experienced it.
- Who can and does administer baptism in your spiritual setting? Why?

17

"I Have Come Home!"

In 1991, there were approximately 150 MBBs in Somalia, a country classified as 99.9 percent Muslim. Seven years later, only four of those MBBs were alive and still in Somalia. Another brother has since died of disease. Persecution in Somalia is almost nonexistent today, because there are few believers left to persecute.

Historically, persecution had always been severe among people groups in the Horn of Africa, but this level of persecution among this specific people group seemed to be something more evil. As civil society deteriorated, a more fundamentalist Islam emerged, which led to the persecution of local believers even beyond the historical norm. Without question, those who were martyred were followers of Jesus Christ. Even so, the timing of most of these "martyrdoms" was not directly linked to an individual's relationship with Jesus. Typically (and tragically), the martyrdom was more closely related to the individual's relationship with Christian workers from the West than to any focused attempt by these MBBs to be positive witnesses to their families and neighbors.

In depth, on-site interviews with both believers and persecutors indicate that the "trigger" or antecedent for many of these deaths was related to secondary issues.

Several types of examples illustrate the point:

- In some cases, MBBs were murdered specifically because they worked for Christian relief agencies headquartered in the West. Mistakenly, some Muslims believed that the removal of local believers would lead to greater access to relief funds and commodities. Therefore, removing MBBs from the scene (it was believed) was a prerequisite to acquiring these goods, monies, and opportunities for themselves.
- In other cases, MBBs were killed for worshipping regularly (and sometimes openly) with outsiders. Simply being seen with Westerners or spending significant time with Westerners often invited the hostility of the host community.
- Other MBBs were persecuted when they were found in the possession of a Bible or other written discipleship materials, often materials written at a level significantly beyond their own ability or educational background. Others, persecuted for possessing such materials, were illiterate. Others were Muslims who were persecuted for receiving a "gift" from an outsider, not knowing that it was the Westerners' Holy Book.
- Finally, those MBBs who were employed by Westerners specifically to evangelize their friends and neighbors (often in culturally inappropriate ways) found themselves subject to even more intense and immediate persecution. As far as I can remember, all of these were killed.

There is, of course, no way to establish a direct connection between a particular event or relationship and the martyrdom of an

MBB. No single event or relationship can be identified as "the cause" for martyrdom, unless it is clearly for witness to the resurrection of Jesus Christ. It is clear, however, that the involvement of Western workers and their leadership created a mission culture that inadvertently placed local believers at risk. What is perhaps most significant is that this risk was typically *not* the direct result of a positive witness for Jesus.

Martyrdom remains a possibility for all who follow Christ. The road to resurrection led through a gruesome crucifixion. God the Father has used, and continues to use, the sacrificial deaths of His children to usher in a deeper and broader faith and to anchor the church within salvation history. *As central as martyrdom is to the story, however, it is not to be sought.* Persecution, and ultimately martyrdom, is simply a reality for those following the Son of God in a fallen world.

Tertullian's words were mentioned earlier in our conversation: "the blood of the martyrs is the seed of the church." It is possible that people who have not yet experienced severe persecution sometimes speak those words flippantly. While God uses even persecution for His ultimate purposes, martyrdom also leaves children without fathers, spouses without mates, and believing bodies temporarily void of leadership.

Martyrdom is tragic wherever and however it happens, but it is especially tragic when it happens because of secondary reasons. Looking back on the recent history of Somalia, it appears that severe persecution visited the young and emerging Somali church at a delicate time in her history. And, sadly, it appears that the persecution largely arose for reasons other than witnessing to the life and resurrection of Jesus.

Of course, God's story in Somalia is still being written. But at this point, and from a human point of view, it seems that our generation has witnessed the almost complete annihilation of a reproducible faith within the land and among the peoples of Somalia. God always uses the blood of those who die for Christ to increase and deepen witness. Yet when the death of believers occurs more for their relationships with outsiders than their positive witness to the saving grace found in Jesus, then the positives that come from that "martyrdom" will likely be severely reduced. Perhaps the most positive lessons learned are to never do what we did there again, in Somalia or anywhere else. Perhaps that would be a way to honor what is written in Romans 8:28?

Few functions of the faith will lead to persecution more quickly than that of a believer's baptism, especially baptism encouraged and administered by an outsider. Still the most common baptism for Muslims is secretly administered among and by Westerners, in the Westerners house, in their bathtub, and inside the most unclean room in anyone's house.

This chapter will reflect on the issues surrounding the baptism of MBBs within cultures of persecution and violence. It will outline some of the unique challenges related to baptism and then suggest some missiological perspectives that could reduce the frequency of persecution *for secondary reasons.*

In keeping with our earlier claim, the goal of this chapter and the goal of the mission enterprise itself is not the elimination of persecution. In fact, as we have stated, the only way to eliminate persecution is to eliminate conversions to Jesus. So our goal is not to bring persecution to an end but to make certain that persecution is a by-product of faith and witness. The goal is to be certain that, when persecution comes, it is grounded firmly in an individual's walk and witness as a follower of Jesus. Being put to death because of employment practices or because of worship circumstances or because of possession of certain discipleship materials is not the same thing as being martyred for a positive, culturally sensitive witness to the death and resurrection of Jesus.

Simply stated, *Islam generally equates baptism with conversion.* From the perspective of Islam, to be baptized is to be saved. A repeated emphasis throughout our interviews with MBBs was the intensification of persecution immediately following the believer's baptism. Up to that point, it was not unusual for a "seeker" to be allowed to study the Bible, listen to Christian radio programming, attend a CBB church (if welcomed), and even to meet regularly and openly with Western workers. All of these behaviors can be explained as a desire to understand Christianity for debating purposes.

Obviously, in some cases, there was significant resistance to such practices. But this often low-key persecution paled in comparison to the overt and intense persecution that began to surface immediately after the MBB experienced believer's baptism.

Islam is convinced that it is at baptism that its sons and daughters have become separated from their former way of life. Islam identifies baptism as the time when the believer has died to the old way and embraced a new worldview. Though the image might be uncomfortable, it might even be suggested that baptism, given the worldview of Islam, is to a new believer in Christ what strapping on a belt of explosives is to a suicide bomber.

For Islam, baptism is the point of no return. Though Western believers might be repelled by such an image, it seems that Islam (perhaps more than the Western church itself) has truly grasped the weight and significance of baptism!

Most practitioners of the Christian faith, regardless of background, would agree at this point: baptism is critically important. Baptism is central to the expansion of the kingdom of God and is, therefore, crucial to the mission enterprise. Baptism is extremely important in identifying the new believer with the faith community and all that it has to offer (including mutual support and nurture, accountability, creation of a new family, a setting for service, and an environment for corporate worship, among many others).

When overseas workers belittle, misuse, or misunderstand the power and impact of a believer's baptism, defined and practiced locally, they can unintentionally hinder emerging faith. It is ironic that workers can baptize literally hundreds of MBBs, and yet those baptisms rarely result in a church that can survive the departure of the foreigner. What our interviews suggest is that baptism is profoundly significant, but that an MBB and a Western worker will understand that significance in radically different ways.

Those who are sent out are often captive to the doctrinal formulations of their sending bodies, compelled to produce measurable results (often represented in the statistic of "baptisms"), and desperate for some kind of observable "success." Given that worldview, they would quickly agree that baptism matters. What can be easily neglected, however, is the transforming impact of baptism within a culture of persecution and violence. The MBB will agree that baptism is staggering in its importance but for entirely different reasons.

Within Islamic cultures, workers will generally encourage MBBs to embrace believer's baptism approximately three to six months after an MBB professes faith in Jesus. That statistic holds true regardless of how the process of conversion occurred. When a MBB baptizes another MBB, however, baptism might follow a declaration of faith by as much as three to five years. At this point, the difference in timing is not easy to explain. Westerners will suggest that their desire to baptize quickly is an effort to be biblically obedient. MBBs will suggest that the delay allows a stronger grounding in the faith before the crucial step of baptism. MBBs suggest that to deny one's faith is normal before baptism and causes less harm to the emerging church. But to deny Jesus after baptism is catastrophic. This is clearly an area that calls for ongoing and candid dialogue.

Another highlight of the interviews focused on the connection between baptism and the planting of new churches. When a Western worker baptizes an MBB, persecution of that person is often swift and devastating. Despite the fact that baptism of an MBB by an outsider can be administered in the dark of night and outside of the local community (perhaps even in another country), the family and friends of the MBB will learn of the baptism almost immediately. Regardless of whatever attempts are made (and leaving for now the question of whether or not secrecy is advisable), there is simply no way to keep a baptism secret. The rapid rate of communication in an oral culture rivals the speed of the Internet. The only exception to this reality happens when an MBB is extracted for baptism and then never returns home to family and friends. The motivation behind such a choice is, of course, easy to understand. Workers might be compelled by genuine love and concern for their newfound brother or sister in Christ, but the implications for the birth of CPMs are profound. Unfortunately, the way that baptism is often administered can, in fact, lead to *reduced* rather than *increased* witness.

Given the seeming direct relationship of baptism to persecution, workers often seek to baptize MBBs in secret. Despite the good intentions, the worker inadvertently models fear and insecurity that will hinder the new believer's faith for months and perhaps years to come.

When the persecuting family or community is asked about why they treated their child or neighbor so harshly for being baptized, the reply is often, "He has participated in a secret, foreign religious ritual at the hands of a foreigner. He has been bought with foreign money. He has become a Westerner and has taken sides against our own people."

The missiological implications are clear. Persecution becomes a socially responsible (and even necessary) reaction to a "foreign ritual" or even a perceived "foreign invasion." Couched in these terms, it is impossible for the local community to so much as consider the claims of Christ or the process of faith. Protection of the community from foreign influence is the main concern; faith questions are seldom considered. The entire experience has been reduced to the inappropriate influence of an outsider and the community's response to it.

As important as baptism is—*and it is utterly crucial*—it becomes apparent that even baptism is a secondary matter. To be persecuted because of baptism (regardless of how or by whom it is done) is not the same thing as being persecuted for who Jesus claims to be.

The interviews also reveal that most MBBs, within five years of their declaration of faith in Jesus (regardless of whatever process they have been a part of), may have been baptized and re-baptized three to five times. In countries where overseas workers representing different agencies are beginning to partner and share statistics, it is clear that the number of annual baptisms of MBBs is significantly inflated as MBBs are baptized time and time again within different mission bodies. Seldom, due to security issues, will these mission entities realize that a particular MBB has already been baptized by a sister organization. The baptism of one MBB might be counted by a number of different groups. It is not unusual to read that there are, for example, a thousand followers of Christ in a particular country, while in personal interviews it is possible to account for only two or three hundred. The difference can be explained by the fact that many MBBs have experienced repeated baptisms through several different groups. What's more, each *time* the MBB is baptized, the potential for severe persecution escalates.

One of the motivations behind multiple baptisms is the connection of baptism to the opportunity for employment within a mission organization. Whether implied or explicit, the step of baptism is understood to be an entry requirement for a job, and MBBs willingly submit to that expectation, especially in places where unemployment tops out at 90 percent. Additional pressure sometimes comes from workers themselves. It is difficult to delay baptism when home churches and sending agencies are evaluating the number of baptisms as a measure of missional effectiveness.

The matter is complicated further by the theological, historical, and doctrinal differences represented by various mission organizations. It is not unusual for a MBB to receive believer's baptism by immersion at the hands of a Baptist worker who explains to the believer the symbolic nature of baptism. Yet, sometime later, either because of spiritual struggle or the opportunity for a new job, the MBB may gravitate to an Assembly of God worker, receiving another baptism along with detailed teaching about being filled with the Holy Spirit. This same MBB might then be drawn to a Lutheran relief agency or, perhaps, one supported by Presbyterians.

This pilgrimage might be the result of honest seeking, or it might be motivated by a desire for employment, education, a spouse, or a chance to live in America. Whatever the motivation, this MBB (in a relatively short span of time) could have been repeatedly baptized by outsiders who use immersion, sprinkling, *and* pouring—every mode of baptism that the Western church has practiced over its two thousand years of life.

For many MBBs, generally speaking, the mode of baptism is not especially significant. The theological setting for baptism is also likely to be confused. MBBs do not come to Christ in a vacuum. In some cases, they have already been exposed to the church. In fact, in many cases, this historical church can pre-date Islam. As if by osmosis, these seekers and incipient believers have already been affected by different theologies and traditions regarding baptism. The impact on both the MBBs and their faith is deeply significant.

Imagine a man named Mohammed. He has experienced dreams and visions that have sent him on a spiritual pilgrimage. This season of searching has lasted from three to five years. During this time, he has interacted with the Bible; he has read it and studied it. He has also had between twenty and thirty spiritual encounters with the gospel.

The Holy Spirit, time and again, has sent believers to Mohammed. The process repeats what happened often in Scripture: Joseph was sent to Pharaoh, Ananias was sent to Saul, Philip was sent to the Ethiopian eunuch. In the same way, many different people have been sent to Mohammed.

As a result of this good and godly witness, Mohammed makes a declaration of faith in Jesus. He then receives believer's baptism.

At this point in the story, it does not really matter who administers the baptism. Remarkably, when MBBs baptize each other, with a minimum of outside participation, the greatest influence on the *mode* of baptism does not come from Bible studies or even from discussions with other MBBs. What influences Mohammed and his friends the most is whether or not they have seen *The JESUS Film*. The most common mode of baptism comes from a movie.

So Mohammed receives a *"JESUS Film"* baptism. Often, he will describe his faith pilgrimage and speak of this baptism (which has come several years after his declaration of faith) using symbolic words concerning his relationship with Jesus. If Mohammed is married, he will go home to his family. Within three to six months, Mohammed will make a proclamation to his wife: "Woman, I am now a Christian. That makes this a Christian home. Therefore, you are now a Christian."

Of course, his wife is shocked, as already mentioned. Because of his terrible indiscretion, she can divorce him or betray him to his family. But often, her dependence on her husband and her desire to obey him is so deeply ingrained that she will accept the fact that faith has been declared for her by her more informed husband. A few months later, he will baptize her.

In the interview, Mohammed will describe his own faith and the faith of his wife in different ways. In fact, he might say that his wife is not yet a "true believer." She is married to him, however, and her baptism (he will say) represents a *sign* that one day she will believe in her own right. One day, she will become a "true believer."

Mohammed is not quite finished. His faith has not been birthed within a vacuum. The religious environment surrounding him often includes Catholic and Orthodox churches. He has been influenced by the teachings of these groups also. He gazes with love at his three-month-old son. He knows the difficulties that lie ahead for this child. He knows the struggle of being educated in an Islamic system. Mohammed may have many theological questions, but he is willing to take a chance that perhaps the Catholics and Orthodox are correct. So Mohammed will baptize his infant son, praying that this time baptism is actually salvific.

Notice that baptism has gone from symbol to sign to sacrament *within one family and within a very short span of time.* Perhaps Mohammed has been immersed. Perhaps his wife has had water poured over her head. Perhaps their infant son has been sprinkled. Mohammed has very little interest in the theology of baptism or in the proper mode of baptism. He has different and deeper concerns.

It is also likely that each of these baptisms has taken place with the participation of an outside community. Regardless of their level of theological or biblical understanding, Mohammed and his family experience increasing persecution with each step of the process. Quickly, they become outsiders within their own community. If they happen to live in an environment where violence is common, workers will typically offer to extract them to a country of safety. Often, the persecution that Mohammed and his family will experience will be precipitated by multiple baptisms with the involvement of outside workers as well as with those within the CBB church.

Perhaps Islam understands what the West has forgotten. Perhaps Islam understands the meaning of baptism more profoundly than the church does. Baptism represents dying to sin, dying to self, and dying to an old way of living in community. Baptism represents a new alignment with the kingdom of God and a new way of relating to family and friends. Quite simply, baptism represents a new life. It is startling to realize that Jesus never extracted one person from his or her country of origin. In every case, submission to the lordship of Jesus (and sharing in the experience of baptism) was a local experience.

There is also a growing theological corruption that surrounds baptism when an MBB receives baptism by Western hands. The interviews record numerous instances where godly workers have faithfully witnessed, led Muslims through a process or experience of salvation, and then baptized them. Rarely does this result in a church being planted, even when the worker has performed in culturally appropriate ways and fulfilled the expectations of the sending Body.

Why?

The interviews suggest that many MBBs have experienced serious persecution when their faith pilgrimage and baptism were traced to the ministry of the outsider. In some settings, scores of MBBs went to jail and were severely beaten. When asked why they did not simply meet with other MBBs, evangelizing and administering the ordinances or sacraments of the church themselves, several trust issues and several theological corruptions were noted in almost every case.

MBBs will typically meet with one another, but only if the Westerner is present. If the worker is reassigned, goes on a furlough, or even takes an extended vacation, the MBBs refuse to meet together. When the foreigner is absent, the MBBs simply will not meet together.

When a group of MBBs was asked why this was so, especially since all of them went to jail *for their association with the outsider*, the reply was, "We cannot trust a person from our own country."

"Who do you trust?" I then asked in my interviews.

"We trust the foreigner," the MBBs responded.

"But it was because of your relationship with the Westerner that you went to jail!" I pointed out.

"Yes. That is true," they answered. "But, still, we only trust the outsider."

Missiologically, understanding this apparent contradiction makes cultural sense. *MBBs will trust the one who brings them to Jesus.* "Timothy" will trust "Paul." And "Paul" will trust the "Timothy" who he has come to know well. He has observed "Timothy" struggle through the faith process. He has watched "Timothy" begin to endure persecution. This trust is based on shared experience. MBBs will meet as a church with the people they trust. Interestingly, the *greater* the role that outsiders play in bringing MBBs to faith, the *less* trust those MBBs will have for other MBBs.

Though they experience serious persecution as a result, most MBBs will come themselves and they will bring scores of other people to the outsider in order to pray the prayer of salvation and receive believer's baptism. Why? Why is it necessary for the foreigner to be involved at this point in the process? Almost without exception, MBBs will say, "My baptism is *better* at the hands of a Western worker who has known Jesus for years, comes from a Christian country, and has such deep religious training."

John 3:22 is perhaps the most definitive reference to the *possibility* that Jesus Himself baptized. But John 4:1 indicates that Jesus quickly delegated this task to His disciples. There, Scripture makes it clear that "it was not Jesus who baptized, but his disciples" (v. 2).

The apostle Paul addressed this issue of baptismal corruption in 1 Corinthians 1:13–17. He concludes with this telling word: "For Christ did not send me to baptize, but to preach the gospel."

More damaging is the almost universal statement from MBBs that is so painful to hear, "My salvation is better at the hands of a foreign worker who knows Jesus so much better than any local person." This is a theological corruption. Unknowingly, the worker can give credence to the development of a "first-class MBB" and a "second-class MBB" within a group of first-generation believers. And, significantly, such a desire to receive these blessings and functions at the hands of the foreigner often leads to increased persecution.

When these MBBs are arrested, the arresting authorities seldom question MBBs in regard to issues of their personal faith. The persecutors demand information concerning the involvement of outsiders in the lives of local believers. They want to know from where the Bibles originated, who gave them *The JESUS Film*, who provided Christian witness, materials, and money. It is very common for MBBs to be arrested simply because of their relationships with outsiders. Issues of personal faith are seldom raised during the course of the persecution event. Ideally, this persecution moment would be a time for bold witness, but bold witness is made more difficult when personal faith is not even part of the conversation.

Several concluding observations are in order.

First, the interviews suggest that baptism should be practiced in and among the host, believing community. Workers from the West seldom, if ever, make up that host, believing community. Clearly, baptism in the New Testament took place in local community. Baptism outside of a local community, if present at all, was a distinct exception to normal practice.

The story of the Ethiopian eunuch in Acts 8:26–39 might be cited as the classic exception to the norm. But the comments that persecuted believers make about this story and the cultural setting are telling. In the view of persecuted believers, it is significant that this Ethiopian was "an important official in charge of all the treasury of Candace, queen of the Ethiopians" (v. 27). They point out that he was traveling in caravan and was, therefore, surrounded by community. They suggest that this man was riding in a chariot that was likely driven by a servant. Other people were traveling with this man. And that entire community, *his* community, was able to observe what he experienced.

To people in the West, the story suggests isolation and separation. But through MBB eyes, the baptism of the Ethiopian eunuch was clearly within community. The biblical norm is baptism within community. The biblical norm is a setting where an individual's family members and friends are baptized together. In the New Testament, there is no evidence of secret baptism by outsiders in their bathroom, in their bathtub, in the middle of the night, and certainly not in another country. John's baptism of Jesus, the baptism of the household of Cornelius, and the baptism of the Philippian jailor are representative of being baptized inside the culture by insiders. If, as a near-culture believer, the Holy Spirit places you beside the Ethiopian Eunuch miraculously, be sure to lead him to Jesus and do not hinder his baptism! Then be ready for the Holy Spirit to move you away from this Ethiopian.

Ignored and rejected by Western workers is the evidence that many MBBs experience psychological dysfunction *after they come to Christ*. This might include alcoholism, multiple marriages, sexual voyeurism, or depression. Why might these things happen at that point?

Islam informs an adherent how to live life, how to exist in community, how to fill every moment of every day. It defines when to wake, when to pray, where to pray, the direction to face during prayer, and even the words to pray. It regulates life between genders. Islam touches on every aspect of daily life.

Often when a young Muslim comes to Jesus, baptized by an outsider, he or she loses family, as well as social identity. This new believer has indeed died to, and been thrown out of, the old culture. But, because there has been no immersion in real, local, believing community, there is no place of belonging within a new Christlike culture. This new believer and the one who has helped him or her come to faith live in two distinctly different worlds. This new believer has lost the entire structure of life, but that lost structure has not yet been replaced with anything else. Without community, this MBB is "lost" even though salvation has already been experienced!

Second, reflecting on both the interviews and the New Testament record, it is clear that ideally an in-culture or near-culture believer should baptize MBBs. The more the baptizer is viewed as an outsider, the more likely it is that intense persecution and theological corruption will result. In the West, the baptizer is generally set apart by seminary degrees, education, title, and ordination. Right or wrong, there is a clear delineation between clergy and congregation. Within environments of persecution, however, community is formed most quickly when local hands lovingly administer baptism: husband to wife, father to children, neighbor to neighbor. As in-culture and near-culture believers baptize, persecution for secondary reasons is sharply reduced and old communities of faith are transformed into new communities in Christ.

In this case, when persecution *does* arrive, it is in direct response to who Jesus is and to the kind of transformed community that He is creating. And when persecution arises, an incipient community of support has already come into existence. This is not to suggest that Islam has the right to persecute those who turn to Jesus if a Western worker happens to be involved in that conversion. What is suggested is that sent out ones need to work and minister with greater sensitivity and wisdom.

It is not uncommon for MBBs to plead with believers from the outside to baptize them, even outsiders temporarily passing through their country. If MBBs are evangelized, baptized, financed, and gathered together by outsiders, what is their motivation to be in community? The interviews suggest that MBBs need to be locally accountable for witness and behavior among their family, friends, and neighbors.

Clearly, a sound theology of baptism is important. The church for centuries has debated and divided over whether baptism represents a symbol, sign, or sacrament. The church has persecuted itself over who has the authority to perform baptism and which mode of baptism is biblical. These are heavy and important issues. At the same time, these issues of theology and mode, as defined by the Western church, were seldom, if ever, raised by MBBs or others in hundreds of interviews globally!

MBBs will experience multiple baptisms as they pass from one Western mission family to another. They will usually receive something useful from each doctrinal experience, even if they acquiesce to multiple baptisms for the sake of employment. MBBs will pass from one agency to the next; expressing the feeling "something is still missing." Generally, they will be baptized again and again, until they receive believer's baptism at the hands of another MBB within their own community. Then they will weep with emotion saying, *I have come home! I have found our true New Testament family. This is my real Body of Christ.*

MBBs, in environments of persecution and violence, are primarily concerned about only one doctrinal issue regarding their baptism. These are their questions: Have I been baptized into Christ and into a local community? Will this church care for me, hold me daily accountable, and share all things common? Will this new spiritual family care for my family and me if I lose my job, if we are excluded from my extended family, or if we are thrown into prison or martyred for our faith?

Unfortunately, that concern is not always the central issue for Western workers and their sending bodies concerning baptism in cultures of violence. *Sometimes, workers are more consumed with counting baptisms than with making baptism count.*

At the point where baptism, MBBs, and workers converge, the overwhelming foundational issue is the nature of local community. What is church in its essence? What is church stripped of property, buildings, and all of the possessions collected throughout the centuries? What does it mean to belong—*to belong!*—to the Body of Christ?

Baptism is at the heart of church planting in environments framed by violence and persecution, especially in places where faith is emerging. At its heart, baptism is the midwife to the emerging church. What we suggest here is a revealing and wonderful insight: when baptism is truly New Testament and culturally sensitive, it will always leave a church behind.

Among first-generation believers, baptism is often the birth of a new church. At the very least, baptism is into a local, believing community. Baptism defines where and to whom they belong.

He had listened and listened to the Bible stories on the radio and fell in love with the stories and eventually with Jesus. He found a Bible and devoured it daily. He gave his life to Jesus but was terribly troubled when he read about believer's baptism, including the baptism of Jesus. He knew of no other believer like him. He was walking alongside the largest lake in his country, one of the largest in Africa. Pacing back and forth for a long time, he kept looking over the cliff at the water 15–20 feet below. Suddenly he walked ten yards away from the cliff, began to run faster and faster until he jumped off the cliff. Falling through the air he shouted, "I baptize myself in the name of the Father, the Son, and the Holy Spirit!" Then he hit the water.

I met him two weeks later and heard his story for the first time. In the midst of telling me his story he stopped, fear clouding his eyes, and he asked, "Did I do something wrong? Was my baptism OK?" "Well," I replied, "it was the deepest baptism I have ever heard of!"

Yet hear his heart. Biblically, intuitively, he knew something was missing. We were able to introduce him to a house church close to where he lived, among his own people. He met with them, received baptism by that community. Following his baptism he wept and cried out, "I have come home, I have come home."

To me, the mode of baptism is an important issue. Do we sprinkle, pour, or immerse? For me, the theology of baptism is crucial. Do we view baptism as a symbol, sign, or sacrament? Yet what the Western church has forgotten, maybe forsaken, is this irreplaceable truth of baptism; does it define where I belong? Is this community flesh of my flesh and bone of my bone? Will we willingly bring all things common and care for all the parts of our body? We will die for Jesus and with each other.

Dare I say it? The Western church may have the mode of baptism and the theology of baptism figured out. Yet where is the sense of belonging, of being part of the Body, and of being in real biblical community?

I had to sit at the feet of the Body of Christ in persecution to learn what I had never experienced in the Western church.

Jesus was baptized of John. Why? He had no sin needing forgiveness. Jesus was baptized of John because He desired and needed a community from which He and the Twelve would launch His ministry. He needed a place, a family to which He belonged. Afterwards the Holy Spirit ascended as a dove and God said, "You are my beloved son, I take delight in you!"

"As I Go Down to the River to Pray . . ."

- Describe what it means to you to belong to your local church.
- Comment on the fact that in persecution baptism is often the birth of a new church.
- Why did Jesus and the apostle Paul resist baptizing? Why do Westerners overseas rush to baptize?

Part IV

Practical Matters

18

Wise Servants, Tough Places

In our interviews, we were often able to talk to believers in settings of persecution about Western workers. Over time, we began to ask about this near the end of our interviews. In many cases, we had already been talking for hours with a deeper trust emerging with those whose stories we were hearing.

As our time grew to a close, we would ask, "Tell us about Western workers. What do you value in us? What do we do that is especially helpful, and what do we do that is especially harmful to the growth of faith? What should we stop doing? What should we start doing? How can Western workers best assist believers in getting to reproducing house churches?"

After looking at each other, as if to ask, "Should we tell this foreigner the truth?" they would candidly, sometimes cautiously, offer advice. The responses were both insightful and profoundly honest.

The first observation we would make is that it is not enough for lost people to be the *focus* of Western workers. As good as that sounds, it is essential to go beyond that. Lost people must not be merely the focus of Western workers; instead, lost people must become their *family*. A staggering depth of commitment and compassion is absolutely required. Beyond that, the insights of believers in settings of persecution suggest several other essential characteristics.

Competence in Language and Culture

We have made the point that persecution can happen for a variety of reasons. Ideally, if persecution is to come, we want to make certain that it comes because of who Jesus is. Much persecution, however, comes for secondary, lesser reasons. The primary way for the Western worker to reduce persecution for secondary reasons is to be adept in language and culture. Tremendous damage is done when outside workers are unwilling or unable to master the nuance of culture. Believers in contexts of persecution insisted that Western workers commit to competence in language and culture. There is a direct correlation between language and cultural acquisition in regard to persecution for secondary reasons. As one's ability to handle the local language with efficiency increases, persecution caused by the Westerner diminishes. Sadly, the opposite is also true. As outsiders' ability to communicate cross-culturally remains low, persecution related to the outsider escalates.

Everyone who came to Jesus in the New Testament did so in a local or regional language. When the Holy Spirit visits unreached peoples through dreams and visions, He always speaks to them in their heart language. Those who would take Jesus across the oceans, *or across the street,* must commit to learning the language of those with whom they are attempting to share the Good News of Jesus Christ, even if these lost souls dwell in Western countries! This is a very challenging observation for the thousands of Westerners who go on short-term mission trips. Thousands provide great service to God's kingdom. In persecution, the short-term worker must serve under the supervision of someone with credible language and cultural skills. Perhaps their largest contribution is in the care of the long-term teams in tough places. We want to give Satan as little opportunity as possible to turn our good intentions into unwarranted persecution. Becoming a "missionary tourist" engaged in spiritual "drive-by shootings" is unacceptable. This is meant in love, as we all desire what is best for those still outside the kingdom of God as we lift up those who are local believers and long-term workers.

Mutual Trust

The relationship between outside workers and believers within a certain culture is potentially intimate and close. It is obvious to expect trust in that relationship. Importantly, that trust must be mutual.

As we have shared already, but bears repeating time and again, to use the example of Scripture, it is essential for Paul to trust Timothy, and it is equally essential for Timothy to trust Paul. It is easy to see how this trust can grow. Timothy sees that Paul is willing to sacrifice for his ministry and that Paul has left behind family and friends for the sake of the gospel. He observes firsthand how Paul is utterly committed to God's command, and that Paul demonstrates his love in concrete, consistent, and faithful ways. In light of that, it is almost a given that Timothy will come to trust Paul.

On the other hand, Paul can see that Timothy is serious in his embrace of the faith, that Timothy is working hard to grow and learn, that Timothy strives to be worthy of trust, and that Timothy sees himself as a part of Paul's ministry. In light of that, Paul will come to trust Timothy.

That trust is mutual. And it is a crucial part of the relationship between these two individuals who are part of the mission endeavor. Interestingly, however, sometimes the nature of this unique

234 / THE INSANITY OF OBEDIENCE

relationship can lead to problems. In fact, we found many cases where the trust (or dependence) between the worker and the in-country believer was so strong that it was difficult for the local believer to trust other *insiders* because trust in the outside worker was so great. In fact, that strong trust can inhibit the emergence of church. And it at least partly explains why the Westerner is sought out for baptism, counsel, instruction, and relationship.

Even further, this profound and growing trust can lead to several dangerous theological corruptions. The first one was mentioned in the previous chapter and suggests that baptism, in the eyes of local, first-generation believers at the hands of a Western worker is superior to baptism at the hands of a local believer. In missiological terms, baptism at the hands of a local believer would actually be preferred and desired, but, in actual practice, baptism administered by an outside worker is normally seen to be superior.

The second corruption is similar but perhaps even more dangerous. It is common to conclude that a salvation experience that has come through a relationship with a Western worker is superior to other salvation experiences that come through the faith of local believers. To see how this would matter, imagine a believer boasting about the fact that he or she had been "led to the Lord" by a well-known outside worker. The implication is that his or her salvation experience is more valid or more legitimate.

Both Jesus and Paul addressed this very issue. As noted above, we are told in John 4:1 that Jesus did not baptize at all. And Paul, in 1 Corinthians 1:14–17, thought that it was important to point out that he had baptized very few people. Evidently, this sort of problem is not a new struggle. And evidently, it continues to be a problem even today.

Trust is an important component in partnering with God to see families come to Jesus and reproducing house churches planted. Such trust must be primarily between local believers, not only between local believers and the outsider.

A Commitment to Stay among the Lost

Believers in settings of persecution highlight the commitment of overseas workers to stay—and not simply to stay, but to stay among the lost. Once believers enter the picture, the tendency is for Western workers to devote most of their time and energy to these believers. It is a rare worker who works hard to stay among the lost, especially when believers begin to surface. Often, Western workers will evangelize just long enough (often until ten or fifteen believers emerge) until they have a small group to "pastor." Once enough believers emerge to constitute a flock to pastor, the overseas worker ceases to keep evangelism central. In my lifetime, what has caused workers in persecution to come to the attention of the persecutors is not due to too much sharing of God's stories and talking about Jesus. Where workers come to grief is when they assume the role of a pastor, doing the functions of the church, rather than intentionally staying among those lost as an evangelist and church planter.

The context of Jesus' own ministry shows Him using the vast majority of His resources outside of any established religious structure or community. He modeled a lifestyle that fulfilled His statement, "For the Son of Man came to seek and to save what was lost" (Luke 19:10).

Believers in persecution cry out for the sent-out ones to model for them how to reach their neighbors. They need examples of how to evangelize a corrupt policeman and the old man behind the fruit stand. Local believers strongly believe that they can shepherd the sheep, and they are seeking models for doing just that. What they ask of the overseas worker is to model staying among the wolves.

The Ability and Desire to Express the Faith in the Local Culture

Believers in settings of persecution repeatedly mentioned the importance of workers expressing faith within the local culture. Their desire was not to import a post-Pentecost faith from the outside, but to allow a culturally appropriate faith to develop and grow as the Spirit led. Customs of dress, indigenous music, even sitting on the floor rather than in chairs or church pews are symbolic of faith going deep in the host culture, not simply mirroring the faith and culture of the outsider.

In addition to these specific characteristics, the ability to foster and model community is also crucial. Outsiders are always under a microscope. Aware of it or not, they are modeling community—good or bad. In our experience of working with teams for decades, we have identified four types of people in terms of how they relate to the growth and health of community. It is critical to pay attention to these types of people as teams among workers are formed, developed, and sent out. Churches and institutions that send workers to the field must deliberately send their very best from among their sons and daughters and from among those interviewed for overseas service. Here is some advice for the senders.

First, some people build community wherever they go. This ability is a spiritual gifting, and it is a precious skill in relationships. Wherever these people go, community simply emerges. People with this gift are indispensable to teams and indispensable in reaching those with little or no access to the good news. Ruth, my wife, is such a soul. I have heard counselors say that if Ruth were left alone in the desert, she would simply gather rocks around her and community would blossom!

Second, some people love community and easily live within it. These people will not quite have the community-creating gift of the first group, but they are good in community, they enjoy it, and they make it better. These people are good within teams and they contribute to healthy community. My current favorite definition of church is, *"Church is the place where, when you fail to show up, they come looking for you!"* Those in these first two descriptions are people who are committed to community and accountability. Yet, sadly, we are not finished.

Third, some people drain the energy from community. These people find relationships difficult or they regularly require special attention. They are draining for teams of workers. As with the first two types of people, they are always present whenever and wherever the "doors" of the church are open or whenever the mission team meets. Yet they demand hours of care, nurture, and intervention. In most cases, they arrive on the field with huge personal needs and they require great attention. And the attention that they require is drawn from the higher priorities of the team.

Finally, some people destroy or damage community. Candidly, they leave dead bodies wherever they go! Quite simply, it is best not to have these people in a mission setting. They not only require special attention, they also seem to work against the goal of good and healthy relationships. The presence of these people will work against the commitment of the group to serve the needs of the lost; they will divert significant energy and time from the ultimate goal of the team. In addition to damaging the team, these people model dysfunctional spiritual behavior to new believers among unreached and unengaged peoples.

Ideally, teams of workers will be composed primarily of people from these first two categories. Churches and agencies who send their sons and daughters as sheep among the wolves need to send their very best. We can expect that great harm will come to sheep as they labor among the wolves. But sending unhealthy sheep into the overseas challenge is harmful to healthy teams and will impact the work in negative ways. They will keep local people from the kingdom of God.

It's on Our Shoulders

- List those who have been sent out from your church long term? How are they doing in learning the language and culture? Were they healthy in healthy community before going overseas?

- Who in your Western church is learning another language for the purpose of reaching internationals?

- How do you deal with unhealthy, dysfunctional people in your church?

- How many hours a week do you intentionally spend with those who do not know Jesus? How often are they in your home or you in theirs?

19

On Our Faces before God

It is axiomatic to point out that we cannot bring into existence what we do not already know and do ourselves. It is simply not possible to model what we have not yet experienced. As obvious as that sounds, this truth has profound implications when it comes to the significant role of worship in the cross-cultural enterprise. If Western workers are expected to model for others the essence of worshipping God (and they are), it is essential that they know how to worship God themselves. It is not enough simply to "enjoy" worship or to "participate" in worship when other people create a setting where worship can take place. Given the almost certain isolation of life within a context of persecution, Western workers must be adept at their own personal worship, able to lead their families in worship, and able to model healthy worship for new believers.

As simple as that sounds, it is not easily done. Many Western workers are ill equipped to do this basic and essential task, and the consequences for this inability are devastating. The Western church seldom prepares its members to create worship for themselves as individuals, parents, team members, and leaders. In the West, worship is often the purview of the professional clergy. In the West, believers can have most of their "worship needs" met at one place and during a few hours on a special day of the week. But the dangerously unreached often dwell in environments where there are no places set aside for prayer or worship.

All too often, the result is workers who become dry, spiritually powerless, and unable to lead local people to the throne of God and model "church" for those around them who are carefully and eagerly watching.

Perhaps the best picture of the early church is found in Acts 2:42–47. As God drew these new believers together, they experienced a Spirit-filled and Spirit-empowered life. The resulting life included the meeting of needs, rich fellowship, a desire to learn and grow, a commitment to prayer, and a deep and abiding passion for worship.

Essential components in the life of a worker (and, indeed, essential components in the life of any believer!) would include the following six elements.

Daily personal devotions. This is a spiritual discipline that, we suggest, should be learned early and practiced throughout life. Perhaps it is a naïve expectation, but our assumption is that workers who serve overseas should be committed to daily time with God. Strangely, and much to our disappointment, we have found this not always to be true and needs to be modeled for new workers.

Family worship time. Again, it is our position that this is a basic discipline that, sadly, is not always practiced within overseas workers' families. Why? Because worshipping as a family was not taught and modeled within their home churches. In many settings, it is simply not possible to gather with a broader Christian community for worship. In those cases, it is even more essential for families to worship together on their own. We have discovered that many families do not know how to do this and, in some cases, they are simply not willing to try. Some families resort to playing a DVD, or watching worship through the Internet, of a worship service from a sending church, and they presume that the playing of that electronic tool has been "worship" for them. This substitute for worship, however, is severely lacking. When there is no opportunity to gather with a group for worship, it is essential for the family to worship on its own. We have been surprised how difficult this is for most families. This must be a daily practice for any group or family desiring to serve cross-culturally, especially in environments of persecution.

Worship with team members. Again, as obvious as this sounds, it can be rare in many groups. For some reason, absent the traditional forms and trappings, we do not always know how to worship alone, with our families, or in small groups. Perhaps we are accustomed to having this provided for us.

But, if we are not involved in worship at all of these levels, learning to do this, or at the very least *desiring* to do this, how will new believers (especially believers in settings of persecution) know how to worship in groups? What will they learn from our behavior? And how will they discern that corporate worship is important and necessary? Again, it is impossible to model what we are not already doing. Sadly, our failure at this point demonstrates that corporate worship is not always an essential component in the faithful living of a believer.

Healthy teams often have three core practices. First, they worship together once a week. When dissension arises on a team, and that is always a real possibility, they should worship twice a week! Second, teams deal with their business decisions (for example: cars, housing, budgets, children's needs) separate from worship. Third, teams set aside time every month when they can play together as a team. They get away, they spend time "off duty and out of uniform," and they find ways simply to be family and friends for one another.

Fellowship with and among international congregations, other Great Commission believers, and national believers. Overseas workers should seek these opportunities whenever possible and whenever appropriate. Even if this happens only three or four times a year, these gatherings to worship among the broader Body of Christ are crucial. Often there is an international church in a country. Typically, its focus will not be on the unreached. Instead, its focus will likely be on the English-speaking expatriate community. Given that focus for this international congregation, a worker who is committed to reaching the unreached can hope to have about 10 percent of his or her worship needs met in this type of setting.

Shadow worshipping and modeling community. When possible, Western workers should share in the worship experiences of already existing groups and build long-term relationships within those communities. Ruth and I attempt to worship with MBBs and others as often as possible. All the same, we seldom, if ever, worship with them in their home environments or where we are known. We go out of our way not to fall into regular and predictable patterns while we worship with a myriad of house churches globally. Often we both will meet in a city where neither of us is known.

The ongoing role of the sending church in ministering to and with those who are sent out. Sending churches have a specific responsibility to nurture the spiritual well-being of those who are sent out. It is not enough simply to pray for them or to provide financial support. Real supporting churches are encouraging spiritual health and providing inspirational worship as one way for sending churches to minister to their sons and daughters while holding sent-out workers accountable. *It almost goes without saying, but must be said again and again: sending churches should provide short-term teams to lead worship experiences with those who are on the field.* This must be a shared experience a few times annually.

One of the outcomes of vital worship in the early church was specifically evangelistic in nature. As this new community lived and worshipped together, "the Lord added to their number daily those who were being saved" (Acts 2:47). We should never forget the evangelistic impact of worship. Within their home church in the West, workers had "one-stop shopping" and were able to have all of their spiritual needs addressed. In a ministry field defined by persecution, workers, families, and teams may need to go to four or five different places to have their worship needs met. Without this, workers will soon become spiritually empty and will then feel guilty about being empty! It is better not to begin that downward spiral.

God has made us for worship and we must get on our faces before Him as individuals, as teams, and within the larger believing community.

A life of worship is vital to personal spiritual health, family health, team health, and the health of the work. In addition, its impact on those who become new believers is incalculable. There is no way, of course, for the worker "to get everything right" but, surely, we will want to be modeling behaviors and disciplines that we consider indispensable for life in community. Clearly, both individual and corporate worship would be high on that list.

Where Are You, God?

- Do you have a pattern of personal devotions?
- Does the Body you "belong" to model for you worship as a family? Men, are you leading your families in worship?

- What is the minimum number of people needed for a team in a hard place for healthy team worship and dynamics to be available?

20

Jesus and Money

At this point, some brief words about the sensitive matter of money are in order. Traditionally, the use of money in overseas mission enterprises has been a delicate and troubling area to discuss. We could spend our time talking about the shockingly small percentage of giving in churches that actually ends up addressing the needs of the lost, but we might be better served putting our focus in another place. However much money is given, and however decisions about money are made, we need to make certain that the resources that God has placed in our hands are used to impact the lost. While it is obviously biblically wise and helpful to assist existing believers and the historical church, and while we will do such in love as much as is possible, *the highest priority is reaching the lost,* and that priority should inform every decision that is related to strategy and budgets.

The story of Ananias and Sapphira in Acts 5 is revealing. In addition to the problem of lying and misrepresenting their actions,

Ananias and Sapphira acted in a way that threatened the very existence of the church. While the community was committed to meeting needs by having all things in common, Ananias and Sapphira's behavior threatened the fragile makeup of the gathered believing community. By lying to the Body of Christ, lying to the Holy Spirit, and withholding their resources, Ananias and Sapphira put others' lives at risk. Their actions threatened the very existence of the emerging church. Among other things, the story in Acts 5 assures us that the Holy Spirit will protect Christ's church.

What are some guiding principles when it comes to the use of money in the overseas enterprise? How can wise workers use money in such a way that it will give the peoples of the earth access to Jesus? How can decisions to follow Christ remain focused on Him alone and not on "Jesus-plus" issues?

1. Making sure that our agenda is a kingdom agenda. This kingdom agenda is not necessarily the agenda of those who send the money, and it may not even be the agenda of local leaders. We will want to use God's resources in a way that will carry out the agenda of the kingdom of God. Sadly, denominational identification in emerging churches where persecution is widespread can have more to do with dollars than doctrine.

2. Striving for financial independence and enlarged witness. Many Muslims who come to faith in Jesus believe through contact with an outside worker; in most cases, they come to faith through being employed by an outside worker. While their decision might be genuine, there is always the chance that this decision to follow Jesus includes the hope of continued employment that could perhaps also lead to other benefits (financial or otherwise). Certain matters need to be addressed early in those conversations.

First, it should be pointed out to them that persecution will follow their decision to trust Christ.

Second, it should be made clear that there will not only *not* be financial benefits but also that the current job will likely be lost! Working for "outside Christians" and becoming a believer is a doubly dangerous environment for the new believer. It usually paints a target on their backs. Now, who would make such a choice to follow Christ and, through this choice, lose a job? Clearly, only someone who truly desires to follow Christ!

Instead of continued employment (which marks the new believer for persecution), it is perhaps better to use funds to set up a small business (perhaps using micro-enterprises) and even better to do this for both believers *and a host of nonbelievers within the same location.* In fact, the best model is to include ten to fifteen lost families for each believing family. This leads to tremendous goodwill, and it specifically does not lead to the believing family being set apart for persecution. Instead of saying, "These Western workers take care of their own and you have to become a Christian to get a job," people will say, "These Western workers certainly love Muslims!" which is, of course, completely true. *The goal is to always seek to help local believers to be financially independent from outsiders.*

If our resources only serve to make believers (and especially new believers) financially dependent and are not used to impact lostness, then we will fail in two ways. We will contribute to a long-term sense of dependence and entitlement on the part of believers, and we will neglect the needs of the lost. Both mistakes are tragic, and both mistakes carry devastating consequences.

3. Comparisons with Western workers. Often new believers and other Western workers will react to the large financial needs of new believers in persecution by pointing out that, after all, the Western workers are paid! The question might sound like this: "If you are paid for serving, then why am I not allowed to be paid for working?"

Insisting on local financial independence for a church (and for new believers) will be the best way to make it possible for a young church to support its own sent-out ones. The biblical model for this is the early church using its own resources to send out and support Paul and his companions. We want for local believers exactly what we have: an aggressive desire to bring thousands of people to Jesus and plant churches that can send us anywhere the Spirit leads us around the globe.

4. Reminding people that the book of Acts did happen. We often feel captive to strategies, budgets, and resources. We often believe that, with the right mix of people and (Western) resources, we will be able to accomplish God's purposes. And there is nothing wrong with resources, especially when those resources are used in God-honoring ways. The book of Acts, however, stands as a testimony to God's power to accomplish His purposes with or without human (Western) resources. It is wise and helpful to remember that the book of Acts really did happen. Against all odds, and without a wealth of resources, God's power was more than sufficient. God acted this way once, and God can act this way again.

We would be wise to study the New Testament church, and we would be wise to relearn the lessons of vital worship, submission to the Spirit, humble obedience, sharing of things in common, relying on God's Word, and Spirit-empowered giftedness. Western-styled churches with paid clergy and buildings are expensive. Not so with house churches and bi-vocational leadership. Their overhead is tiny and the time they have to remain among nonbelievers significant.

We would also be wise to pay attention to the New Testament reality where significant suffering and costly sacrifice was shared by every part of the faith community. Churches sacrificed to send out workers. Workers sacrificed in going. Communities receiving those workers sacrificed in caring for them. And, when needs were discovered in any part of the faith community, resources freely flowed in every direction. Even those who lived in extreme poverty begged for the opportunity to give and share. When one sector of the community sees itself always as the "giver" and another sector sees itself always as the "receiver," the entire community and the work of Christ is damaged and diminished. Church becomes a shadow of itself.

I went to a strongly Muslim country to interview MBBs in five different settings. The interviews were rich and varied. They understood their faith in the context of local history and culture. After the first set of interviews, I asked a final question, "Would you be willing to share with me what makes a good worker from the West?"

After the normal hesitation, one of the men said, "We cannot tell you what makes a good worker, but we can tell you about the worker we love." I prompted them to continue and they told me a Westerner's name. I asked them again to tell me what he did to deserve such an emotional response and they replied, "We don't know why, but we just love him."

In my notes, I wrote down, "They love him."

I went to a second location and interviewed some men and women believers. Later that day I asked them the same question about Western workers. Surprisingly, they answered my question in the same way. "We don't know what makes a good worker," they said, "but we can tell you who we love." Then they proceeded to tell me the same man's name.

Again, in my notes, I wrote down, "They love him."

I traveled to five different locations to interview MBBs. In every setting I asked the same question about Western workers. I wanted to learn what makes workers successful and welcome in local eyes.

As I moved from place to place for my interviews, I heard the same man's name and the same words of description: "This is the man we love."

After hearing these words over and over, I found myself becoming jealous. After all, I had never been loved this deeply. I was intrigued and felt compelled to figure out what these words meant.

Finally with the fifth group, I refused to budge. After finishing another set of interviews, I moved on to the familiar question: "What makes a good Western worker?" True to form, these people mentioned the same man.

I stubbornly crossed my arms, sat back in my chair, and told them that I was not leaving until they told me why so many people in this country loved the same worker from the West. Finally, one of the men leaned aggressively across the table, looked me in the eye, and tapped me on the chest with his finger.

He said, "I'll tell you why we love him. He borrows money from us!"

I thought to myself, *Well, that's nothing. I could do that!*

Yet I knew there had to be more to the story, so I began to draw them out. Finally, they began to share the details. They said to me, somewhat aggressively and with pride, "When this man's father died and he did not have enough money to go home to bury his father, he did not go to the other Westerners to borrow money. He came to us and we took up an offering so that he could go home and bury his father. When his family had given away so much of their money that they had trouble putting meat on the table, paying their rent, and raising the school fees necessary for their children, this brother did not go to the Westerners for money; he came to us. And we loaned him what was needed."

"So this is why we love him. He needs us. The rest of you workers have never needed us."

My heart was broken as they went on to explain how most Westerners treat local people as if they are objects of salvation and reports . . . and not real people. They listed the ways that Westerners seemed to treat them as passive partners in this thing called salvation ministry: "You give us Bibles. You bring the gospel. You bring materials for discipleship. You rent places for us to meet. You bring your songs from America. You bring the baptism. You bring everything, expecting us to sit passively and simply appreciate everything that you give us. It is as if we are not worthy of contributing anything of value ourselves. It is all about your giving. And we feel like we should simply sit quietly and receive."

"He needs us. The rest of you have never needed us."

The apostle Paul would have understood these brothers' and sisters' hearts. He said to the church at Corinth that they were correct in understanding that they had received the gospel through his hands. But then he reminded these first-generation believers that for everything he had given to them, he had received a multitude of things in return.

My soul was shaken to its very core as these words continue to echo through my mind, "Do you want to know why we love him? He needs us. The rest of you have never needed us."

Money, Missions, and Me

- What is your church's mission budget for the unengaged and unreached?
- If house churches in the book of Acts are the norm, what must we change in the Western church world?
- Are mission trips about us giving with them passively receiving?

21

Being Midwife to the Body of Christ

To this point, we have raised many issues and we have asked dozens of questions. This is probably a good time to step back and explore how this all fits together. Our over-arching question is: "How can we, as Westerners, partner with the Holy Spirit, seeing reproducing house churches emerge in environments of persecution? What does it look like to be tough people in tough places?" If we minimize our mistakes and if we get a few things right, is it possible to help lost people to come to Christ and, furthermore, is it even possible that we might play a positive role in that? Our answer to both parts of that question is . . . *"Absolutely!"*

In light of all that we have talked about, and along with a lot of advice from believers in persecution, let's describe how that might happen.

For this part of the book, let's imagine a sent-out couple with their children and team. We will call this couple John and Joan. Ideally, a team will have young and old couples, some with children, some without children, with single people fully integrated into the team. Short-term volunteers rotating in and out of the team are an asset as they work under the teams' strategy.

(Warning! Do not triangulate people on your team. Do not have two single men and one single woman as a team or vice versa. Do not send a young woman or a young man to join a young couple on a team. Ninety percent of all adultery in business, as well as in churches, is a result of such triangulation. If you find yourself in such a situation as you are reading this book, take deliberate and immediate steps to add other healthy members to your team.)

John and Joan know enough not to go out on their own. Not only do they need one another, they also realize they need a team. In building their team, they try their best to include a number of different kinds of people; they want their mission mirror to be both genders and biologically broad enough to reflect a large portion of their people group. When people look at these believers (and, in this setting, they will quickly be known as believers), people will be able to see themselves reflected in the witnessing mirror. As a result, in selecting their team, John and Joan include older and younger team members, married people and single people, men and women, families with children and families without children. So, really it is not just John and Joan; it is an entire (and diverse) team committed to reaching a particular people group in a particular area. Jesus always sent by twos, and a couple is not two, they are one in Christ. Couples placed in the hard places by themselves is not sound mission strategy. Placing two single women or two single men on the edge of lostness alone is a recipe for burnout, immorality, or worse. Why do we attempt challenges Jesus Himself did not condone?

John and Joan do not go by themselves.

In the traditional worker model, we would find John and Joan and their team members building relationships with people, looking for opportunities to share their faith. They would carry their denomination identity with them along with their post-Pentecost baggage. Then, as people respond to Jesus through the witness of this team, new believers would be gathered together into a "church." In all likelihood, John would lead that group who meets in the traditional church building.

But this is not the model that we are proposing.

In fact, we are suggesting something quite different. John and Joan have laid a good foundation. *They, their team, and their children are constantly growing in the local language and culture. Their children have local friends.* They are living, hopefully, where they can walk out of their door and meet their people group. They are tentmakers, committed to a job that is acceptable and understandable among local people. They, too, begin with the building of relationships. John and Joan and their team members build scores of relationships. In fact, this is easy to do. People will be drawn to these Western workers simply because they are different and because this difference will be seen by the way these team members live. (We sometimes wonder how we will "find" those without Christ. In fact, these are the people who will find us!) And, ideally, those encounters will eventually include conversations, which is sometimes scary for new workers—like this:

> Muslims approach a Western worker and ask aggressively, "Are you a missionary?" Experience will be evident in the worker's response. *We have learned from believers in China and also from Jesus Himself that the best answer to a question is often to ask a question in response.* So this worker responds with a question: "Why would you ask me a question like that?"
>
> The local people will likely reply to the worker's own question with something like this: "You are different from the other Westerners. I've noticed that you live a moral life. You

don't drink alcohol and you don't eat pork. We've watched the way you treat your wife and children. We have listened to you talk. You seem to be kind and caring. You are learning our language. You don't cheat on your wife. Why are you so different?"

Now that's the question we want to answer! When such a question is asked, we know that we have reached a deep starting place for spiritual conversations.

The relationships continue to grow, John and Joan find themselves in the homes of their new friends and neighbors almost overnight, and they intentionally invite their friends into their home. And, almost incidentally (at least it will seem incidental!) John and Joan will begin to model house church for their new friends *long before* their new friends ever express an interest in Jesus. What John and Joan will model might look like this:

> At mealtime in their home with new friends, John might say, "We are so happy that you are here to share a meal with us. We don't want to embarrass you, but, like you, we believe in one God so in our home we pause before meals to thank God for His blessings. We are so thankful for God's good care and we want to thank Him. We're going to pray and thank God. By the way, is there anything you are thankful for? We would love to include your thanks in our prayer too."
>
> John will ask his wife and children for things they are thankful. In societies where women are second-class citizens, this simple question before prayer models the worth of a woman's soul before the visitors. The fact Joan is even included in this conversation will be startling to them.
>
> Obviously, this cannot be artificial. Rather, this practice of prayer is simply an ongoing family discipline which others, now, have been invited to join.

Perhaps another local family would visit later another evening. At bedtime, John might say, "We normally have a family devotion before we put our children to bed. Please, we don't want you to leave. Excuse us as we'll spend a few minutes here in our living room getting the children ready for bed. We don't want to embarrass you, but we would love for you to share this time with us."

Then Joan and John will ask their children about the Bible story they shared the previous evening, and the children themselves will retell the story. Then the family will talk about another Bible story. John may ask Joan to tell the next story! The children may request the singing of a simple children's song. And then John and Joan ask, as usual, the children to pray as the family devotional time comes to an end. Beware! This is a dangerous practice. John and Joan may pray a more culturally sensitive prayer, as do the older children. Then comes the moment for six-year-old Susie to pray. She boldly prays, "God, You know how much we love Uncle Libaan and Aisha. God, You know we have been praying for them to know Jesus for months. God, would You bring them to Jesus tonight? Amen."

John and Joan are rigid with fear. Little Susie has outed them! They glance over at their guests and Libaan is weeping as NO ONE has ever called his name out to God.

Imagine how powerful it will be for these new friends to watch and listen as this normal practice unfolds. They are hearing stories from the Word of God. They are watching believers pray. They are fixated on the relationships between a believing husband and wife and between parents and children. They are being prayed for by name before God in their own hearing!

Essentially, this family's life together is house church, and it is being modeled to people who are not yet believers. In fact, this is the

THE INSANITY OF OBEDIENCE / 257

ideal time to model house church! If we wait to model house church with believers, corruptions will likely already be assimilated. But, at this point, a purer model of worship can be presented.

In case we haven't made the connection, this is another reason why it is essential for the workers' families to be able to worship together and why such a holy task cannot be left to some larger group. A family at worship in the presence of unbelievers will be the most powerful expression of evangelism that we can even imagine! But remember, we don't use family worship as a show. It is vital to our relationships within the family and it expresses our obedience to worship God as a family.

As time goes on, these relationships will grow. More and more time will be invested, and faith will simply be lived out in the presence of these new friends.

Throughout the whole process, though, notice the role of John and Joan. They live out the prayer of John the Baptist when he asked for his own role to decrease in relationship to the role of Jesus. John and Joan are in the background. *Perhaps their greatest task is to find those men and women in their host culture who already believe in Jesus and who also want everyone to have access to Jesus within their own people group.* As their new friends come closer to Christ, John and Joan will seek advice from these older, homegrown disciples—the potential Simon Peters and Esthers whom God is raising up within the local culture. They will seek out these local believers and tell them confidentially about other couples and single people they have met.

John and Joan will do their part in drawing these people together. If these non-believing friends and contacts of John and Joan are on a serious pilgrimage toward Jesus, these local believers, with John and Joan's help, will quietly meet them, begin a relationship and help them come to faith in a matter of months, if not weeks. As more new believers come to faith, they are gathered into existing house churches or they will start one in their home. *This is perhaps the hardest task*

*a Western worker will ever attempt—handing off a seeker to a local
believer who is better situated to lead them to Christ, baptize them, and
then assist them in planting a new church.*

John the Baptist did talk about decreasing so Jesus could increase.
The Western worker must pray daily this same prayer in regard to
local believers. It is a hard prayer to pray. It is an even harder prayer
to live it out.

In places where persecution is acute, John and Joan will never
be present in local house churches; local believers who mentor new
believers will lead this new group. John and Joan will encourage, pray,
and provide background support, but their role will be a decreasing
one. While this is happening with a first group of friends, John and
Joan will be developing similar friendships with others, and the same
dynamic will potentially happen over and over again.

Notice some of the dynamics of this process. John and Joan will
never take on the role of the apostle Paul. In fact, they will be on the
lookout for people in the local culture who can begin to shoulder such
a role under the leadership of the Holy Spirit. We want to be very
clear at this point that the local leader is the emerging "apostle Paul."
John is not the leader, certainly not the pastor. At the most, he is a
"Timothy," taking on the role of encouraging and praying for Paul.
John and Joan will never be the focus.

Because of their chosen role, John and Joan will be able to remain
with non-believing people the vast majority of their time. John and
Joan will choose not to *lead* the movement, but to *serve* it.

Believers in persecution suggest how this might take place. They
say to us, "You come to our country with a Western plan on how to
fish for lost souls. As a Westerner, you choose your fishing rod, the
fishing line, and the size of fishing hook. You even choose where to
fish. Can we suggest a different approach? We know our people. We
can choose the best fishing pole and the right weight of the line, and
we know what size hooks to use.

"As we fish here in our own culture, can we use you as fishing bait?" That is a crucial and important question.

They go on: *"Are you willing to give up the central role that traditional workers have modeled and allow us to fish with you? People in our culture do not know whom they can trust when they have dreams and visions; they don't know who to talk with when God has touched their hearts. They see you as safe people with whom they can share their spiritual dilemma and pilgrimage. You can have hundreds of spiritual conversations while a local person could possibly have a dozen. So are you willing to be bait for Jesus and allow us to gather in a harvest of local souls?"*

I love to fish. I did not say that I am good at fishing; I just love to fish. One thing I do know about the sport of fishing is that it is very dangerous for the bait. Are we willing to be bait for Jesus?

Notice how John and Joan will avoid those theological corruptions that seem to suggest that a salvation experience and baptism at the hands of a Western worker are somehow superior. In fact, in this model, it is possible that John and Joan will seldom actually lead someone to Christ or administer a baptism. They will choose, instead, to trust the Holy Spirit, the Bible, and local leaders with the spiritual leadership and life of this emerging family of faith.

This is clearly not a traditional workers' approach. But it is an approach that can lead to a church planting movement more quickly within environments of persecution. It will demand that our overseas personnel rethink roles and expectations, and it will require Western sending churches and agencies to rethink their approaches and expectations as well. It is not about us, the Western worker. It is about seeing the gospel broadly sown and rapidly reproduced.

Again, let's be clear. If the Holy Spirit picks you up like Philip and places you beside the Ethiopian eunuch, it is imperative that you help him find Christ. It is crucial for you to help him obey God's command to be baptized. But if that happens, be sure to read to the end of the story. As quickly as the Holy Spirit brought Philip into the Ethiopian's life, the Holy Spirit took Philip away before the outsider could possibly corrupt the Ethiopian's new faith.

The model we are suggesting might also call for some dramatic lifestyle changes. This might sound odd, but research suggests that most Muslims who come to faith in Jesus actually make those commitments *after 10:00 at night!* After repeatedly hearing stories about these late-night conversions, we began to ask more questions. We struggled to discern what that might mean.

And, after listening to a multitude of stories, here is what we think. In many Muslim cultures (especially in the Arab world), the first meal of the day is around noon. The second meal of the day is late afternoon. And the third meal of the day is late at night. This late meal is the setting when many Muslims (men, in particular) are ready and willing to talk about important things like politics, sports, and spiritual matters. We have had many of our workers shift their own schedules so they might be able to be with their Muslim friends when these kinds of conversations are most likely to happen. It perhaps seems like a small concession, yet it is huge. For families, lifestyle changes are the most challenging. Yet why would we not be willing to change our own schedule if doing so would provide us with greater opportunities to be with people who are hungry for the good news? If Muslims are willing to talk about spiritual matters late at night, then perhaps we should choose to be with them late at night! Moms are changing the times their kids nap and sleep. They are, as a family, with their neighbors in the parks until 2:00 a.m.! Their lives mirror the rhythm of the local culture. Lifestyle changes are hard, yet we must acknowledge there is nowhere in the Bible where home school has to start at 8:00–9:00 a.m. each day!

So what, exactly, is the role of workers in this model? It turns out that workers will do many of the things we have already talked about in this book.

They will keep their lives centered within their people group.

They will commit to staying among their people group and they will live among those without Jesus with a bold witness. They are evangelists and church planters each day. They are not pastors.

They will work hard to be competent in language and culture. Workers who thrive cross-culturally increasingly learn language and culture. Those who stay the longest have children who learn local languages and have local friends. These workers do not "cocoon" with Mom spending a lot of her time protecting her kids from lost people! Be assured, lost people are messy. Many a conversation will have to be debriefed once lost people exit the scene. This worker's family will look for culturally appropriate ways to live out and share their faith as a family, as team together. So . . .

- They will change their habits and schedules in order to be with people who have had little or no access to Christ.
- They will be willing to serve the process rather than lead it.
- They will witness and worship as a family and as a team.
- They will become shadow pastors and shadow evangelists, serving in the background.
- They will sacrifice traditional roles in order for mutual trust among new believers and local leaders to emerge.
- They will avoid the theological corruptions that come from elevating the overseas worker to a spiritually higher place than local leaders.
- They will model house church to spiritually hungry people simply by living out their faith in the presence of others. They will invest heavily in sharing meals with families who have never heard the Good News. They will break bread with their neighbors both in their own home and in the homes of others.

- They will worship privately in their homes and with their teams, and their worship will serve as an authentic example of devotion to Christ.
- They will decrease so that new believers and the Lord whom they serve can increase.
- They will choose to see themselves as "bait" that Jesus can use to build His church. Their very presence in the community will draw people to Christ, but they will have no need to be seen as leaders of the movement that will unfold.

Being Bait for Jesus

- In order to model personal and family worship for lost people, what changes do we need to make?
- How would you intentionally prepare to cross the street in your location based upon this chapter?
- Muslims, Hindus, and Buddhists tell us universally that, "America is the loneliest place they have ever experienced." How will you change their perception?
- Can you allow local leaders the privilege of leading lost people to Jesus, baptizing and gathering them into house churches?

22

Recognizing and Equipping
Local Leaders

In general, believers take an *unintentional* approach both to evangelism and discipleship. What this means is that even if we are devoted to those crucial tasks, we generally include in those processes people who simply happen to appear. Often, we include people in those tasks who seek us out. Typically, leaders within the evangelical West do not intentionally select people to evangelize and, typically, they do not intentionally select people to disciple.

The standard for evangelism is often, "Is this person open to the gospel?"

The standard for discipleship is often, "Does this person want to be my disciple?"

We certainly do not want to be misunderstood at this point. Especially when it comes to evangelism, believers should be willing to share their faith with anyone and everyone. At the same time, at least when it comes to introducing the gospel in resistant areas and, hopefully, to the point of reproducing house churches in persecution, thoughtful strategy should inform our choices and relationships. Rather than merely engaging in "passive evangelism" and "passive discipleship," we must be more intentional in those important efforts.

Candidly, this chapter will suggest that those who hope to see a movement of God among an unreached people group will intentionally choose who to evangelize and who to disciple.

In fact, intentionality must be central in both evangelism and discipleship. This chapter will focus on leaders and potential leaders within settings of persecution. The heart of this conversation is people. We have no interest in setting forth a "program" of leadership development. What we are interested in is figuring out how to find the people who will transfer truth effectively through a particular culture. If our goal is "to get to church," can we identify—even before they are evangelized—people who can best help that happen? How did we come by this information? We watched and listened to those who were already leaders in environments of persecution. While not exhaustive, we pulled out those qualities and activities of leadership which emerged in a host of cultures and settings.

Before describing what those leaders and potential leaders will look like, we want to share some basic facts about leadership within environments of persecution in general.

First, believing leaders in persecution will want to understand that evangelism is their most effective survival tool. Even more, evangelism is the answer to most of the problems and struggles they will potentially face.

For example, what is the best way to deal with persecution? The answer: Evangelize the persecutors! What should we do when there is a need for believing wives for believing men or vice versa? The answer:

Evangelize more women and men so more potential spouses will be available. How do we handle the horrible problem of grandparents trying to take away their grandchildren who are being raised in a believing home? The answer: Evangelize the grandparents.

This idea might seem overly simplistic, but it reveals a profoundly important truth. The spread of the faith is, in itself, a solution to most of the problems a believing community will encounter. And leaders and potential leaders will come to understand this central truth. Ask whomever is considered a "normal" member in Western churches how many people with whom they have shared the Good News, or how many people they have played a significant role in seeing them come to faith—the answer is horrific. We are not an evangelizing people in the West outside of those being born within the Body of Christ.

Second, the goal of life together in a believing community is just that: *life together*. As important as the conversion of the individual is (we have already noted the norm in persecution is to be a midwife to families embracing Jesus altogether), the ultimate goal is community. This is a hard word for those of us who live in highly individualistic cultures, but it is a crucial word nonetheless. In persecution, we are not really looking to bring another person to Christ; instead, we are most interested in reaching entire families and social units for Jesus.

Consider this comment, quite popular in some circles: "If I had been the only person in the world, Jesus would have still come and would have died for me." While that statement might be a powerful testimony to Jesus' profound love for each individual, it short-circuits the ultimate purpose of redemption. Biblical references for such a theology will be scarce. From Abraham and his family to Cornelius and his household, God calls and Jesus redeems entire communities. Jesus died to bring a redeemed community into being. What Jesus ultimately desires is redeemed groups gathered together in community. Western cultural theology is woefully lacking here. The Body of Christ is always described in the plural; its setting is always community. Leaders and potential leaders in persecution will grasp the importance of community, and they will give their lives to seeing it transformed. Western workers need not struggle to re-create community if they do not shatter community through sowing the Good News primarily to individuals secretly, baptizing them secretly and mentoring them secretly.

Third, betrayal within the community will simply be a given. We have already talked about betrayal and about wise ways to deal with Judas. It is important to remember that these difficult realities are not rare or even avoidable. Of course, believers should be wise and careful. At the same time, even with great wisdom and care, people within the movement will betray the movement and inform on other participants. This is simply the way things are. Leaders will not lie down and die simply because Judas shows up. They know Judas is a reality and prepare for betrayal.

Fourth, evangelism/discipleship is best done the way Jesus modeled it. His model was living in close community twenty-four hours a day, seven days a week. Jesus was always with His disciples. They walked together, they ate together, they dealt with crises together, and they studied and prayed together. Today, the best discipleship, especially within persecution, will adopt that same approach. Leaders who are more spiritually mature will handpick disciples and they will pour their lives into these people.

Contrast this model with our typical approach. We might say to a newer believer, "Let's get together for two hours every Tuesday for discipleship." Or we send the "disciple" off to a Bible college or seminary almost totally separated from the Body of Christ through which they were raised or to whom they will be sent to minister. In contrast, for three years Jesus lived closely with His disciples; they essentially spent every moment of every day together. It is foolish for us to imagine, in any setting, that we can accomplish discipleship in a couple of hours a week or even in a few years in environments devoid of daily discipleship and accountability.

Jesus' model of discipleship is twenty-four hours a day and seven days a week. This kind of discipleship will be difficult to do cross-culturally. For this reason alone, we can see why it is so important for the work of "life-together" to be in the hands of local believers as quickly and as completely as possible. One of the most common experiences within persecution is for new believers to be kicked out of their homes for a season of time, and they then move in with the evangelist who brought them to Jesus.

How many people do you want to lead to Christ if they all come and live with you in your personal space? Yet this kind of intimate and close relationship is what we see as Jesus walked with and worked with His followers. *Most Western-based discipleship programs are essentially information transfer.* Increasingly, we think we can disciple someone through the Internet. Discipleship in settings of persecution is based on relationship. New believers are asked how they are treating their wife and their children. New believers are asked if they are sharing their faith. New believers are asked about their use of money and about their time on the Internet.

In the Western world, a believer can go to a denominational college and get multiple degrees from a seminary and never be asked these kinds of questions! Discipleship is about building character, not simply transferring information.

Fifth, leaders and potential leaders will come to understand the importance of multiplying their ministry by mentoring others as leaders. Effective leaders duplicate themselves as they pour their lives into the lives of their disciples.

Several historical episodes illustrate this point. When severe persecution came to the church in North Korea, the church was almost immediately brought to a point of crisis. In North Korea at that time in history, there was tremendous love and respect for the pastor/leader. Most of the church authority was invested in such a leader. Therefore, when pastors were imprisoned and put to death, the North Korean church found itself without equipped and prepared leaders and, very quickly, churches died. Of course, when such events happened, it was too late to call out and equip new leaders. When the pastors were taken, there were no leaders. Perhaps we should remind ourselves that Jesus is the head of the church, not the pastor.

The situation in Russia and in China was quite different. Perhaps because of lessons learned from earlier days (when there were not many lay leaders), Russian and Chinese evangelists, church planters, and pastors developed a pattern of involving three or four disciples with them in every part of their ministry. As they shared their faith, they would invite these disciples to come along and learn. As they traveled, these disciples would travel with them. As they counseled, these disciples would listen and watch. These disciples became companions in ministry. Through their close connections, they were being shaped and taught.

When persecution came to the church, something very different happened than what we saw in North Korea. As pastors were imprisoned and put to death, other leaders simply stepped into their place. While this kind of training lacked the formal institutions and diplomas of Western theological education (especially in China), it was very effective training. It was life together as well as character-based.

By the time a person became a "leader," character had been clearly revealed. These new leaders had already been mentored and trained effectively. Their "education" was character-based and not simply the transfer of information. The Russian and Chinese churches, even in seasons of severe persecution, never found themselves without strong leaders. And the church in these countries often thrived in persecution. I have talked with hundreds of seminary graduates the last three decades. It would be rough, but close estimate, that 90 percent of them have never entered the homes of their seminary professors nor had one of them in their homes.

The Western pattern of training does very well in capturing the "content" of the Bible. Where we are lacking is matching the content with its "context." The context was with Jesus 24/7. The context was in the marketplace. The context was in the homes of Mary and Martha and numerous others. Dare we say that the content and context are equally important?

The model described here is Paul's approach with his "Timothy." Paul understood, regardless of how productive his own ministry might be, that it could be multiplied by pouring his life into the life of young Timothy and many others. And we would fully expect, immediately, Timothy would take that same approach with other potential leaders. This is what Jesus—and growing churches—have always done.

With those basic leadership truths in mind, what will a leader in an emerging church movement look like? What qualities will be important? What kind of person will be able to carry truth in a particular culture? (It might be obvious, but there might be some slight differences from culture to culture. Still, overall, these qualities will probably be common from culture to culture.) Behind these questions is the important idea that we will intentionally choose to seek out and evangelize people with these characteristics. It is not true that we will avoid evangelizing others without these qualities. Even so, if our goal is to start house churches which rapidly multiply, then we will intentionally focus on those who are most likely to help such a movement explode.

We have identified five cultural qualities and three spiritual qualities that will generally be present in the lives of leaders in persecution. These five cultural characteristics would be true whether one was a politician, a military leader, or a medical innovator. The question we are seeking to answer is this: Through whom does truth travel the most quickly within any given culture?

The Five Cultural Qualities

1. Leaders in settings of persecution will generally be male.
2. Leaders in settings of persecution will generally be over thirty years of age.
3. Leaders in settings of persecution will generally be married.
4. Leaders in settings of persecution will generally be employed.
5. Leaders in settings of persecution will generally have status in the community.

If, indeed, our goal is to transfer truth rapidly, for the most part we will choose to evangelize people who embody as many of these cultural characteristics as possible. Again, we want to be clear that the point is *not* to avoid evangelism with people who do not have these qualities. Believers should be eager to share their faith broadly and widely. What we are calling for is a strategic choice when it comes to discerning potential leaders, identifying people who might best carry truth in a particular culture, and being willing to effectively evangelize/disciple them.

Our suggestion is to intentionally evangelize people with at least three of these five cultural qualities. Someone with four of these qualities would be an even better choice. And someone with all five of the qualities would be ideal. Everyone must have access to Jesus. Yet this discussion is how to identity, evangelize, and walk with game-changers, those who can effect social change in regard to God's kingdom. Can God use women to impact the kingdom and accelerate the growth of the church? Absolutely. We are not entering into the discussion concerning what gender should become pastor of a church. We are asking how does truth travel. Women with three or four of the cultural characteristics above are greatly used by God.

For purposes of illustration, consider Jesus. As a leader in a setting of persecution, what measurable, cultural qualities did He possess once He began His earthly ministry? Looking through our list above, we see that Jesus was male, He was over thirty years old when He began His public ministry, He was trained as a carpenter, involved in the world of employment, and Jesus possessed at least the first-born-son status in His community. Obviously, because of His unique role, Jesus was not married. In sum, Jesus fulfilled four of the five cultural qualities on our list. This is the Bible in its content and context. While not obvious to most Western believers, our brothers and sisters in persecution see these characteristics as normative.

Perhaps it is even more telling to consider the choices that Jesus made when He began to select His inner circle of disciples. Among many people who followed Him, He intentionally chose twelve for a more intimate life together. Essentially, He was, with purpose and insight (and prayer), selecting people who would be able to carry truth in His culture. What cultural qualities did these chosen followers possess? They were male, they were over thirty years of age, they were (at least in some cases) married, they were employed, and they had status in the community. Perhaps there would be differences from culture to culture, but in Jesus' culture during His earthly life, these were the kinds of people who could assist Him in beginning a movement.

Again, we realize how easy it would be to misinterpret these claims. Clearly, God can use anybody. And God often uses very unlikely people to accomplish His purposes. We certainly do not want to call into question the power of God to do His work His way. In this chapter, we are not *prescribing* what must happen. On the contrary, we are *describing* what we have seen. These are the kinds of people who have been able to carry truth in settings of persecution in our time. Could God use other people to do the same thing? Of course. But these are the trends and patterns that we have seen. The reader's task is to determine how truth travels the most quickly in a host culture. While not wanting to be prescriptive, these five cultural characteristics bear investigation. The deeper truth for a cross-cultural worker is to discover within their host culture, how does truth travel, seeking these people out for the sake of the kingdom, even before they are in the kingdom!

How we wish to have known these cultural realities when we began our ministry in Malawi in 1984! How we wish we had known these insights before going into Somalia in 1991!

In a similar way, in addition to these five cultural qualities, we have discerned three specific spiritual qualities present in the lives of leaders in persecution.

The Three Spiritual Qualities

1. Leaders in settings of persecution exhibit the filling and the fruit of the Holy Spirit. These leaders clearly exhibit *gifts* of the Spirit, but those gifts are also demonstrated in or nested in the Fruit of the Spirit (Gal. 5:22). Interestingly, we are taught in Scripture that the Evil One can duplicate (counterfeit) the gifts of the Spirit, *but the Evil One cannot duplicate the Fruit of the Spirit.* Leaders in settings of persecution live lives under the increasing control of the Spirit, and the Spirit produces His fruit in their lives. For example, the more Timothy exhibited the Fruit of the Spirit, the more the apostle Paul allowed Timothy freedom for increased ministry opportunities. The more Timothy depended on his innate gifts but was green and unripe in regard to the Fruit of the Spirit, the apostle held him close to himself. Until the Fruit of the Spirit in the life of Timothy was clearly evident, he continued to work in close proximity to his mentor. In the West, we often choose leaders based on the presence of gifts in their lives. As important as that may be, perhaps we should pay more attention to the presence of the Spirit's fruit in their lives! In persecution, rushing green fruit into leadership is a recipe for disaster if not actually laying the groundwork for a Judas to emerge.

2. Leaders in settings of persecution naturally multiply themselves in others. Desiring to be an evangelist and church planter is a part of the DNA of house churches within church planting movements. Leaders in settings of persecution invariably multiply themselves in the lives of others. It is almost as if they cannot help it! In some of the places we visited in China, leaders were allowed to lead Bible studies only *after they had led at least ten people to faith in Christ outside of any formal worship setting—in other words, they did this in the marketplace and homes.* Leaders in China, in our snapshot within history, are invited to pastor house churches only *after they had led twenty to thirty people to faith in Christ.* The commitment to multiplication and the expansion of faith is unquestioned. If evangelizing scores of people, outside of any formal church setting, were the prerequisite for serving as a pastor, how many pulpits would be empty this Sunday in Western cultures? Again, these cultures highly elevate evangelism no matter one's position within the Body.

3. Leaders in settings of persecution mentor new believers through at least one cycle of denial within a persecution context. Be assured: every follower of Jesus, then and now, will deny Jesus! The most common denial is a failure to share the Good News within the opportunities given by God. A wise leader is walking close enough to a new disciple that, when denial comes, the leader can provide an opportunity for the confession of sin, encouragement, forgiveness, instruction, and damage control.

Empowered by the Spirit, leaders in persecution not only know how to endure persecution themselves, they also are able to lead others through that experience.

There are other essential spiritual qualities needed in the lives of leaders in persecution, but we have seen these three qualities present without fail.

Tough Leaders Who Are Marketplace Savvy

- How are leaders chosen within your faith environment?
- What are the cultural characteristics of a leader? Please compare and contrast the five characteristics listed in this chapter.

Part V

A Victorious Faith

23

If the Resurrection Is True, This Changes Everything

We often assume that we know exactly what God is doing. We tend to believe that we have a good understanding of both His methods and His purposes though it often turns out we are mistaken about both. When Ruth and I began interviewing believers in settings of persecution, we thought we understood our purpose. In fact, we would have told you we were interviewing these believers to assist us in developing discipleship materials for believers in persecution. This was our expressed goal; we were asking these believers who were suffering to share their wisdom so we could help others in similar situations. It was a good and worthy goal.

But this was not God's agenda for us, and it was not even what we were actually seeking. When we started our interviewing, we were utterly broken. We had experienced failure and heartache in ministry. We had recently buried a son. We had serious questions and doubts about God and about ourselves. We would have said that we were working on the development of discipleship materials, but we were really seeking something more.

We traveled the world to figure out if God really is God. We wanted to discern for ourselves if Jesus really is who He says He is. We wanted to know if the stories of the Bible were simply old stories or if those stories described the living, active, and ongoing activity of God. We wanted to know for ourselves if this life with Christ is real.

Of course, for mature believers and veterans of mission life, those might seem like childish questions. But those were our sincere questions. And, in God's grace, the people we met in our travels around the world nurtured our faith and restored our hope. They challenged us to believe all over again. In fact, we did discover some wonderful resources for discipleship materials. But we also received much more than this meager goal; we learned what it meant to be a follower, a disciple, of Jesus.

Perhaps we found the best answer to our struggle in the story of Dmitri.

I had already done several days of interviews in Russia when Viktor, my translator, insisted that we visit a man who lived in a faraway village. Early the next morning, Viktor and his friend picked me up. We began a four-hour drive through the countryside north of Moscow. On the way to our destination, Viktor told me what he knew about Dmitri, this fellow believer who had suffered much for the faith. For the rest of the trip, I listened to Viktor and his friend recount their faith journeys and life stories.

We finally arrived at a small Russian village. We stopped in front of a tiny dwelling. Dmitri opened the door and he graciously welcomed us into his tiny home.

"I want you to sit here," he instructed me. "This was where I was sitting when the authorities came to arrest me and send me to prison for seventeen years."

I settled in and listened with rapt attention over the next few hours as Dmitri related his unforgettable personal story.

Dmitri told me that he had been born and raised in a believing family; his parents had taken him to church as a child. Over the decades, he explained, communism slowly destroyed most of the churches and places of worship. Many pastors were imprisoned or killed.

By the time he was grown, Dmitri told me, the nearest remaining church building was a three-day walk away. It was impossible for his family to attend church more than once or twice a year.

"One day," Dmitri told me, "I went to my wife and I said: 'You'll probably think that I am insane. I know that I have no religious training whatsoever, but I am concerned that our sons are growing up without learning about Jesus. This may sound like a crazy idea, but what would you think if just one night a week we gathered the boys together so I could read them a Bible story and try to give them a little of the training that they are missing because we no longer have a real church?'"

What Dmitri didn't know was that his wife had been praying for years that her husband would do something like that. She readily embraced his idea. He started teaching his family one night a week, reading from the old family Bible, then struggling to find the right words to explain what he had just read so that his children could understand.

As he relearned and retold the Bible stories, his sons soon began helping with the task. Eventually, the boys and Dmitri and his wife were telling the familiar stories back and forth to each other. The more they learned, the more the children seemed to enjoy their family worship time.

Eventually the boys started asking for more: "Papa, can we sing those songs that they sing when we go to the real church?" So Dmitri and his wife taught them the traditional songs of their faith.

It seemed a natural progression for the family not only to read the Bible and sing, but also to take time together to pray. And they began to change a Bible study into real family worship.

Nothing could be hidden for long in small villages. Houses were close together and windows were often open. Neighbors began noticing what was going on with Dmitri's family. Some of them asked if they could come and listen to the Bible stories and sing the familiar songs.

Dmitri protested that he was not trained to do this; he explained that he was not a minister. His excuse, however, didn't seem to dissuade his neighbors, and a small group began gathering to share in the reading and telling and discussing of Bible stories and to sing and pray together.

By the time the little group grew to twenty-five people, the authorities had started to take notice. Local party officials came to see Dmitri. They threatened him physically, which was to be expected. What upset Dmitri much more was their accusation: "You have started an illegal church!"

"How can you say that?" he argued. "I have no religious training. I am not a pastor. This is not a church building. We are just a group of family and friends getting together. All we are doing is reading and talking about the Bible, singing, praying, and sometimes sharing what money we have to help out a poor neighbor. How can you call that a church?"

(I almost laughed at the irony of his claim. But this was early in my pilgrimage. I could not easily appreciate the truth that he was sharing. Looking back now, *I understand that one of the most accurate ways to detect and measure the activity of God is to note the amount of opposition that is present.* The stronger the persecution, the more significant the spiritual vitality of the believers. Surprisingly, all too often, persecutors sense the activity of God before the believing participants even realize the significance of what is happening! In the case of Dmitri, the officials could sense the threat of what he was doing long before it even crossed his mind.)

The communist official told Dmitri: "We don't care what you call it, but this looks like church to us. And if you don't stop it, bad things are going to happen."

When the group grew to fifty people, the authorities made good on their threats. "I got fired from my factory job," Dmitri recounted. "My wife lost her teaching position. My boys were expelled from school. And," he added, "little things like that."

When the number of people grew to seventy-five, there was no place for everyone to sit. Villagers stood shoulder-to-shoulder, cheek-to-cheek inside the house. They pressed close in around the windows on the outside so they could listen as this man of God led the people of God in worship.

Then one night as Dmitri spoke (sitting in the chair where I was now seated), the door to his house suddenly, violently burst open. An officer and soldiers pushed through the crowd. The officer grabbed Dmitri by the shirt, slapped him rhythmically back and forth across the face, slammed him against the wall, and said in a cold voice: "We have warned you and warned you and warned you. We will not warn you again! If you do not stop this nonsense, this is the least that is going to happen to you."

As the officer pushed his way back toward the door, a small grandmother took her life in her hands, stepped out of the anonymity of that worshipping community, and waved a finger in the officer's face. Sounding like an Old Testament prophet, she declared, "You have laid hands on a man of God and you will *not* survive!"

That happened on a Tuesday evening, and on Thursday night the officer dropped dead of a heart attack. The fear of God swept through the community and at the next house church service, more than 150 people showed up. The authorities couldn't let this continue, so Dmitri went to jail for seventeen years.

I knew, because Dmitri was sitting right in front of me in his own home, that this particular persecution story was ultimately a story of survival and victory. This story would obviously have a happy ending. But that didn't mean that the story was going to be "nice" or easy to hear.

Indeed, it was a painful story. Dmitri spoke quietly of long, heart-wrenching separation. He spoke of sweat, blood, and tears. He talked about sons growing up without their father in the house. He described a poor, struggling family enduring great hardship. This was not the kind of inspirational testimony that we love to celebrate; this was raw, biblical faith. This was the story of one man who refused to let go of Jesus—one man who refused to stop telling the good news to his family and neighbors.

The authorities moved Dmitri a thousand kilometers away from his family and locked him in a prison. His cell was so tiny that when he got out of bed, it took but a single step either to get to the door of his cell, to reach the stained and cracked sink mounted on the opposite wall, or to use the foul, open toilet in the "far" corner of the cell. Even worse, according to Dmitri, he was the only believer among fifteen hundred hardened criminals.

He said that his isolation from the Body of Christ was more difficult than even the physical torture. And there was much of that. Still, his tormentors were unable to break him. Dmitri pointed to two reasons for his strength in the face of torture. There were two spiritual habits that he had learned from his father, disciplines that Dmitri had taken with him into prison. Without these two disciplines, Dmitri insisted, his faith would have not survived.

For seventeen years in prison, every morning at daybreak, Dmitri would stand at attention by his bed. As was his custom, he would face the east, raise his arms in praise to God, and then he would sing a heart song to Jesus. The reaction of the other prisoners was predictable. Dmitri recounted the laughter, the cursing, the jeering. The other prisoners banged metals cups against the iron bars in angry protest; they threw food and sometimes human waste to try to shut him up and extinguish the only true light shining in that dark place every morning at dawn.

There was another discipline that Dmitri told me about. Whenever he found a scrap of paper in the prison, he would sneak it back to his cell. There he would pull out a stub of a pencil or a tiny piece of charcoal that he had saved, and he would write on that scrap of paper, as tiny as he could, all the Bible verses and scriptural stories or songs that he could remember. When the scrap was completely filled, he would walk to the corner of his little jail cell where there was a concrete pillar that constantly dripped water—except in the wintertime when the moisture became a solid coat of ice on the inside surface of his cell. Dmitri would take the paper fragment, reach as high as he possibly could, and stick it on that damp pillar as a praise offering to God.

Of course, whenever one of his jailors spotted a piece of paper on the pillar, he would come into his cell, take it down, read it, beat Dmitri severely, and threaten him with death.

Still, Dmitri refused to stop his two disciplines.

Every day he rose at dawn to sing his song. And every time he found a scrap of paper, he filled it with Scripture and praise.

This went on year after year after year. His guards tried to make him stop. The authorities did unspeakable things to his family. At one point, they even led him to believe that his wife had been murdered and that his children had been taken by the state.

They taunted him cruelly, "We have ruined your home. Your family is gone."

Dmitri's resolve finally broke. He told God that he could not take any more. He admitted to his guards, "You win! I will sign any confession that you want me to sign. I must get out of here to find out where my children are."

They told Dmitri, "We will prepare your confession tonight, and then you will sign it tomorrow. Then you will be free to go." After all those years, the only thing that he had to do was sign his name on a document saying that he was not a believer in Jesus and that he was a paid agent of Western governments trying to destroy the USSR. Once he put his signature on that dotted line, he would be free to go.

Dmitri repeated his intention: "Bring it tomorrow and I will sign it!"

That very night he sat on his jail cell bed. He was in deep despair, grieving the fact that he had given up. At that same moment, a thousand kilometers away, his family—Dmitri's wife, his children who were growing up without him, and his brother—sensed through the Holy Spirit the despair of this man in prison. His loved ones gathered around the very place where I was sitting as Dmitri told me his story. They knelt in a circle and began to pray out loud for him. Miraculously, the Holy Spirit of the living God allowed Dmitri to hear the voices of his loved ones as they prayed.

The next morning, when the guards marched into his cell with the documents, Dmitri's back was straight. His shoulders were squared and there was strength on his face and in his eyes. He looked at his captors and declared, "I am not signing anything!"

The guards were incredulous. They had thought that he was beaten and destroyed. "What happened?" they demanded to know.

Dmitri smiled and told them, "In the night, God let me hear the voices of my wife and my children and my brother praying for me. You lied to me! I now know that my wife is alive and physically well. I know that my sons are with her. I also know that they are all still in Christ. So I am not signing anything!"

His persecutors continued to discourage and silence him. Dmitri remained faithful. He was overwhelmed one day by a special gift from God's hand. In the prison yard, he found a whole sheet of paper. "And God," Dmitri said, "had laid a pencil beside it!"

Dmitri went on, "I rushed back to my jail cell and I wrote every Scripture reference, every Bible verse, every story, and every song I could recall."

"I knew that it was probably foolish," Dmitri told me, "but I couldn't help myself. I filled both sides of the paper with as much of the Bible as I could. I reached up and stuck the entire sheet of paper on that wet concrete pillar. Then I stood and looked at it: to me it seemed like the greatest offering I could give Jesus from my prison cell. Of course, my jailor saw it. I was beaten and punished. I was threatened with execution."

Dmitri was dragged from his cell. As he was dragged down the corridor in the center of the prison, the strangest thing happened.

Before they reached the door leading to the courtyard—before stepping out into the place of execution—fifteen hundred hardened criminals stood at attention by their beds. They faced the east, and in what Dmitri told me sounded to him like the greatest choir in all of human history, those men raised their arms, and began to sing the heart song that they had heard Dmitri sing to Jesus every morning for all of those years.

Dmitri's jailers instantly released their hold on his arms and stepped away from him in terror.

One of them demanded to know, "Who are you?"

Dmitri straightened his back and stood as tall and as proud as he could. He responded: "I am a son of the Living God, and Jesus is His name!"

The guards returned him to his cell. Sometime later, Dmitri was released and he returned to his family.

Now years later, I listened as Dmitri told his story of his own unspeakable suffering and God's steady faithfulness. I found myself thinking of a time in Somalia when I envisioned creating some discipleship materials that might help believers in places of persecution, believers like Dmitri. What a ridiculous idea this seemed now. What could I possibly ever teach this man about following Jesus? Absolutely nothing!

I was overwhelmed by what I had just heard. I held my head in my hands. I cried out in my heart: *Oh God, What do I do with a story like this? I have always known of Your power, but I have never seen Your power on display like this! If this man represents a biblical faith, who am I? How small is my faith.* Dmitri's story was more dangerous to me than all the bullets in Somalia. Somalia endangered my life. The quality of Dmitri's faith endangered my soul. How can I, with my small faith, watch and listen as Daniel, Elijah, Moses, and Simon Peter burst forth from the pages of the Bible? It was as if the Bible became present active tense for me for the first time. Its pages were flung wide and there was no escaping a God who is doing what He has always done.

Lost in my own thoughts, I realized that Dmitri was still speaking. "Oh, I'm sorry," I apologized, "I wasn't listening!"

Dmitri dismissed my concern with a small shake of his head and a wry smile. "That's okay," he told me. "I wasn't talking to you."

He went on to explain, "When you arrived this morning, God and I were discussing something; your visit interrupted that. So right now, when I saw that you were busy with your own thoughts, the Lord and I went back to finishing that conversation."

In that moment, I knew what I had to ask next.

"Brother Dmitri, would you do something for me?" I asked. I hesitated to continue, but his eyes moved me forward: "Would you sing that song for me?"

Dmitri pushed himself up from the table. He stared into my eyes for three or four seconds. Those seconds felt like an eternity to me. He turned slowly toward the east and stiffened his back to stand at attention. He lifted his arms and began to sing.

I don't know Russian, so I didn't understand a single word of his song. But I didn't need to. The words probably didn't matter. As

Dmitri raised his arms and his voice in praise and sang that song that he had sung every morning in prison for seventeen years, the tears began to flow down both of our faces. Only then did I begin to grasp the meaning of worship and the importance of heart songs.

I had tentatively arrived in Russia looking for answers and wondering if faith could survive and even grow in the world's most hostile environments. Dmitri became one of my first guides on my journey. I began to sense that this journey was not about developing discipleship materials, *but it was about walking with Jesus in hard places.*

I felt drawn to this life Dmitri had lived: knowing Jesus, loving Jesus, following Jesus, living with Jesus.

Our question, now, is this: Is it possible to live a victorious life in the midst of persecution? Dmitri's story tells us plainly that victorious living is possible. If so, then how can such a life be lived? How can a believer have a victorious faith in a setting of suffering and persecution? In truth, the remainder of our interviews sought to answer this specific question. And through those interviews, we identified a number of common essential spiritual truths and practices present in the lives of believers living victorious lives in persecution.

Our question also was this: *Is it possible to live a victorious life in the midst of a Western world that seems to suggest that followers of Jesus are entitled to everything?* In persecution, things are often black and white. In persecution, evil and good seem clearly delineated. In the West, however, there is so much "good" it is almost impossible to surrender some of those "good things" so that we might choose the "pearl of great price." We would never presume to suggest Dmitri had it easy! But the interviews clearly show a frightening truth: When believers in persecution are rescued and resettled in the West, the faith they fought to express so vigorously in persecution diminished greatly (and quickly) under the noise of Western consumerism.

Could it be that serving Jesus in the Western world might be even harder than serving Jesus where persecution is the norm?

In either setting, we are convinced the need for victorious living, though difficult, is possible for one who seeks to be a true follower of Jesus and not just a member of a church. And we are also convinced that believers in settings of relative freedom have the most to learn from believers in persecution. These are just a few of the lessons we can learn.

1. Believers living victorious lives in persecution know Jesus. Their faith is neither distant nor abstract. Their faith is real, and Jesus is real. The relationship between Jesus and His followers is rich and vital and alive. Believers in persecution know Jesus and they live daily with Him. These believers have not traded a relationship with Jesus for a religion, a denomination, or a political party. Believers we have interviewed reveal their close walk with Jesus in their voices, on their faces, and through their body language.

These believers model for us how we have little need to attack governments or denigrate other religious figures. Our task is to simply lift up Jesus. When Jesus is "lifted up," people are drawn to Him and to His kingdom. Our interviews have reminded us of something we already know well: There is no one like Jesus!

2. Believers living victorious lives in persecution know firsthand the power of prayer and fasting. Dmitri's seamless transition from conversation with another human being to conversation with God illustrates the power and the reality of prayer in his life. We noticed this same seamless transition repeatedly in our interviews. Both talking to and listening to God are vital, daily realities for those who live victorious lives. These believers speak to Jesus as a trusted friend who listens; they commune with a God who answers. They submit to His leadership when He says, "No," "Yes," or "Wait."

I was asked to leave a day early from a southeastern Asian country because a believer I was to interview felt he was being followed. I readily agreed to his security concerns. Some other believers would be taking me to the airport. As we were driving to the airport early the next morning, the driver of the car began driving erratically through various back alleys.

Seeing the look of concern in my eyes, he smiled and told me not to worry. He had heard through the spiritual grapevine a leader from the hill country had returned to the capital city late the night before, and he wanted me to meet him. We drove through many back streets until we came to a ramshackle apartment with wooden stairs attached loosely to the outside of the apartment. As the three of us climbed to the third floor, poised to knock on the door of the apartment, the door suddenly opened and there stood the believer from the hill country.

The man said, "While I was praying this morning, the Holy Spirit told me you were coming. So I fixed breakfast." We entered the room and there was the breakfast table with food prepared and four place settings already arranged.

We want to pray like that! As we have heard from scores of interviews, we want to pray and set the table in obedience to what God says to us. We want to pray and then travel to the airport to pick up the visitors the Holy Spirit has told us were coming. We want to pray simply to see God glorified. We want to pray and then find ourselves standing beside the Ethiopian eunuch's chariot. We want to pray and believe God hears and answers us through our conversations with Him!

The spiritual discipline of fasting is also important. We met some believers in persecution who practiced fasting as much as four days a week. It is not clear whether the prayer and fasting resulted in the intimate relationship with God or if the intimate relationship with God resulted in increased prayer and fasting, but it is clear to us the two things are closely tied together. It is hard to deny believers in persecution their food for the day as punishment when believers are already fasting! This practice of focusing on God through fasting is virtually absent from sermons and the daily lives of Western believers.

3. *Believers living victorious lives in persecution can re-create large portions of the Bible from memory.* Believers in persecution love God's Word. They memorize it. They meditate on it. They devour His Word. They have re-created large portions of the Bible orally; God's Word is written on their hearts. As important as God's written Word is, believers in persecution know their oral Bible is all they will be allowed to take into prison with them. Believers in persecution suggest the Bible you know by heart is in actuality, your Bible. God's Word is so much a part of who they are, it can never be taken from them. Believers in persecution have learned from Jesus and from each other how to handle the Bible orally. When witnessing opportunities arise or when persecutors are attempting to extract information from a believer, these believers often answer each and every question with a Bible story. When they are asked a question about the story they have just shared, they will simply tell another Bible story.

Persecutors of God's children do not allow Bibles in prison. It is the Word of God deeply imprinted on a believer's heart and mind that allows the believer to thrive through persecution. Followers of Islam sometimes complain, when they ask us a biblical question, believers have to find our Holy Book, look up a specific verse in the concordance in the back of the Bible, and then answer their question.

Eight believers came from a harsh Central Asian country. All of them were oral communicators and they had led thousands of people to Christ. Together, these eight believers knew about twenty stories from the Bible. Somehow, they had encountered just enough stories to hear about Jesus, to believe in Him, to be baptized, and then to form hundreds of house churches.

We were able to visit together for five days. During this time, whenever they asked us a question, we would answer with a Bible story. They would then discuss this story among themselves. Then they would retell the story to each other several times while telling their own stories which seemed to parallel the biblical accounts. This went on for five days. They left our time together with fifty or more stories from the Bible. One in their group could read. He had a Bible in hand and he would authenticate the Bible stories that were being recited from memory. After the telling of each story, he would look at the story in the Book and then confirm what they had heard was actually recorded in Scripture and accurately shared.

Possessing the Bible in literate forms is nonnegotiable. Freeing the Bible, through the power of the Holy Spirit, to be shared in oral forms is also nonnegotiable. The main debate here is not between literacy and orality. The main point is the power of the Holy Spirit and the utter centrality of Scripture both oral and literate forms. In settings of persecution, though, often only an oral Bible will suffice for the majority of believers, backed up by the Bible in literate form.

4. In similar fashion, believers living victorious lives in persecution have committed large amounts of indigenous music to memory. Believers in persecution rely on their heart songs—the music of faith that speaks to them and tells their story. They sing their songs as expressions of faith and as acts of worship. The songs belong to them, and they are not imported from other cultures. This music is vital for the survival of faith in situations of persecution.

An MBB was arrested by his government because of his faith in Jesus. In jail, he continued practicing his faith daily by praying, reciting Bible stories to himself, and by singing his praises to God. There were eight guards responsible for him, sharing shifts of eight hours apiece, two guards at a time. After about ten days, one set of guards came to him. They were quite angry and a bit afraid. They said to the believer, "You must stop singing those songs."

Puzzled, he asked why they were making such an unusual request.

They explained: "The songs you are singing are so powerful they are going to convert us. Then we will become Christians also and we will be in the same cell with you!"

There are few disciplines in the life of believers more vital than singing God's praises, especially singing God's Word back to Him.

And the songs must be in the local language, locally written, and set in the local style. Christian music transliterated from the outside seemingly does not give one victorious living in persecution. Developing heart songs from within the local culture is extremely important, nonnegotiable.

If, during an interview, local believers shared with us the songs they sing in worship and in their own prayer time, and if those songs were imported from outside, we knew one of two things. Either these believers had not been through enough suffering to write their own heart songs, or they had gone through persecution armed only with Western, outsider music. In that case, we knew they had probably stumbled and fallen without experiencing victorious living in their persecution. Personal, indigenous heart songs are simply this important. Each and every culture needs to sing their own hard-won heart songs to Jesus.

Each generation also needs its own heart songs. Churches in the West must stop fighting over whose heart songs to sing in corporate worship. Believers in persecution have taught us that each and every generation must have their own heart songs.

5. Believers living victorious lives in persecution know that they are prayed for and they were not forgotten. We were constantly overwhelmed to see the reaction as believers in persecution learned they had not been forgotten, other believers knew of their suffering, and thousands of believers around the world were praying for them. This awareness was more than encouraging; it was life giving and, sometimes, faith saving.

Often when we finally reached a clandestine location for

interviewing believers in persecution, their initial reaction was one of shock, disbelief, and then tears. They were moved to the depths of their souls when they heard we had not forgotten them, that believers in other places had never ceased to pray for them. Please take this to heart. Believers in persecution *do not make it through persecution by themselves.* Victorious living in persecution is experienced when the Body of Christ carries on their prayerful shoulders those suffering parts of the Body to the throne of God. Believers in persecution are victorious often through your prayers. Can it be that you may decide if a believer is victorious in another part of the globe, as they languish in a dark jail cell or as they are beaten, due to your prayers on their behalf? What a challenge. What a privilege. This is the Body of Christ.

6. Believers living victorious lives in persecution are certain the local believing community will care for their families. Even in prison, persecuted believers have absolute confidence their families will be cared for while they are not able to do so. This is not merely a hope; it is a certainty. And our interviews indicate how the local faith community proved itself time and again to be faithful at this point of need.

When a pastor, elder, deacon, evangelist, or church planter is visited in prison, the first question asked by their visitor is typically: "How are you doing?" Strangely, such a question is never answered. Instead, the prisoner shifts the conversation emotionally in another direction: "How is my wife? How are my children?" Visitors who represent the Body of Christ reply to the imprisoned believer, "Your job is to be obedient to Jesus while you are in prison. Our job is to take care of your family as long as you are in prison. Please, you do your job and let us do ours." Knowing their families are taken care of gives imprisoned believers confidence to stand firm.

7. Believers living victorious lives in persecution understand their suffering is for Jesus' sake. They understand their pain is not something they have taken on themselves. Rather, they understand in their innermost being their suffering is for Jesus and for His gospel.

Some Westerners went to a very restrictive country. Though very new to the whole persecuted world, they did their best in a hostile setting. Though doing their best, they were arrested by Islamic fundamentalists and placed in a primitive prison. Western media, even some Christian organizations, turned on these young women, blaming them for their persecution at the hands of the fundamentalists! The suggestion was even made to those who had been arrested that their sending organization should apologize to their persecutors for what had happened. This is neither God's will nor God's way. *Even if we make mistakes in our witness, we must remember that the only witness God cannot use is no witness!*

Ultimately, there is no such thing as a worthless or bad witness. At the same time, what we are trying to do in this book is to suggest we give Satan as little opportunity as possible to take our good deeds and turn them into something destructive. Whenever a brother or sister is persecuted, *no matter how such persecution has come about,* we look our brother or sister in the eye, we hold them in our arms, and we say, "What has happened to you is for Jesus' sake and we are so proud of you."

We can then stand back and watch how the Holy Spirit strengthens our brothers or sisters in persecution and grants them renewal, hope, and strength. We can never blame those persecuted for what the persecutors do to them! We simply invite the Holy Spirit to teach those in persecution how to become wise partners in evangelism and church planting.

8. *Believers living victorious lives in persecution accept the fact that their persecution is normal.* Persecution for them is not an indication they have done something wrong. In contrast, persecution can well be an indication witness has been shared powerfully! Faithful living and faithful witness lead to and result in persecution. Persecution is the inevitable result of faithfulness. Believers in persecution expect persecution and they see it as normal, predictable, and unavoidable. They

do not seek persecution, but they are not surprised when it comes. Persecution is simply a by-product of faith. Often, if we notice unexpected and unusual persecution, we discover unexpected and unusual faith has exploded in that location.

9. *Believers living victorious lives in persecution have claimed their freedom.* They understand they are always free to share their faith in any setting. They also understand there are consequences for their witness, but they know no one can take their freedom to share their faith away from them. The freedom to share their faith is a freedom God Himself grants, and believers in persecution will relinquish their biblical freedom to no one.

It was one of my worst days in Somaliland. I needed a word from the Lord. His answer came through the strange medium of a BBC radio broadcast, by a woman who was single, a member of the British Parliament, and Jewish by faith. She was speaking on the Ten Commandments, specifically the one which says, "Remember the Sabbath day by keeping it holy" (Exod. 20:8). It was her suggestion the Western world does not understand this commandment and that we have virtually neutered the power of this chiseled-in-stone word of God. In a strong voice over the shortwave radio she proclaimed, "When Moses read the commandment on remembering the Sabbath day, a shout, a cry of exquisite joy, would have rung out throughout the land from all of the Jews." Her point was this was the first time in human history where Almighty God had proclaimed that His people were to be free, because only those who were free could choose to have a Sabbath day!

No more could Israel blame Egypt for not worshipping the one true God. It was now their responsibility to claim their own freedom and set aside a day for worship—a day that declares for all time that God's people are free. Have you claimed your freedom?

10. *Believers living victorious lives in persecution refuse to be controlled by fear.* Fear of consequences and fear of persecution do not

prevent them from obeying Jesus and being faithful. They have already given their lives to Christ, so they refuse to fear those who can *only* kill the body (Matt. 10:28). In some cases, these faithful believers simply choose not to be afraid. In other cases, they are very afraid but choose to be faithful and obedient regardless.

Believers in persecution understand that fear of persecution is often worse than the persecution itself, and they determine not to let such fear inhibit their obedient response to Christ's call.

Victorious believers in persecution refuse to be defined by fear. They desire to be defined by faith and obedience. Two MBBs, one old and one younger in two different countries, claimed there are 366 verses in the Bible related to fear. This was their testimony, "God has given us a verse for each day of the year and an extra verse in case we have a really bad day." God took a great risk in the Garden of Eden when He gave humankind a choice between good and evil. At times, we have not made the best of choices. Yet the one thing Satan can never take from us is our ability to choose. *We can choose not to be afraid, we can choose joy, and we can always choose Jesus.*

Our fear is perhaps the greatest tool in Satan's arsenal. Satan cannot be everywhere at once. He cannot know everything. He does not possess all power. Through our fear, though, Satan can hold us captive. Our fear allows him to be in many places at one time. Our fear provides him with knowledge and power. Believers who are victorious in persecution have claimed their freedom in Christ and, because of that freedom, are losing their fear.

11. Believers living victorious lives in persecution have a genealogy of faith. Hearing story after story of faithful obedience, biblical in proportion, I cried out, "Where did you learn to live like that? Where did you learn to die like that?"

The answer was always the same: "I learned it from my father, my grandfather, my great-grandfather. I learned it from my mother, my grandmother, my great-grandmother."

They beat him, starved him, and humiliated him in prison for seventeen years. His experiences included all the physical and psychological tortures that history records. Yet he sang every day in prison even while bloodied and discouraged. He was imprisoned right up to the disintegration of the USSR.

Today, his son is a chaplain in the prison where his father was held for almost two decades.

Where did this young man learn to live and die as a follower of Jesus?

He learned it from his daddy.

Obviously, first-generation believers from largely unreached areas will not have such a genealogy of faith. Pentecost-like movements have not come to their people and churches have not been birthed. They have little Bible and few songs of the faith. They might be scattered, alone, and afraid. They have no one to pray for them, to visit them in jail, or to take care of their families. They face persecution alone. They are first-generation believers with no genealogy of faith.

In those settings, it is our responsibility and privilege to do two things.

First, we have the responsibility to proclaim a genealogy of faith for them from Scripture. This is a nonnegotiable, biblical genealogy of faith that links them to the faithful and obedient people of God from the beginning of Genesis to the end of Revelation. Our message would be something like this: "This is how the people of God have always lived and died, and this is now how you will live and die as one of God's people."

Second, we have the responsibility to show them, from our own lives, how to live and die. Like the apostle Paul encouraging others to imitate his life, we should have the courage to say to first-generation believers: "If you want to know how God's people live and if you want to know how God's people die, look at me. Watch me. Imitate me." It would be difficult to imagine a higher calling or a greater responsibility. But this is at least a significant part of our calling.

These are the common characteristics for believers living victorious lives in persecution. More than simply being "characteristics for other people," this list becomes for us a challenging call to victorious faith in our own setting. *This list turns out to be a convicting and challenging tool for self-evaluation in our lives and churches.* These pages are not meant to simply be a monologue of victorious living in persecution. They are meant to be a biblical imperative, guiding believers in Jesus for all times and in all places. Believers in persecution have paid huge prices to share with us their lives' lessons above. Shall we handle this holy material with the respect it deserves?

"Oh Victory in Jesus"

- Using the 11 signs of victorious living listed above, how many of these characteristics are to be found within the Body of your church?
- Using the 11 signs of victorious living listed above, how many of these characteristics are to be found within those sent to serve as cross-cultural workers from your church and denomination?
- Using the 11 signs of victorious living listed above, how many of these characteristics are to be found within the lives of your family, your children?
- Using the 11 signs of victorious living listed above, how many of these characteristics are to be found within your life?

24

Our Marching Orders

This is a challenging book. It is a challenge to read, and it is perhaps an even greater challenge to apply. As we draw our conversation to a close, let's revisit a few of the core convictions that define the world of persecution.

Followers of Jesus in all places are called to embrace a lifestyle that includes suffering, persecution, and martyrdom. This life of faith is built upon a number of important truths.

1. If we are obedient to Christ's call, persecution will come. One of the chief causes of persecution is people accepting Jesus as their Lord.
2. The suffering that follows should come for the sake of Jesus and for the sake of witness, and not for lesser, secondary reasons.
3. Safety cannot be our primary concern. The goal of life with Jesus is not to remain safe, but to sacrifice our lives for a lost world.

4. We must find ways not to model fear. Fear cannot be our dominant response to the evil around us.

5. Spiritual and psychological strength will be required to suffer the consequences of obedient faith. We must discern when to leave Joseph in prison.

6. A genealogy of faith is essential and it should be modeled through our witness.

7. We must choose to share the risk of suffering with believers all around the world. The burden of suffering is not a burden for certain believers but a burden that must be shared by every believer. This is the privilege of witness, and witness is to be extended to all peoples at all times.

8. We are free to share our faith in every setting and in every place. There will always be consequences for our obedience, but we are always free to obey.

9. Somehow, within the context of eternity, God will use suffering for His purposes, and we can trust Him to do so.

10. Through God's power, our faithfulness is always a possibility.

11. Above all else, this is about Jesus and His kingdom.

Afterword

Fifteen years ago, we sensed an invitation from God to sit at the feet of believers in persecution around the world, learning from them. In the process, God restored our faith and convinced us of His power to accomplish His purposes. We can walk with Jesus in the tough places.

As we listened to our suffering brothers and sisters, our lives were forever changed. In some cases, our convictions were strengthened. In other cases, we were challenged with brand new insights. Some of our assumptions were affirmed and some were revealed to be completely wrong.

Beyond the lessons learned, however, is this vital truth: God is at work in His world. And even in a world filled with persecution and suffering, God is building His church. Though it seems impossible, God is drawing people to faith in Jesus Christ, and those people are responding with courage and faith. Despite strong opposition, God's kingdom is growing and God is revealing that His power is more than sufficient.

The questions which remain are personal.

Will I play a part in what God is doing? Am I willing to take the clear command of the Great Commission seriously and personally? Am I willing to go across the street and around the world?

Having gone, am I willing to stay? Will I choose to be an obedient partner with God? Am I willing to sacrifice for Christ's cause? Regardless of the cost, will I choose to obey?

The testimony of our brothers and sisters thriving in persecution globally is compelling, and their testimony reminds us we are always free to obey Christ. It is our high privilege today to act on that freedom.

Clearly, God will find a way to accomplish His purposes. In His grace, we have the opportunity to play a part in what He is doing. May God Himself give us the courage to obey.

Notes

1. The book *You Lost Me*, by David Kinnaman, provides more sobering assessments of the spiritual health of churches in America

2. The more complete story of our lives is told in our earlier book entitled *The Insanity of God: A Journey of Faith Resurrected.*

3. Paul Marshall, *Their Blood Cries Out* (Nashville: Thomas Nelson, 1997), 249–50.

4. Ibid., 250–51.

5. David B. Barrett and Todd M. Johnson, *World Christian Trends, A.D. 30–A.D. 2200: Interpreting the Annual Christian Megacensus* (Pasadena, CA: William Carey Library, 2003), 228.

6. Ibid.

7. David Garrison, *Church Planting Movements: How God Is Redeeming a Lost World* (Monument, CO: WIGTake Resources, 2004), 59.

8. Kevin Greeson, *The Camel: How Muslims Are Coming to Faith in Christ* (Monument, CO: WIGTake Resources, 2007).

9. A good source for information concerning today's pre-Pentecost world is http://www.joshuaproject.net/great-commission-statistics.php. The statistics are often so overwhelming that they easily lose their meaning, but these numbers represent actual people. Today, between 1.5 and 3 billion people do not have enough knowledge to become followers of Jesus. What would we call that kind of a world? Clearly, that world might be called the world of the Old Testament. In any case, these numbers represent billions of souls with little or no access to Jesus.

10. Samuel M. Zwemer, *Across the World of Islam* (La Verne, CA: Old LandMark Publishing, 2008), 135.

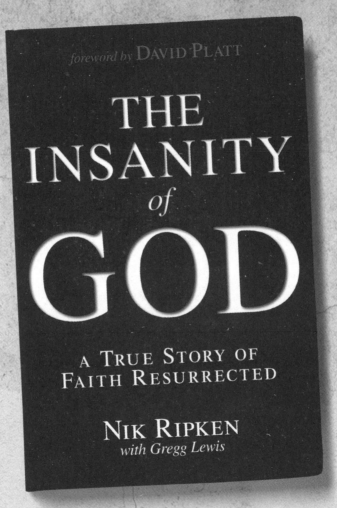

UPSIDE DOWN

YOUR WORLD

IT WILL TURN

GOD'S
INSANITY

GODSINSANITY.COM

1-888-524-2535

Open*Doors*®
Serving persecuted **Christians** worldwide

A multitude from every
language, people, tribe and nation
knowing and worshipping
our Lord Jesus Christ.

Nearly 5,000 workers around the world, supported by Southern Baptist churches, working to make disciples of all peoples.

Connecting churches with the unreached
Connecting the unreached with the Gospel

imb.org

continue the journey at...

nikripken.com

if the resurrection is true... that changes everything!